THE NOTE BOOKS

A THINKER'S NOTEBOOK

Posthumous Papers of a Buddhist Monk

Bhikkhu Ñāṇamoli

Buddhist Publication Society
Kandy • Sri Lanka

Buddhist Publication Society
P.O. Box 61
54, Sangharaja Mawatha
Kandy,
Sri Lanka

First edition: 1972 (Forest Hermitage, Kandy)
Second edition: 1980 (BPS)
Third edition (including *Pathways of Buddhist Thought*, earlier published under the same title as Wheel Publication 52/53): 2008

National Library of Sri Lanka - Cataloguing in Publication Data

Bhikkhu Nyanamoli
Thinker's Notebook: Posthumous Papers of a Buddhist Monk/Bhikku Nyanamoli.-
Kandy: Buddhist Publication Society Inc., 2008.-
p.256; 21cm

ISBN 978-955-24-0312-5 Price: Rs.

i. 181.043 DDC 22 ii. Title
1. Buddhist Philosophy

Typeset at the BPS in Garamond BPS.

Printed by
Ruchira Printers
Kandy—Sri Lanka

A THINKER'S NOTEBOOK

POSTHUMOUS PAPERS OF A
BUDDHIST MONK

BHIKKHU ÑĀṆAMOLI

EDITOR'S PREFACE

> "I shall never be able to compose my biography; but let no one else have the presumption to do so; for this would amount to theft. —Don't worry, no one will think of it."
>
> (*Note Books* § 268)

Thus a Buddhist monk, the late venerable Ñāṇamoli, the author of the following pages, wrote in one of his note books. And in deference to his wish, only a few bare facts of his life will be given here, just for 'identifying' him. Even for such bare identification he would hardly have cared: "It is my ambition to attain to obscurity" (§ 75; see also § 339). Those who knew him are aware that these words were neither 'false modesty' nor any other posturing.

Though the present publication seems to go counter to his 'ambition,' he might not have minded a circulation of his ideas after his death as this left him uninvolved and unencumbered. Hence the Editor, a Brother-in-Order of the author, felt that the rich store of thought seeds and thought fruits found in these pages should be made accessible to some appreciative readers, at least within the modest range of a private publication.

Osbert Moore (as the author was known in lay life) was born on the 25th of June, 1905, in England. He graduated at Exeter College, Oxford, and during the Second World War he served as an army staff-officer in Italy. It was at that time, by reading an Italian book on Buddhism, that his interest in that Teaching was roused. This book—*The Doctrine of Awakening* by Evola—was later translated into English by a friend and fellow officer, Harold Musson, who in 1948 accompanied Osbert Moore to Sri Lanka. In 1949 both received Novice Ordination as Buddhist monks, at the Island Hermitage, Dodanduwa; and in 1950 the Higher Ordination as Bhikkhus, at the Vajirārāma monastery, Colombo. Osbert

Moore, our author, received the monastic name of Ñāṇamoli, and his friend that of Ñāṇavīra. Both returned soon to the Island Hermitage (an island monastery situated in a lagoon of South Sri Lanka), where the venerable Ñāṇamoli spent almost his entire monk life of eleven years. Only very rarely he left the quietude of the Island Hermitage, and it was on one of these rare occasions, on a walking tour undertaken with the senior monk of the Hermitage, that he suddenly passed away on 8th March, 1960, through heart failure (coronary thrombosis). He had not yet completed his 55th year. His death took place at a lonely little village, Veheragama near Maho. Though he seemed to be in vigorous health, his end will not have come unexpected to him as his note books show (§ 209), and, without doubt, it found him inwardly prepared. (§§ 555, 556)

Personal reminiscences of his lay life have been published by Maurice Cardiff, in a short article "Osbert Moore, A Character Sketch" (in *Visākha Puja*, 1968; publ. by The Buddhist Association of Thailand, Bangkok). A slender memorial pamphlet was issued in 1960 by the Buddhist Publication Society, Kandy, Sri Lanka.

The author's own scanty contribution to his biography is contained in a single note in this book. (§ 267)

* * *

What was known of the monk life of the venerable Ñāṇamoli to a wider public in Sri Lanka and abroad, was his outstanding scholarly work in translating from the original Pali into lucid English some of the most difficult texts of Theravada Buddhism. These translations, listed at the end of this volume, were remarkable achievements in quantity as well as in quality. Some more unfinished work of that nature was found among his papers, and he might have completed it in years to come. His translations showed the highest standard of careful and critical scholarship and a keen and subtle mind, philosophically trained. His work in this field is a lasting contribution to Buddhist studies.

It was characteristic of him that he had limited his publications to that scholarly field, so that his "public image" was that of an able scholar and an exemplary monk, which left him enough of his cherished 'obscurity.'

Very few knew, or even suspected, those other facets of his rich and profound mind, which in the present volume appear in such an astonishing variety. And even the contents of these pages do not exhaust the entire range of his knowledge, his interests and his capacities.

Yet, there were still other 'layers' of his mind (and still not the deepest), without which the picture of his personality as presented by this book and in his scholarly work would be incomplete and even misleading. These other features of his character, however, manifested themselves only in his way of life and in his human relationships. From his unrelentingly realistic world-view as appearing in his note books—undeceived by the deceptions and self-deceptions of life and of our own minds—a reader could possibly gain the impression of a harsh if not cynic character with a rather contemptuous view of mankind. But this would be very far from the deep humanity and friendly composure of his nature, which made his self-effacing reticence still more unobtrusive. He had a natural affinity with the Buddha's detachment as well as with his compassionate outlook. In his detachment and reticence he was not "forbiddingly aloof," but quite relaxed and natural. His friendliness and compassion was unsentimental and undemonstrative, but of a simple human warmth. His quiet and friendly smile will be unforgettable to his companions. Though not of an 'out-going' nature, he was always willing to help when approached, and he was also quite skilful in practical tasks. Though he rarely took the initiative in conversation and discussions, he was quite willing to speak and discuss at length when spoken to in a worthwhile manner; and whenever asked he gave to the younger monks help and guidance in their studies. The simplicity and frugality of a Buddhist monk's life came quite natural to him. As he himself wrote to a friend, he had found great happiness in his new life as a monk (see Maurice Cardiff, l.c.). In the Buddha's Teaching on reality and man's situation in it, he found ever-fresh inspiration for his own thought, and the Buddha's practical path to deliverance being the solution of the human predicament, was the guiding and directing force in his inner life.

* * *

When after the death of the venerable Ñāṇamoli the Editor looked through the posthumous papers, he found two little note books, the contents of which fill the bulk of the present volume. As one of these note books was badly bound and near disintegration and pencil writings in it would have become illegible soon, a typewritten copy of almost the entire contents of the two books was made by the Editor, first for the sake of preservation and for perusal by a few friends. Matters rested at that for some years when inquiries made from knowledgeable friends abroad made it improbable that a publisher could be found for a book of that nature. But finally the Editor decided to prepare the book for printing as a private publication, and he added other representative material taken from the posthumous papers.

It hardly needs mentioning that the title of this volume was not given to it by the author who probably did not think of having these note books published as they were, but perhaps of using some of the ideas in other writings. The numbering of the aphorisms and other pieces was done by the Editor for facilitating reference. Personal circumstances, however, did not allow the Editor to add an Index to the book.

Nyanaponika Thera
The Forest Hermitage
Kandy, Sri Lanka.
April 1971

Note to Third Edition

In this expanded and newly typeset edition, the essays contained in *Pathways of Buddhist Thought,* Wheel Publication No. 52/53, have been included. Like the other material contained in *A Thinker's Notebook*, they were collected from the posthumous papers of the venerable Ñāṇamoli by Venerable Nyanaponika. *Pathways of Buddhist Thought* was issued in 1963 in commemoration of Venerable Ñāṇamoli's death.

Another paper called "The Sukkavipassaka" on "dry insight" meditation in relation to tranquillity meditation has also been included in this edition. It is also one of Venerable Ñāṇamoli's posthumous papers, but was not published earlier.

Bhikkhu Ñāṇatusita
Editor
Buddhist Publication Society

Table of Contents

The First Note Book 15
The Second Note Book 37
Addenda 117
General 117
Notes on Philosophy 120
Ontology and Buddhism 139
Miscellanea 165
Poems 167
Tale 169
Story 171
Dialogues 172
Words 175
Today's Fallacies and Half-Truths 175
Impressions 176
Canticle 177
From Letters to Venerable Ñāṇavīra 179
I 179
II 185
III 188
The Essential Relation in Observing 189
Pathways of Buddhist Thought 198
Buddhism: a Religion or a Philosophy? 198
Does Saddhā Mean Faith? Part I 205
Does Saddhā Mean Faith? Part II 211
Cessation of Becoming 220
Consciousness and Being 224
The Sukkhavipassaka 232
Appendix I 242
Appendix II 248
Works of the Author 251
The Venerable Bhikkhu Ñāṇamoli 251

The First Note Book

1. Civilization is the art of living in contact with other persons with the minimum of discomfort. (1945)

2. A thought for this Damocletian Age: the trouble with justice is it just isn't it? (1946)

3. For every man killed by man for the sake of facts, twenty or more are so killed for the sake of opinion. (1946)

4. Worms look out of the eyes of the very rich and all the platitudes about them are true. (1946)

(Later addition:) And the poor—how poor they are!

5. I was the future and shall be the past—I am a timeless, everlasting Now, so short I have no end, so long I have no duration.

6. If I insist on having only beauty before me I know only horror will be behind me, therefore I shall not dare to turn round. (1947)

7. Madness is sometimes said to be divine—can the same ever be said of sanity? (1947)

8. The five senses offer us five different ways of shutting out reality. What is intuition and what does it perceive? (1947)

9. As electricity is made up of positive and negative current, so is human life a system of attraction and repulsion.—Turn off the current if you want quiet.—Yes, but where is the switch?

10. Present-day politics rely for their power largely on an efficient battery of quick-firing slogans. (Mar 54)

11. An unsuccessful lie conflicts with truth, but a successful one subverts and seduces it. (Mar. 54)

12. Sing as loud as you will, there is nothing that does not eventually fall into the cavernous lap of ruinous Old Age, the procureuse of death. (1947)

13. Let him who climbs the spiritual ladder make sure he has a sound head before he looks down into the past. (1949)

14. How is it I have the strength to carry my own weakness? (1948)

15. It is in the company of others that one can be really lonely, for then one's personality is forced openly to try to express what its separate individuality is. (1949)

16. If one could continue the calming process after everything has fallen calm one might enter the looking glass world. (1949)

17. Among the inhabitants of Naples there are those who are inclined to cultivate ulcers and deformities on their bodies which they display while begging, in order to induce others to give them money. Among the inhabitants of a much wider area there are those who cultivate ulcers and deformities of the mind which they display, in company, in order to induce others to give them attention. (Sep. 49)

18. The so-called seven colours of the spectrum together go to make up what is known as light—what, in other words, the scientists say is no more than a mere fractional band in the whole range of electro-magnetic waves—the only section of the wave-range which the visual sense can directly grasp. Indeed each colour is experienced as a particular limitation of light; light itself appears to be a particular limitation of the electro-magnetic wave-range. So would the five senses seem to be five specific limitations of the infinite—five exclusive ways of screening off, of shutting out the rest. In fact, the "outer world," as known through the senses, seems to be conditioned by—shall one say our knowledge of it depends on—the limiting and sifting qualities of our five senses. By means of sifting and excluding, form could be said to be created from Chaos and thus our five senses are at the same time five creators and five ways of being partially blind. We live, as it were, in a cathedral with stained windows whose, to us, magnificent colour patterns let in a little of the light which the sun sheds indiscriminately outside. (1947) (Later *addition*:) But the "sun" would then stand for Chaos in our simile and how would that be wrong?

19. If I had a child what could I say to him? "My child," I could say, "you are here in this world because of my own pleasure and incontinence. I can offer you nothing better than become another 'little man' like myself whom it is the present fashion for

politicians and the like to idolize *en masse* and exploit and ignore as an individual. If you succeed in 'improving' your position this can only be at the expense of others and will increase its instability. If your position deteriorates it will be at your own expense. In a few years time you will, no doubt, be repeating these very words." (1949)

20. Heaven is where (it is supposed) we may enjoy what other people consider we ought to enjoy. (Apr. 1948)

21. History is bones daubed and plumped out with the clay of opinion. (1949)

22. The waves that die on the shore—where are they born? (Amalfi—Sep. 45)

23. For a long time—over many years indeed—the atmosphere continued to echo the clanging of evil times as multitudes fell upon them.

24. Some say "Jones has gone up in the world." Others say "the world is upside down." What has happened to Jones? (1949)

25. Virtue is perhaps covertly disliked as much as it is because it entails refusing frequently what other people want one to do. (1948)

26. One is, as it were, on the 20th storey of a burning house, and from the window there is a narrow plank leading across the street to the balcony of an—apparently—safe building opposite. (The Building Opposite whose blinds are always down, whose chimneys never smoke, whose doors never open, where no light is seen at night, about which there has been one's frequent yet always inconclusive speculation.) To stay is to be burned for certain. By attempting the plank one will probably fall—still one knows one will have to walk that plank or burn. (Nov. 48)

27. The journey through life is fingered by sign posts indicating routes whose bridges are found, on exploration, to have been breached by floods or wars. (1949) (*Later addition*:) The new "*Autostrassen*" have no signposts.

28. It is spring, as the sun comes back north again, and, obediently, out come the bright leaves. In summer they will weary and darken under his rays; in autumn, as he retreats south, he abandons them to themselves; worn out they will die and fall to the

ground. Observing her own peculiar disciplines the moon watches monotonously throughout the seasons; waxing and waning she is occupied with herself—only when she is full do her three expressions reveal three phases of the boundless ennui she must feel watching all this for so long.

* * *

28a. The restless river slides by day and night intent only upon the sea. (Turin by the Po, May 1948)

29. A function of art—of contemporary art—is to explore, to send scouts ever further into the wilderness of unclaimed discord. The advance-guard is in continuous touch with the enemy, fighting the unnamed, capturing the formless. Sometimes patrols fall into enemy hands; then, from their prison camps where madness rules, they send back reports, some of which seem half intelligible. (1947)

30. Art is a reminder and, to some degree, illuminates. In my prison cell it serves as a screened window—which lets in a little light from which I infer the existence of the bright outside world. Were I to go and live out there, art, the screened window, would no longer serve any purpose at all. (1947) (*Later addition*:) But how do I know there is anything to live on out there?

31. To say "The politicians have failed, the philosophers have failed, religion has failed or is out of date, science has failed and is not what it was thought to be," and so on are not these all ways of saying that we, ourselves, have failed? The Govt. Treasury has no revenue unless the people work and are taxed (how taxes are levied and revenue spent is another question). Unless we put something in our bank account it remains empty. And so with religionists helpfulness depends upon what we put into it and continue to put into it. We may spend wisely or foolishly thereafter. After all, does not each community get the government it deserves or the religion it deserves, and so on? (Jan. 50)

32. Certain water creatures delight in adorning their shells with other shells, pebbles, leaves: often they will stick on another living creature without regard to its preferences or to the position it dislikes.

In the building of systems of relationships among humans, one may often see someone build into his scheme of things—his psychological house, or shelter, as it were—the personality of another. That other personality may, on occasion, scream and kick against finding himself used as a brick to build another's house, a tile to keep out the rain from another's room, a bronze ornament on another's chimney piece, more especially if he has been stuck on upside down out of disregards for his feelings, or to please the aesthetic sense of the first-named. That you are a brick in my house, or that I am one in yours is largely a matter of view point, once the building process has set in. (1947)

33. Philosophies are to experience as maps are to the countries they represent. They should help one to find one's way about, but even in this respect each is no more than symbolic. Philosophies have an ornamental value, too, just as maps have; and the latter are often elegant when framed and hung on the walls of rooms—used thus they serve quite another purpose. The prettiest are mostly those drawn to fancy on the basis of hearsay and those which are out of date. (1946)

34. A party was once given to which Charity was invited as a guest of honour. However as she had only the rags of humility to wear and came to the front door on foot, she was turned away by the footman when she asked to be admitted. Nobody noticed she was not there. (May 50)

35. When "duty" (as with "objective good and evil" and other such concepts) is brought into a discussion, beware! Mostly it is a means of getting you to work for some one else's benefit without repaying you for it. "Jones is not doing his duty by society," usually means: "I think if Jones were to do so and so instead of what he is doing, I should benefit. If you help me to persuade him we shall both benefit." (Apr. 50)

36. The food rotting in my guts provides me with the energy to play the harpsichord.

37. The humanitarian needs an oppressed proletariat. The ministering angel lives by suffering. Meekness only shines forth when abused by the angry. (Mar. 50)

38. What person or place or thing has benefited rather than

suffered by commerce and relations with me? But has anyone in their senses ever asked such a question? It can only be conducive to depression or complacency—and there is no conclusive answer. (Undated; 1950?)

39. What does one say to one who has lost all he ever valued—to a cripple—to one who knows he must die within a brief period? (1950)

40. Wandering in deserted places there are found many traces and tracks from which we deduce the movements of heroes and gods and so we weave history. Yet were our vision to become a little clearer we might discover that all these tracks are merely made by ourselves during our own earlier wanderings. (Mar. 50)

41. One can judge people's nature more reliably by the way they treat their immediate associates than by the feelings they voice towards humanity in general. (Aug. 50)

42. For someone who would like to get on* but cannot, the next best thing is to teach others how to do. (Aug. 50) *(*The insertion has been cancelled*:) or make spiritual progress.

43. It is impossible to please everybody, they say. And so that is perhaps why Saints who should be, one supposes, good enough to please everybody, are always dead. For then only the skeleton is left and everyone is free to make of them what he, in person, likes, and the Saints do not appear to confute such opinion. (Aug. 50)

44. The recognition of a saint (and not only of a saint) requires two things: that the saint should be held to behave within certain prescribed limits of behaviour, and that people should have the will and capacity to recognize such behaviour. (Aug. 50)

45. If you owe one a debt of gratitude, as in the case of any other kind of debt, it is better to avoid him until you can pay it off. (1950)

46. Those who set themselves a final goal secretly—may be unconsciously—dread the attainment of it. (Aug. 50)

47. Much of what is asserted as true is so asserted, not as a declaration of what the speaker knows but rather as a defence against doubt in the hope that the opposite proposition may be thereby excluded. (Nov. 50)

48. You will never meet with a saint by walking round the world looking for one; but you may do so if you sit in one place

and consider the matter. (Nov. 50)

49. One may suspect that people whom one sometimes meets on their trapsings from continent to continent, "looking for truth" are really like the man who searches his house for his spectacles which are all the time on his nose. But if he takes them off to look at them, he cannot see them for shortsightedness. (Nov. 50)

50. Suppose boredom is a backstairs to liberation—insignificant, and so often overlooked. No one who has not known its higher degrees can claim to have lived. Not the Relative Boredom of long waiting at junctions for railway connections on the way to visit friends—or the rashly accepted weekend with acquaintances—the reviewing of a dull book. In such Relative Boredom the "wasting-of-time"—feeling only heightens the enjoyment of the coming escape, the anticipation of which sustains us meanwhile.

Absolute Boredom is rather the pain of nausea, it is the loss of one's livelihood as for the pianist who loses his hands, the insatiable desire for what we know makes us sick, it is the Great Drought, the "Carnal physic for the sick soul," the Dark Night of the Soul after the climbing of Mount Carmel, it is the pillar of salt, the exile from the land which is no more, the Sin against the Holy Ghost, the break-up of patterns, the horror that waits alone in the night, the entry into the desert where Death mocks by serving one one's daily food and one cannot bear but to keep the darkness of one's own shadow before one for the very brightness of the light that reveals the universal emptiness. Do not try to turn back now—here in the desert perhaps there are doors open—in the cool woods they are overgrown, and in the busy cities they have built over them. (Mar. 50)

51. *Palliatives.* Such thoughts about death as: 'The end of it all,' 'Those whom the gods love die young,' 'a merciful release' etc; then such small dividends from the bankrupt estate as: work (I am always busy, you see), helping others (before learning how to help oneself or them), art ("it helps"), collections, Fitzrovia, Mont Martre and Parnasse, Via Margeritta, Bloomsbury and the Pheasantry, drink, travel, kindness to all except the human animals, kindness to humans one does not know personally, politics, utopias, teaching what one would like to, but cannot practise. (1950)

52. In the long run mostly one is not measured (either by others or by oneself) so much by one's best actions or by one's worst (though the latter are the more likely of the two to be remembered). It is rather the average level of all one has done and one's general tenor and tendencies and ways of reacting, the compass of one's moods and the emotional, moral, ethical, aesthetical and productive range that count, that censor all one's thoughts and acts. One can always try to leap to greater heights (and thereby risk coming down to earth more heavily). But what desperate work it is to try and displace in any direction the dead weight of one's average conduct. (1950)

53. Sometimes it is more difficult to sin than to be virtuous; though ability to do either does not ensure greatness, inability to do either is one of the signs of mediocrity. (Dec. 50)

54. From the 18th to the 20th Century it was the boast that human thought had at least come out of the dark woods of medieval superstition, credulity and obscurantism, into the sunshine of clear thinking where the dry breezes of scepticism blow unhindered. 'Fell the trees and level the hills that still obscure the view; let the winds drive off the mist.'—they said. But now that much of this work has been accomplished it is beginning to be felt that there is no shade in all these flat plains of perpetual, parching wind and sunshine, and through this desert no flooding Nile flows. There are those who, secretly, would like, if they could, to reconstruct the dim, wet, haunted woods before they die of thirst. (Mar. 50)

55. When people relate their symptoms to me I think of trees and of the cows that unscab their itchy backs on the bark of those trees.

56. Maturity seems to be merely a name for the doorway that leads out of adolescence into old age. (Jan. 51)

57. We have apparently to drink the wine of pleasure out of the cup of pain—and the cup remains. (Dec. 50)

58. Religion is the organization of hope. (Oct. 51)

59. Hope is killed by attainment. (Jan. 53)

60. The world is like a zoo where there are no spectators, only animals in cages—some can move their own cages from inside and

sometimes they play at being spectators. (Oct. 51)

61. People are often aggressively assertive in proportion to their inward doubts about the truth of their hopes. Here fear lends strength to rally to the defence of the hopes suspected to be illusory. (Oct. 51)

62. Wandering across a city—walking often quite alone, down dark alleys, through unfrequented districts and debouching suddenly onto main thoroughfares where for a spell one follows the main stream, is adopted by a group "he has come where we come from, wants to go where we want to go." For a while it is true but the side streets are there. Pause in one of them for a moment, and the stream has moved on. So, as there is no catching up with the group, there is no more reason to return to the main street than to wander away from it... more alleys... more thoroughfares.... Where shall we be sleeping tonight?... And those odd encounters of eyes in lonely alleys... (May 51)

63. When one brings out one of one's favourite paradoxes with the cliché, "I can never understand why ...," it is disconcerting when someone knows the solution and one is made to understand it, for a mental prop has been removed, a domestic mystery debunked, a painted window shown to be a mere piece of wall in the rational jail. When one asks (not wanting an answer) in some strange suburb, "I wonder what is round the bend?", it seems possible that there *might* be a forgotten palace or a volcano there, or the back stairs to hell, yet people are mostly only too anxious to show you how homogeneous and respectable the suburb is. (May 51)

64. Let us define religion as the organization of hope in such wise that all hopes are arranged as lesser hopes subordinated to one supreme hope which is of such a nature that, while it *seems* realizable, it cannot be realized now. In communism the "fading away of the state," and in the old religions "heaven" and "the life to come" are like a rainbow (it has a treasure hidden at its base), clearly visible, but moves away as you approach. In fact the very essence is unrealizability *now*. As far as the average man is concerned, the realization of the final aim means existence without hope which is shunned as futile despair and a horrible living death. Yet scarcely any one asks himself why he drags his heavy load of

hope around. (Oct. 51)

65. Like the drop of ink in the glass of water and the drop of water in the glass of ink, an evil doer does not purify his reputation with one good act, but the virtuous man ruins his reputation by one bad action. So evil would seem more effective than good. Odd that the world is not worse than it is. (Apr. 51)

66. A man went to a theatre, but when he thought it was time to leave he found that the real audience was elsewhere and he was part of a show containing the piece he had come to see. (Nov. 50)

67. Charity and a party of other virtues went for a trip to heaven. They got hungry and were served in a cafe with ambrosia and nectar. Now the virtues live on special diets. Charity looked at her plate and said: "I must be served with poverty or I shall starve. But there is none here." Love said he needed separation. Hope wanted privation. Patience wanted adversity. Humility abuse, etc., etc. "Come," said Charity, "We shall all starve here as we can't get our special diets." The others agreed and they returned to earth where there was a plentiful supply of special food for each. (Nov. 50)

68. Pursuit of the "fascinating" difference of people leads to the discovery of the "appalling" sameness of people. "Fascinating" because one always hopes to meet the marvellous person who will be "radically different," and eventually one's search establishes the fact that people are but slight variations on the same human theme and it is "appalling" to find that the search was simply a flight from the monotony. (Nov. 51)

69. So much can be done by teachers for others—but what can others do for teachers? (Apr. 52)

70. Greek and Roman pagan thought is like the dry light of noon between dark nights. Early Christian thought is like a burning(?) fire in a vast moonless night. The Roman Catholic Church today is like a gas-lit street at mid-winter dusk in a foggy city. (Oct. 50)

71. Funny how many claim to have the key to unlock the secrets of the universe—but where are those who will show, by example, where is the keyhole for their key? (Dec. 51)

72. Europe has been kissed by History with a sore upon her lips. (May 51)

73. The average man's compulsive urges mostly pay him

enough wages to live on. (May 52)

74. Intellect is like the dry land—by itself, without the rain drawn from the sea, it is like a barren desert. Feeling or emotion, is like the ocean—by itself also a desert of waves. They may cooperate as where Western Europe meets the Atlantic, or they may remain aloof and indifferent as on the shores of the Sahara. (1951)

75. It is my ambition to attain to obscurity. (Jan. 52)

76. All these things one gets attached to are continually letting one down by changing or dying or getting destroyed, or if it seems not, it is because one has oneself let them down by oneself changing or falling sick or dying. (Mar. 52)

76a. What does one get from company? Two things apparently, firstly more stable and certain conditions of living than man as constituted can get by himself (mostly man dies by starvation or something if entirely isolated), and secondly a certain shake-up of ideas which is brought about by signs coming to one from "outside" (other people) in a different order than one is able to think up for oneself. That would seem to be all. But one has to pay through the nose for these. (May 52)

77. The beauty of the world sometimes seems to hang about it like the shapes fancied in the pale coils of vapour exhaled by a midden on a still autumn evening. (May 52)

78. There was never any time when the mortality of physical infants was as low as now—yet with present-day enthusiasm for throwing away bath water, the mortality among metaphorical babies was probably never so high. (May 52)

79. If one has not attained any superiority over the average it looks silly to run down average people—and if one does obtain superiority there is no need to do so. Carping is the last desperate attempt at self-justification. (Apr. 52)

80. It has been discovered that the flowering and fruiting of plants depends upon the right proportional length of night to day—and so too one might say that for a man's personality to flower and fruit there is needed the right proportion between the daylight of reason and the night of emotion. (Apr. 52)

81. Though we are often willingly exhorted by moral biologists to despise the parasitism of cuckoos and mistletoe and

tapeworms, the unprogressive and reactionary outlook of king-crabs, lamp shells and club moss, the antisocial venomenousness of snakes and nettles, the contemptuous and hostile seclusion of euphorbiae and cacti, yet it would seem that nature, with all her ruthlessness, is more tolerant here than they. (Apr. 52)

82. A dead dog washed up on the lake shore; a large water lizard (the kind whose skin is made into handbags and shoes) puts its head into the mouth, between the teeth like jasmine buds, pulls out the soft tongue and gulps it down. It squeezes up to the shoulders through rents in the throat and gorges itself on the rotting guts inside. White fragrant flowers fall from the shore trees above. (Apr. 52)

83. I should like to be sure that there was someone I had met or had known, who was, on balance, better off for the acquaintance. But how to know this?

84. I should like to be reasonably confident of dying quietly without remorse for what was done badly or wrong, regarding it as the result of honest mistakes; and without regret for anything at all left behind. (Mar. 52)

84a. Will the Behaviourist view of the mind one day seem as quaint as Cosmas' description of the world seems to us? (Jul. 52)

85. Nobody, I think, has actually said "The Kingdom of hell is within you"—perhaps because it is so obviously true that it does not need saying. The only new factor the idea of hell (the Christian one anyway) adds to the horrors that from time to time make their appearance in the world, is that of everlastingness—which shows nothing but man's vindictiveness. (1951)

86. Under the bushes in the dusk a land rail—not fugitive nor unfriendly. Neatly dressed in sober subdued colours as usual with its kind; this one in dark grey with russet head and striped pants; oversized shanks and toes. Prudent, grave and judicious; middle-class, unafraid, skilfully avoiding the inappropriate and the exaggerated,—the simple, Quaker-like humility a little studied? No use for "art"—see the huge, shapeless but so serviceable nest, and the complacent delight in its "song" which so nearly resembles the cries of a dying pig. (Mar. 50)

87. Are not these tropical bookworms that drill through the

pages from cover to cover wiser than we—better off in knowing only how to eat books than we who know only how to read them? We read and mark—they inwardly digest. (May 52)

88. When all one's associates go away for a holiday and leave one behind, one has a holiday oneself without the bother of travelling. (Apr. 52)

88a The two opposed theories of the course of mankind—the past fall from grace, the present downward drive to the sordid end among the worms in slime and darkness and entropy—or the upward development from the insipid simplicity of grubs with triumphal progress up through the hopeful present to the golden wonders of the future superman (or) superdivine.

If a man believes the first he can die like he who gets his ship and cargo into port before the winter gales set in. If he believes the second he can die like a man who is sent to a concentration camp and sees his bride carried off the day before his wedding. (May 52)

89. Let us say I have come from Camden Town. I am in Oxford Street for half an hour looking for a shop to buy a toy and then I have to go on to a room in Lambeth. What has it to do with me if Oxford Street traces its beginnings in the Bucks and Oxon countryside and if its progress eastwards leads on to the blank walls of the Bank of England?

What actual value or bearing has the progress of the race through future centuries—even if it were true—to a mortal with a hundred years' life span? Is this what they offer for sale now as immortality? (May 52)

90. When we are young the noise of general conversation seems much the most fun. When we grow up we discover the possibilities of the tête-à-tête. In maturity the monologue habit sets in. But now at last there is the chance to investigate the rich depth of the silence when the monologue is suspended. (May 52)

91. If I must believe in something, let me believe in the next world—not in this death's antechamber. For if this world is good and true then death must be horrible—and it is the only thing that is certain. (1948)

92. Man has got bored with prostrating himself before god, so he now indulges his need for self-prostration by doing so to the

state or to the material world of the five senses, worshipping them, according to his new, creed, as his omnipotent master. Men like to worship a master because this gives them authority to exercise power over others in the Master's name. (Aug. 52)

93. The sweetest words are those not spoken. (Aug. 52)

94. The past is full of people who have made portentous and menacing utterances for which they have claimed the authority of god. They do the same now but claim the authority of the people and the state. (Sep. 52)

94a That is mere escapism" they say—but if they were suddenly to believe there really was an escape, are we to suppose they would not take it? (Sep. 52)

95. The bars of one's prison are the people around one—and I, too, am a bar in each of their prisons. Much of the 'help' we give each other is just cement to fix the bars more firmly. (Sep. 52)

96. I cannot see:

why it is better that there are *more* people in the world at a given time (is Belsen *full* better than Tristan da Cuñha?);

that the trend of evolution needs must coincide with the direction I or any one would like it to be taking, nor that its goal (if any) is mine or theirs.

97. What should a compassionate man do who sees a savage tiger about to eat poisoned meat? (Oct. 52)

Or who when walking beside a deep and dangerous river, and unable to swim, sees a man drowning in the middle of the swift current? Ought one to walk beside such rivers?

98. The voices of jungle birds—like concert flutes in the hands of idiot children. (Oct. 52)

99. Worship of an anthropomorphic god is merely a form of narcissism and worship of the state is the same only more of a close-up. (Oct. 52)

99. Worship of an anthropomorphic god is merely a form of narcissism and worship of the state is the same only more of a close-up. (Oct. 52)

100. Autumn hush in an English August. Transparency, loneliness, small distant sounds, stillness of (departing) summer, not-yet-ness of (coming) winter. (Nov. 52)

101. When I have to make up my mind, I am forced, like Mark

Twain, to think I must have a great deal of mind for it to take so long to make it up. But when I give someone even a little piece of my mind, I seem to have not enough left for myself. (Jan. 53)

102. The potentialities of any situation are, as it were, its womb full of litter. When we say "a choice has been made," we are indeed stating that these offspring having matured, one of them has overcome the others and, in order to be able to express itself in the stream of actuality, to get chosen, it has had to kill them and devour their substance. For if once one choice has been made all other potential choices are irretrievably lost. But to suspend choice would be to suspend the flow of becoming. And so this cannibalism seems essential to becoming. (Jan. 53)

103. What bores me is that whenever I look at anything I am precluded for just that amount of time from looking, at anything else. (Jan. 53)

104. The invading platitudes that advance like sand dunes in the desert and bury the oases. (Jan. 53)

105. One's physical body lives inside the protection of its skin; and one's mental body, as it were, lives inside the protection of its skin of fixed concepts. Just as one's physical body heaves earth about with a spade, grows vegetables and cooks itself meals of physical food, so one's mental body heaves ideas around, grows notions and cooks itself mental meals of definitions, purposes and aims which keep it going. (Jan. 53) (Later addition) Then there is the lavatory side of the simile.

106. Eternity is a finite concept which is perhaps why Blake said that "eternity is in love with the productions of time." These oppositions live on the borders, as it were, half beyond the horizon of one's experience and they depend of the fact that I am I, and have an horizon to my field of experience, and that there has to be a beyond to it. (Jan. 53)

107. This age is the age of spring cleaning ... spring after spring, and the furniture gets shabbier and shabbier and has to be replaced, and the walls get filthy and have to be repainted, and the tiles fall off and have to be put back, and the owners grow old and are succeeded by their heirs, and the house falls down and has to be rebuilt, and the state collapses and has to be reformed, and the

world economic system gets out of date and has to be remodelled, and the world sources of supply dry up and new ones have to be found, and the sun cools down and the solar system gets deranged... It is the "progress" which keeps you where you are; and the whole thing is kept going by hope and fear, dangling their carrots and cracking their whips. (Jan. 53)

108. Life and the world and oneself are nothing but a vast tautology. (Jan. 53)

109. There are three ways of feeling low, or levels of fatigue (and they can all happen at once): physical, for which one takes rest and tonics; mental, for which one changes one's environment and habits; and spiritual (which, is perhaps comparable to what the last surviving inhabitant of an oasis being blotted out by sand—in modern parlance, a "displaced person"—might feel), for which one takes time. In all three cases one hopes the remedy will be effective. (Jan. 53)

110. Three kinds of people: Those who seem nicer when absent than when present, the opposite kind, and those who are equal present or absent. (Jan. 53)

111. Dogmas are like stays to sustain a sagging understanding. But as they hold one up so too they hold one back. (Jan. 53)

112. One may distinguish at least five layers in the mental ocean: (1) the public stratum of communicated reasoning and as much of the emotions as is communicable or convenient to communicate, (2) the bedroom layer, private to couples, (3) the evident personally private layer, private to oneself because incommunicable or inconvenient to communicate, (4) the lower personal layer half glimpsed, half inferred, incommunicable, (5) the supposed "unconscious depths" postulated in order to explain inconsistencies,—like phlogiston?

On the surface of it all reason floats like the unsupported layer of plankton. The great Philosophical Systems, the great Religions and Political Civilizations grow like organized mats of sargasso, heaving and drifting with the swell and the currents of the lower layers dissolving away. On the plankton reasoning birds walk, feed and so on. (Jan. 53)

113. One's life is like a jaunt in a car running without brakes

down a long hill towards a chasm. It makes little difference who drives it, for in any attempt to turn it round uphill its own momentum will overturn it and send it rolling down towards the same abyss. Skilful driving, only averts the overturn. (Jan. 53)

114. A man's life is like a day's journey travelled, westwards and facing always the way one has come. In the morning the field of experience is bright, simple and—dazzling. Shadows are thrown by the sun from things already past and known and they need no interpreting—and there is nothing to hinder fancying the future. But after midday the sun gets ahead and there begin to fall—into the field of vision shadows of things before they are seen, some of which can be recognized as similar to things already known, but others not. And now the future journey depends on how these shadows are interpreted before the things which cast them—are encountered. And as the day draws on the shadows get longer and more intricate. And meanwhile, as when looking back from a car travelling down a long avenue of trees that are slipping by, the trees appear to get rapidly smaller as they recede, but distant hills behind in the background, though receding too, seem, by contrast with the shrinking trees, to be getting larger and larger. (Jan. 53)

115. If people's lives were adequate there would be no need for them to go hunting outside themselves and their surroundings by reading novels, going to cinemas, football matches and other forms of hero worship, and, vicarious life. At different times self-discontented people have admired kings and aristocracy, man in the street and workers, farmers, govt. officials, the rich, the poor, the good old times, the good time to come, saints, foreigners, travel, mountains, the sea, the country, the city, this world, the other world, the West End, the East End, round the corner, humanism, satanism, solitude, company—but never what a man is himself now. (Apr. 51–Jan. 53)

116. Why are the rich rich? Because society as it constitutes itself, by consenting to their status, is in fact paying them wages for the qualities it recognizes (the wisdom or folly of society of so doing is not at issue here). But this being so the rich then claim intrinsic worth not based on the society on which their status depends, and they fancy they have independent ownership of their

wealth. Forgetting their position is supported by society they bully it. For a while society seems to like it but later it turns and rends them. But in so doing it seems to be punishing them for its own stupidity and deficiencies—after which it pays others to be rich, and so this process goes on. (Feb. 52)

117. What moved unicellular amoebas to amalgamate themselves into multi-cellular units like hydra and volvox? And multi-cellular units into societies of units like the Portuguese man of war? Was it boredom? And in the transitional stage did they live in loose societies like sponges or like termites or like us? And came to sell themselves to that association for their livelihood? And did they evolve a means of communication by which they exchanged experiences, built up a body of knowledge, and dominated each other, thus excreting a psychological glue in which they got trapped into new emergent complex units from which there was no longer an escape, except by the death of the unit which, as simple cells they had no necessity to know? An amoeba's death is an accident, not a necessity, but to a complex unit death comes both as an accident and as a necessity. Are we heading towards new emergent complexities which will produce a new emergent kind of death? Up to now it has been an instantaneous affair but might we not invent a kind which lasts—a real "living death"? (Oct. 52)

118. What is the matter with edifying poems (Tagore's *Upagupta* for instance)? Does it fail on the highest level because it assumes the necessity (the "rightness") of suffering without which the virtue, say, of unselfish service, collapses for want of anything to serve? No one need deny that suffering will be *lessened* if the sick are helped, and if prisoners help each other (though a study of man's behaviour indicates this solution is less simple than it appears on the surface), but are we to adopt as the ultimate principle that the disease ought to be maintained so that there may be sick to serve—that all people ought to be kept in prison that they may need each others' help; or, on the contrary, are we to adopt the principle that while it is good to help it is better to cure the disease and remove the necessity for prisons, so that help will no longer be necessary. Advocates of the former principle *against* the latter are in fact arguing that all physicians and surgeons should stop their

work and become nurses instead. (Jan. 52)

119. There are those who like distant pen-friends whom they haven't met better than neighbours whom they have. (Jan. 53)

120. Just as one can arrange bits of iron, etc., into a hermetically sealed box which imprisons other pieces of matter, so one can arrange thoughts into a box too, which effectively imprisons other thoughts. (Jan. 53)

121. There seem to be three main kinds of intoxicants or "opiates." The physical ones, and religion, and politics. The former kind is just as popular as ever, but the last seems to be ousting the second (philosophy and works, precept and practice, etc. are subsumed under one of the latter two mostly). The ordinary man absolutely needs one of the three to screen from him the vision of the futility of life and the world. (Jan. 53)

122. It is rather more usual in these times for men to be betrayed by their countries than for them to betray their countries, which is why there are so many "displaced persons." (Apr. 53)

123. In their high chilly palaces in heaven they need the fires of hell to warm them.

If there were no heaven for its whole weight to press down on hell, the fires of hell would expand and cool down, and its inhabitants would have nothing to hate and envy any more. The wardens of hell would be out of a job, displaced persons and the inhabitants of hell would have none to look after them. (May 53)

124. The past is the cesspit of the eaten, digested and excreted future. Like trees well-rooted in their own decayed leaves, we fruit best when deeply rooted in our own past. (May 53)

125. Little boats of thought go fishing from time to time on the waves of the emotions. (Jan. 53)

126. In all the hells that all the religions have described, this sameness and lack of originality is the most striking thing. (Jan. 53)

127. Interpretative thoughts settle on a bare sensory perception like a swarm of blue-bottles on an open wound. (Jan. 53)

128. There is no need to wear one's deeds like medals. One can be just as much mentally nouveau-riche as financially. (Jan. 53)

129. One of the most remarkable facts of this age is the negligible direct personal power which scientists have in the

control of the world's affairs. The marvellous means they so successfully produce are always used by non-scientists against whom the scientists themselves seem to be powerless and even purposeless. What clever sheep they are. (Jul. 53)

130. It is not memory that is the 'positive' achievement but 'forgetting.' It is not strange that we remember so many things—what is strange is that we can forget anything: it is strange and it is an achievement. The moments of happiness in this world are achieved by (consciously or not) blotting out the disagreeable impressions and memories when agreeable ones are present. (Aug. 53)

131. The world as a mass of lies all struggling with each other to become true. (Oct. 53)

132. How much better to be neglected than championed or abused by the wrong people. (Nov. 53)

133. While Continental European Thought favours great philosophical systems built up according to a plan and founded on a central purpose, English thought has favoured the practical, the empirical—bodies of partially coordinated techniques for living and thinking, leaving the central purpose of life unstated—as something almost indecent to inquire into what purpose has been half instinctively referred (when necessity arose) to the Church and the Divine Right of Kings, the individual conscience of a man (the inner voice), the course of nature (progress and natural selection), public opinion, the statistical average, the Great Mathematician, genes—actually these are no more than painted panels on a sealed *cassone* for which there are many keys, but which has no lock. (Nov. 53)

134. The world of what is there, is perpetually haunted by what is not there—what is not, but might be, there; what could not, but ought to be, there. (Nov. 53) (*Pencil note*:—What is there? No answer.)

135. Truth is like the black background behind the stars (because it is ungraspable). Beauty is like the beam that goes out from a search light—because it goes out from the subject and illuminates some objects, leaving others in darkness—and it has no effect on the black background behind the stars. (Nov. 53)

136. Curious that I seem to feel most at home when abroad. (Nov. 53)

137. I have a working principle—which sometimes paralyzes many of my impulses to action—that it is wrong (i.e., will lead only to failure to attain what one expects)—to take any action that is inspired or suggested by or has as its principal motive, opposition to (that is desire to snub or provoke or impress) someone else, (or even in its most general sense perhaps) one of the elements needed to avoid disappointment seems to be action taken for reasons which are "at right angles" to personal agreement or disagreement. (Nov. 53) (*Pencil note:* In brief; don't act out of spite?—I suppose so.)

End of the First Note Book

The Second Note Book

138. Harmony illuminated by consciousness casts a shadow of disharmony. Power illuminated by consciousness casts a shadow of impotence. Non-being illuminated by consciousness casts a shadow of being ... (Nov. 53)

139. Some time this century, I was told, the Houses of Parliament, as the dominant governing body of the Church of England, enacted that Anglicans need not believe in Hell. I have often wondered what happened in the Anglican Heaven after that. Have the heavenly palaces (or clouds), which had till then been conveniently warmed by central heating—they are so high up—from the eternal fires of Hell now put out by man, been growing gradually cold (like London in the early months of 1947 when there was a blizzard and no coal)? And so the Anglican Heaven must now be frozen quite stiff, and no one can get into or out of it. And all the bad people, like the good, have to be reborn on earth again as men—after all they must be reborn somewhere, and if there is no Hell or Heaven any more, where else? And that will then obviously go on forever and ever ... Unless perhaps the British Parliament re-establishes belief in Hell. (Dec. 53)

140. Religion according to Marx is an opiate for the masses; but Marx being more up to date than the old religions gives them morphia instead. (Jan. 54)

141. Facts are the one thing I do not believe in (any way there is no need). I have, admittedly, to "deal with facts" (so has a lunatic with his hallucinations); but that is no reason at all that I should believe in them (like the lunatic). A. N. Whitehead, the great mathematician—who I feel was a Protestant Archbishop *manqué*—often appeals to "stubborn facts" as the last authority, with a sort of unctuous worship. In this he exemplifies, I think, a disease of the modern mind, the tendency to indulge in masochistic orgies of prostration before the whip of its own contradictory sense

experience—another kind of flight from oneself. (Dec. 53)

142. I met a daddy-long-legs today, but not quite the kind one is used to. Though its body and wings were the ordinary size and shape, its legs were a full 3" long, thin as 100% cotton, with a baroque curve, and clothed in black-and-white-banded football stockings. It was like one of those creatures in Dali's Temptation of St. Anthony. A product of natural selection? Nonsense. Made by a Creator then? But why not the third possibility, that its family had always been interested in being different, and had worked it all out themselves? "Let us show them" I can hear them saying. Now, darling, you must do like this always, and get your children to, too... (Jan. 54)

143. The sun sees no shadows. (Jan. 54)
The shadow sees no sun. (Feb. 57)
I see the shadow and the sun—who sees me? (Jun. 58)

144. If I say in the morning "I believe in God" and in the evening "I do not believe in God," I am untrue to my belief and renounce my consistency, but preserve my freedom. If I keep to one assertion, I am true to my belief and preserve my consistency, but renounce my freedom. To be free is to be "untrue." (Jan. 54)

145. A half-truth is more effective—more deadly, says the moralist—than a lie, because the element of truth convinces and with the help of that conviction the false element goes deeper. (Jan. 54) (*Later addition*:) What *is* a half-truth? What is *Truth*?

146. In the 19th century there were the interdependent three coordinates of three-dimensional space, and there was time, and there were conscious observers. In the 20th century there are the interdependent four coordinates of the space-time continuum, and there are the conscious observers. Will it one day be seen that there are only the interdependent five coordinates of the space-time-continuum-observed-by-some-consciousness, and no unrelated extras lying around? It seems unarguable that any event necessitates a position in three-dimensional space, at a moment in time, from an affective-volitional conscious standpoint. The five must go together, and failing any one of the five there is (bar of artificial abstraction) nothing to talk about at all.

"Ah," they say, "but what about records taken of events which nobody was watching? That proves that things happen independently of an observer." Actually it proves nothing of the kind. It only raises a fundamental aspect of conscious experience: that any given experience consists of two elements—what is actually sensed, let us say, and what is "interpreted from" that 'basic sensum.' If I see a tree, shut my eyes and do not see the tree, and open my eyes and see the tree, I say that the tree 'was there' when my eyes were shut, but it 'was there unobserved.' If other people with eyes open or with cameras, tell me it was there, or produce a photograph of it, at the time my eyes were shut, this is simply a new experience which, by inference, I relate to the eyes-open experience of the tree, and which I build into the 'eyes-shut-tree-still-there' concept. A tree that 'is there' unobserved cannot inherently be *known* other than by inferential knowledge, and that is ipso facto on a different level to the knowledge of the direct experience of 'eyes-open-tree-observed' experience. No amount of witnesses or records of a mechanical nature affect this principle at all. They are simply further 'direct-eyes-open-observed' experiences which the mind makes use of to strengthen its inferential (transcendental in the existentialist sense, perhaps) concept. (Feb. 54)

147. What is one going to do if the scientists produce a 'new' and 'superior' species of man?—superior in whose opinion?—And (which is really frightening) if they find the means to avoid the inevitability of death? (Feb. 54)

148. How much of what I think or say or do arises out of agreement with, or opposition to, what other people say or do, and is not spontaneous? (Feb. 54)

148. How much of what I think or say or do arises out of agreement with, or opposition to, what other people say or do, and is not spontaneous? (Feb. 54)

149. If you are not master of the facts they will beat you down with opinions. If you are not master of the void they will beat you down with facts. (Feb. 54)

150. One is constantly encountering the limitedness of universal principles, also the secondariness of first principles. (Feb. 54)

151. There is no *creation*—only conversion of matter over which the mind dances a new dance. (Mar. 54)

152. Just as a flock of geese is led by a gander, so, it would seem, it is a flock of proper geese that is led by propaganda. (Mar. 54)

153. There are two reasons for disliking people (wanting to get away from their society): because they behave objectionably, and because they make one behave objectionably oneself. The opposite holds good too. But there is no 'behaviour' when one is alone. (May 54)

154. It is not, it seems to me, possible to draw a distinction between what is "absolutely new" and what is "absolutely forgotten (and revived again)". Then what is utterly forgotten and has left no trace, never has been? Of course, because it is a contradiction anyway. (May 54)

155. Cats and dogs throw some light on one's relation to others. They are both essentially conscious of others and their behaviour is all influenced by that. They both value others opinion desperately though probably they would not admit it. But there is an essential difference between them. A dog assumes that its welfare depends on others' good opinion of it, so it seeks to find out what that opinion is, it becomes domesticated by trying to sell itself, to serve, and so it is essentially guided and hampered by the concept of duty. Its fundamental anxiety is that it will have failed to interpret what others want of it and that they may consequently abandon it as useless. A dog's sense of dignity is quite secondary. A dog often apologizes. The "good" clever dog is conscientious and earnest. The "bad" stupid dog is resentful and clumsily savage. Dogs do not mind being vulgar by day. Dogs are jolly. I suspect Pekineses know all this, which may be a reason why they are not like other dogs.

A cat assumes that its welfare can be bettered by others' good opinion. It studies how that good opinion can be created and exploited. It pretends to become domesticated by buying one's opinion with systematic flattery. Yet while it actually serves no one but itself and knows it, it puts across a very successful line of make believe about service in catching mice, etc. But no cat will trade or barter or apologize. It is guided by expediency. But it is always concerned about whether the impression it wants to create has been put across successfully and so it is constantly conscious of its own appearance and often anxious about it. It is haunted by the fear of being seen, not as a fraud, which it is not, but in some light which would be incompatible with its own good opinion of itself and undermine its carefully maintained self-confidence and composure. Being ignominiously chased is for it much worse than being killed, and dignity is valued higher than life. The "good" clever cat is skilful and elegant. The "bad" stupid cat is clumsy and dirty. Cats are only vulgar (and how!) at night. Perhaps Siamese cats know all this too, which may be a reason why they are a sort of feline Pekinese. Cats are cosy but aloof. To refer to dogs as "he" and to cats as "she" is very misleading. And cats are not "catty" about each other.

There is another point of difference: a dog is not only concerned to discover its human patron's opinion of it and to "serve" that; but it is also interested that other dogs should know about this, and it is also interested in other dogs' behaviour and personalities: "Smell me and I will smell you." To a cat, on the other hand, other cats are altogether an accidental feature of its world ("love" apart—by day, at least), and unless actively in the way, they form absolutely no part of its life. So a dog may go about as one of a group or a pack either a leader or led; but not so a cat. (Jun. 54)

156. Can one wonder at the picture of confusion man presents. He chooses as his herald of peace the dove, a singularly quarrelsome and disagreeably selfish and greedy bird, as anyone who has kept turtles will know. He takes the bee's honey, mocks them for being "busy," and praises ants, mindless, mechanical, vitriol-throwing, hag-ridden ants, as his ideal of thrift. (Jun. 54)

157. I find puns more important than facts. The Catholic Church, says Joyce, was founded upon a pun (the Rock of Peter). But that apart, there is hardly anything we do or think that has not a double meaning. (Jun. 54)

158. It is our eyes that blind us and our ears that deafen us. (Jun. 54)

159. Let us define suicide as a "half=death"—the death of the object while the subject lives, or vice-versa: an extreme choice, the

result of the extremity of conflict.

Intellectualism or rationalism kills the object by cutting it up with analysis, and so, in the extreme, what is left is perfect vision and perfect darkness. Nothing can escape the eye and there is nothing left for it to see—"the living death of the subject."

Faith kills the subject by refusal to take account of the generality of experience and its trends and contradictions. The light of faith is focussed on one aspect only, whatever it may be, till the eye is burnt out and blinded. Nothing is left unilluminated in that object but there is no eye left to see it—"the living death of the object."

Actually both extremes imply a self-contradiction. But they are not equal. For if we take the two tendencies short of their extremes—the eye that has outgrown its object and the object that has outgrown its eye—the first eye-object relation gives us hunger and the second nausea. (Jun. 54)

160. It is certainly wrong to say pain and pleasure are equal and opposite. For suppose I am sitting feeling neither, I can always (so long as 'the nerves are functioning') be sure of causing pain by sticking a pin into myself. But the same does not apply to pleasure at all.

Suppose we distinguish (a) mental unpleasure and (b) mental pleasure as (provisionally) more or less opposites, and (c) physical pain and (d) physical ... yes, what? ... Well, certain kinds of excitement arising from touch (very provisional). The usual combinations (the obvious ones) are (a) (c) and (b) (d), the other two (a) (d) and (b) (c) also occur (unnoticed) as say guilt and sadism-masochism. The combinations (a present) (a past) and (b present) (b past) are obvious. The combinations (a present) (b past), another form of guilt and (b present) (a past) ... etc., etc. The point is that this analysis which is not carried far enough and is not accurate, is enough to show that the pleasure pain situation is not at all the simple matter it is supposed to be. (Jul. 54)

161. Hallucination I take to be meaningless, unless applied to "five-sense" experience. And on that basis I accept (pro tem) Whately Carington's description of "hallucination" and "genuine experience" as given in "Matter Mind and Meaning"—i.e., a

"genuine experience" is not distinguishable, if analysed, from a "completely organized hallucination." To mental images the term 'hallucination' is inapplicable: it can only signify five-sense experience that is not properly organized. (Jul. 54)

162. He lives in a room hung with luminous curtains by whose luminosity he is able to see: he sees his immediate surroundings, and he sees the curtains themselves moving and agitated, as though by the impact of bodies behind them—but with the raising of the curtains there is nothing but darkness. (Jul. 54)

163. Classical tragedy (according to Aristotle) is played upon the feelings strung between the opposites of pity and to terror. Existentialism seems to use the axis choice a man is forced to choose, terror. Existentialism seems to use the axis of choice—nausea (with the premise that a man is forced to choose to exercise his freedom).

164. If any 'progress' is to be made, it is by continuous vigilance over acts and by continuous re-examination of facts. (Sep. 54)

165. All governments are a symptom of a universal disease, the need to be governed; all governments are bad, and some are very bad. (Sept. 54)

166. With the spreading of the Northeast Asian prison and the American madhouse in this century's second half there will soon be no third choice left. Then there will be the question to decide (the decision perhaps not in one's own hands altogether) whether it is better to be an inmate or a warder—An inmate in America? A warder in Asia? or vice versa? (Oct. 54)

167. As to faith: to make a principle work, that is, to prove it by results—say to swim out of one's depth for the first time—requires absolute faith that the practice learned will preserve one from drowning. (Oct. 54)

Then I can only preserve my faith by not learning to swim. (Jun. 54)

168. The extending of knowledge tends to show that it is not possible to say of any principle 'This is *always* right' or of any generalization 'This is *always* true' though one can say 'mostly' or 'virtually every time.' (Oct. 54)

169. When I pursue the concept of God, the symbol with which the theological systems interpret the Mystic Experience, I

feel as if I were pursuing a rainbow. I see, as it were, the beckoning rainbow inviting the mind to obtain the tangible experience of touching something. But when I walk towards it through the rain, unlike a flowering tree, it recedes and then vanishes. Now for a rainbow I must have the sun behind and the rain in front. If I pursue the rainbow I shall go on getting wet. If I turn round no rainbow is visible. (11 Dec. 54)

170. Overtly wanting to be of use to others seems scarcely distinguishable from covertly wanting others to suffer and need one's help.

171. Heaven must be rather like a museum where our past love's and hope's fantasies are frozen and stored away behind glass, untouchable, in an air parched of the dampness of the suffering and change that lent them the illusion of life and reality. Everything we create for ourselves in this world we mentally kill and store away in heaven. (Dec. 54)

172. We survive in a narrow shifting territory between the dullness of order that drives the mind on towards the nauseating safety of absolute fixity, and on the other hand the excitement of disorder that sucks it towards the vertiginous thrill of being smothered by entropy. (Dec. 54)

173. The sort of person who provides unquestionable answers to unanswerable questions. (Nov. 54)

174. I am not so much interested in arguments that one ought to believe this or that, or to disbelieve it—but rather in the fact that one is forced by the nature of experience to believe or disbelieve (which is only a mode of belief). The octopus sucker must stick to something. (Dec. 54)

175. While every inference still smacks of fact, there is no fact not infected with inference. (Dec. 54)

176. A little chaos in the materialist order is like a drop of oil in a machine. (Dec. 54)

177. Though vision so much dominates our world, we nevertheless do not quite trust it and always seek to confirm it by touch; but when we touch something we look to see what it "is." (Dec. 54)

178. "The five senses are notoriously unreliable" they say; but they always put theory to experimental test.

179. Today's trite thought—so many people have said that the world is a prison, but I can never find out for certain who is supposed to be inside and who outside. (Dec. 54)

180. Any assertion that can be made can be contradicted. It is only by an appeal made to the empirical world (of probability, of things and events) that one side can be established against the other. All syllogistic proof rests on initial assumptions from empirical observation or arbitrary assertion. Where no appeal to empiricism is possible (as in metaphysics) it is impossible to establish one side of a contradiction against the other (unless one counts establishment to be exercise of force and violence and physical elimination of physical opponents). (Jul. 60)

181. It is a mistake to compromise with the Devil and not with man. The alternative is an angry man with compromised principles. (Jan. 55)

182. Just as the word "floating" signifies at its simplest a complex—at least a liquid volume with a surface against a gaseous volume and a solid (or oily) entity to float on the surface between the two volumes: so experience always, even at its simplest, implies a complex—a manifold subjectively organized in or against a manifold objectively organized with a surface dividing them, the surface being indescribable in terms of either manifold except as 'not' or 'nothing.' (Jan. 55)

183. Doing one's duty consists in doing as the majority are supposed to do. (Feb. 55)

184. Faith seems to be the subjective counterpart of Truth, which is objective. Speaking in terms of 'things' they describe 'the same thing' from opposite sides; but I take 'things' to be mental constructs out of the welter of the 5-sense data. (Mar. 55)

185. Absolute Truth would be incompatible with life as absolute light would be with vision. (Mar. 55)

186. The philosopher's function seems to be to substitute for the experiential 'almost' and 'mostly' the words 'entirely' and 'always,' upon which the fiction of the 'absolute' grows. (Jan. 55)

187. Marvellously at variance—the two basic doctrines of today: Evolution and Equality of Man. If man is evolving how can all men be simultaneously equal? (Worship of progress and of the

average). (Mar. 55)

188. Poverty looks bright through rich glasses, and vice versa. (Aug. 54)

189. I have always felt doubtful about those people who try to get one to give up one's own bunkum and accept their debunkum instead. (Mar. 55)

190. The subject is ultimately at the mercy of the objective world: others can kill me without any possibility of my being sure of preventing them; but I cannot ever kill all others however much I might want to, supposing that I did. I exist therefore because others do not bother to blot me out, but the converse cannot be said of others. (Mar. 55)

191. The conventional attitude of 'serious' people to puns (the Utraquistic Device) is hostility: how irrational (it is) has been shown by James Joyce. Perhaps when the psychology of Western philosophy has been worked out a little more it may show why there is this hostility. For the pun reveals an inherent duplicity in the workings of consciousness which the conventional Western moralist is loath to admit. (Mar. 55)

192. It is usual to regard thought and action as having two basic modes: reason and impulse (or emotion or feeling). There is also a tendency to set one against the other and to argue on the lines of 'he who is not with us is against us' in this dualism. But there are at least three such basic modes: reason, impulse and observation. The overlooking of observation (which is the basic motive of the true scientist who has no theoretical or moral axe to grind) is, it seems to me, an absolute block in the way of behaving fairly or neutrally or seeing clearly. For there is nothing so unreasonable as rationalism carried to extremes, and impulse gets bogged down in slush. But how can a bad observer ever hope to get what he wants or even begin to know what he wants? The double conception of rationality/emotionality gives rise to cruel confusions. None is ever quite pure or quite absent, but one usually dominates and exploits the other.

The word "Truth" has a different referent for these three types: consistency for the rationalist, correspondence of idea and the observed for the observer, and perhaps certainty or beauty for the emotionalist. The first tends to 'inject' the objective into the subject and the last to 'project' the subjective onto the object. (Mar. 55)

193. Exercise: Put every statement in this book into the form 'if ... then'; if not already so stated. Where the 'if' is not explicit, find it. —But how difficult! —But how necessary! (Jun. 55)

194. Theistic contemplation seems to be inseparable from disguised narcissism. Advaita Vedanta tries to escape from that by postulating absolute unity and absolute loss of the individual in the whole. But in order to lose personal identity and at the same time save the whole that opposes it, the Advaita Vedanta cheats. Both Christian and other theism and Advaita Vedanta are haunted by the spectre of Nothingness which they cannot cope with. (Jun. 55)

195. Important to be clear and ruthless in one's categories and types, but to remember that no living person is ever a type; for that is impossible from the very fact that he is living, and so both inconstant and with infinite qualities. So no compromise with types, but always compromise at some level with individual persons. (Jul. 55)

We said this of the Devil above; but types are the Devil.

196. Science's dislike of faith is obscene to religion Miracles are obscene to scientists.

It is an error to confound the obscene with the merely sexually indecent. The former includes the latter, but the latter is usually allowed to obscure the profounder and more alarming regions of obscenity that threaten to undermine being. (Jun. 55)

197. The morning weeps tears of dew for the descent of evening. (Jun. 55)

198. At sunset another day bleeds to death. (Jul. 55)

199. While the materialists shout progress the physicists say that the sun will cool down sometime and the earth will become uninhabitable through cold and dark. (June 55)

200. The better I can tell what you do the less I can tell what you are; for by your doing you change and so are no more what you were. (Jun. 55)

201. He is sometimes insincere for God's sake. (Jun. 55)

202. *Love*: The desparateness of separation.
Hate: The desparateness of association.

But I do not see any exact opposites in the world: there is always some little corner of common neutral ground where the spies and traitors can come and go and do their fecund work. (Jul. 55)

203. The essence of conversing mostly consists in throwing disguises to your opposite number and trying to get him to put them on, and vice versa. (Jun. 55)

204. O poverty that blights* the corn / for making bread to feed the hand / that writes the cheque to pay the tax / that funds the cost of all the fees for adolescent education / wars and doles (that keep adults from starving). (Jun. 55) **Superscribed in pencil*: sows? reaps?

205. Pascal provides an example of an intellectual boat constructed in which to sail out on the sea of fever and pain in order to look for a port on a fancied further shore. Pascal's boat was a boat for one; but his plan has served the adherents of the great systems as an inspiration to gang up and build prison ships. We think we have actually seen many boats wrecked, far more *vanish*, but none reach the other shore. (Jun. 56)

206. If I declare on my authority alone I stand small chance of convincing them—why should they choose to be my mental slaves? If I declare on your authority alone or you on mine, or we on ours together, there is likewise not much chance of convincing them. But if I or you or we declare on his authority the situation is quite altered; for it is an invitation to them to be like me or you or us and for all of us equally to be his mental slaves and so each others' slaves. It is the same whether "he" is the expounder of a religion a political dogmatist for "us," or whether for him "he" is God or nature or the state. The structure is essentially the same. (Jul. 55)

207. Pleasure and pain seem to be *opposites* in the sense that crocuses and steam rollers are opposites. (Jul. 55)

208. Social reformers always speak in Universals—and universals are false because all our lives are particular. (Jul. 55)

209. I might die in (the first half of) 1957. (Aug. 55) That hunch was wrong. (1958)

210. It is most difficult to be natural. It is most unnatural to be normal.

211. Authoritative people bore me: but what bores me even more are those swarms of little people who love authority and in

virtue of whom the authority of the authoritative can be exercised. (Aug. 55)

212. One shares some public preferences with an acquaintance. One shares many public and some private prides and preferences with a friend. One shares these and some private hates and shames with an intimate. (Aug. 55)

213. Those who lead public religious lives honestly can have no intimates. (Aug. 55)

214. The Indian mind being brought up in an atmosphere of tropical amorphous jungle, expresses itself in patterns, which repeat. The European mind, being brought up in an atmosphere of open, orderly-patterned vistas, experiences itself in things, regarded as individuals. (Aug. 55)

215. When I laugh shall I think of all the people in the world shuddering at that moment in death? When I am dying shall I think of all the people in the world shuddering at that moment in laughter? (Aug. 55)

216. Which is more "real"?—a bare ploughed field?—a field with cultivated crops? or a field full of weeds? (Sep. 55)

217. At present, the two opposite interpretations of history are: first the classical, which describes events in terms of the deeds of men (kings, generals, etc.), and the Marxian-Hegelian, which describes events in terms of streams and currents, in which individual men are straws without personal influence. There have been some attempts to rejuvenate the old theory (e.g., de Couvey's 'Searchlight on Europe') by describing events as the deeds of race.; and countries; but the result is merely a variety of (1) and no new principle comparable to that in (2) is involved. In (1) the principles are secondary to the man and it is this (which stems from Greek philosophy) which has produced the humanism of Europe, of which the Christian Church has done its best to claim the authorship, falsely enough. In (2) men are subordinated to principles. In (1) the following is possible (the up-to-standard test): individual men can be assessed by application of the principle which is secondary to the individual, and all those who pass the test are all right, no matter what the number. In (2) the opposite is possible (the 'who-will-stand-the-pressure' test): the screw can be

put on till the number falls to so many and the weakest must fall out, no matter what the level of their standard (Sep. 55)

(1) is the basis of security :

(2) the basis of revolution. (Sep. 55)

218. Religions as several, small, discrete (or partly discrete), mutually largely incompatible and wholly antagonistic creedal nebulae of rules held together by metaphysics, which float in an indefinite caustic void of hungry and hostile critical anarchy—a sort of angry magma in whose mass the religious knots condense and on which they surreptitiously feed and excrete. (Sep. 55)

219. Qualified people deserve qualified admiration. (Oct. 55)

220. 'Things' are not 'single' like draughts, but a 'two-fold' (at least) like dominoes—they have (at least) two values or aspects or components always, even if (as in a 'double') the twofoldness is the same; and then they have backs. (Oct. 55)

221. Whatever is will be was. (Oct. 55)

222. In the end you will always get what you want, though you may have to wait very long; but time is very long. And if you are in a hurry, you may have forgotten that you wanted it when it comes; and if you want what is contradictory, you will still get it, but you will be unhappy and unsatisfied. And it is the very hardest thing in the world to discover something uncontradictory to want. (Oct. 55)

223. The virtues can only be distinguished from nothing (or negation) against a background of the respective vices. And so they are only relative and only a means—and the converse is just as valid. (Oct. 55)

224. People tend to fall into two main types: those dominated by feeling and those dominated by intellect. (It is a common notion that women belong to the former and men to the latter). The former being guided by feeling, use intellect as a subordinate means to justify the impulsive feeling, and so tend to be inconsistent logically, self-contradictory and adaptable. Those dominated by intellect tend to use the subordinated feeling as a means to justify choice guided by logical formalism, and so they tend to be ambivalent to things and persons, being more interested in principles than in things. Just as the former try and convince others and themselves that their impulsive choice is right by isolated

logical argument, so do the latter by trying to force what their line of argument had led to upon others and themselves. (Oct. 55)

225. Logical exercise: Suppose we agree that it is morally wrong for you to rob me. And we shall probably agree that right is the opposite of wrong. Then since my robbing you is the opposite of your robbing me, it must: be morally right for me to rob you. (Oct. 55)

226. Philosophy in this period seems most afraid of solipsism. Just through that fear, coupled with an unwitting acceptance of an 'either-or' situation, it has embraced unreservedly *misautic* solalterism, of which the American behaviourists are the most extreme example. But the one is just as much a 'heresy' as the other. (Dec. 55)

227. When I consider "other people" I am driven to the conclusion that in these visible bodies, these visible and audible words of theirs, their material acts, I am merely seeing, as it were, a reflection of part of myself not normally visible to me. I can't see my face without a looking-glass—similarly I can't see certain sides—the perceptive apparatus—of my character unless reflected on the "reflecting material surface" which "another person" presents. The polished surface of a looking-glass reflects my otherwise invisible face: another person's body or speech or acts reflects (serves as a projecting screen for) parts of my personality otherwise invisible to me. What other people's personalities "really are" I have absolutely no way of knowing anymore than a scientist has of knowing what matter "really is." (Jan. 56)

228. The process of life offers two principal divergent aims: (1) involves acceptance of (and placing foremost of) "this world" (including Heaven and Hell, which are only phases of it), and (2) renunciation of it. (1) offers multiplicity and intensity of (sensory) experience as the highest in *theory* with choice in *practice*. Survival involves compromise: compromise between is resort to war to protect the choice made or to get rid of responsibility for it by a surrender to a slave-master situation. Intervals of greater or less anarchy supervene. (Jan. 55)

229. The lowest level of conscious life is like clay, and clay often sticks. Man must enter in creatively to enjoy. His first level of

creative enjoyment is nature (sunsets and all that). Then creative friendships on the level of acquaintance. Much higher comes creative or plastic art, then the discovery of how to make friends. Abstracts (mathematics and such music as Bach or Bartok) and last of all nothing. Nothing is the summit—the meaning of conscious life. (Undated)

230. There is nothing in thought, they say, not ultimately derived from the five senses. So too, one might add in that case, there is nothing in architecture not ultimately derived from mud.

231. A man acts on the (tacit) assumption that his acts will have effects in certain spheres and not in others; that their results will later be evaluated in some lights but not others. Example: a thief discounts the evaluation of his act in the court and an adulterer that of his act in the presence of the spouse—so with rebirth. (Jan. 55)

232. The better I can tell what you do the less I can tell what you are; for by your doing you have changed and are no more what you were.

Now if I describe what you are, when that is done, what you are not but were that. From what you were to what you are is gained by doing. By doing you deny—the present and are not what you were. You are what you will be described (in virtue of your doing, not what you will be or were). (Jan. 55)

233. One tends to have a double standard: (1) what I choose, and (2) what I estimate to be public choice (average choice). Both are essential in the conduct of affairs, but excessive emphasis of the latter gives a vulgar (commonplace, *quelquonque*) tone to all one's thoughts and doings. (Jan. 55)

234. Both hell and love are symbolized by fire—the 'fires of hell,' etc, and St. John of the Cross' 'living flame of Love,' for example. (Jan. 56)

235. 1. I desire—I don't know what = *Angst*

2. I desire *that* (not here, not now) = an ideal

3. I desire this (here, now) = a realized ideal

4. Now there seem to be only two ways of treating a loved thing when confronted with it: either one can unite with it, say, eat it (in which case one has annihilated it, and so lost it) or one can contemplate it and so maintain one's love unsatisfied, in which

case the outlook is perpetual unsatisfiedness (through separation) or supervening boredom (due to change in oneself or the object) turning may be to hate or to forgetting. (Jan. 56)

"Eternal love" and "selfless love" are both equivocations, and utraquisms—that an unstable state can remain unchanged eternally or that self can be eliminated and love retained. (I can set myself before or after yourself, but that is not to say that I preserve or annihilate myself before the world.) (Jan. 56)

236. *Concealment* is concealment from others; *forgetting* is concealment from oneself. (Feb. 56)

237. Definition of a PERSON as a fully-organized continuous focal disturbance in the objective field of *another person*; thus a person is always objective of necessity (my 'person' being 'I' objectivized). (On reading F. W. Myers' *Human Personality*, Vol I, p.457). (Feb. 56)

238. Three characteristics of any experience (however simple, or simplified): it is complex and incomplete and ambivalent. (Feb. 56)

239. I do not believe in facts. (The past a factus).

It is axiomatic that to be conscious is to believe in something, though one may not be actually aware of what (I believe in the next future moment).

Only fictions can be believed in (the future is not a fact).

Fictions produce either good or bad: some fictions contradict facts and produce bad. Some fictions transcend facts and produce good. (vice versa)

240. A man's body is structurally simply a hollow ring. A hollow ring elongated into a hollow cylinder, with the inner potion further lengthened and coiled; and above the upper orifice there bulges a head and between the upper and lower orifices the limbs stick out. The world passes in small portions through the ring, helped in by spoon and gulping and out by pressure and paper. (Mar. 56)

241. If it is agreed by a theist that God has a will and what He wills is absolutely good, that he cannot will evil, and if it is claimed that God made man with free will, then it must follow that man's freedom of will is freedom to differ from the will of God (otherwise he has no freedom), in which case it means simply that

he has been given by God the ability to choose evil. In such a picture man appears like a child left shut up alone in a house with a box of matches and some gun powder by his father. (Apr. 56)

242. Where would *I* be (and what would happen to *me*), if I could see all round me and above and below at once? (Jun. 56)

243. Metaphysic is stamped on the physical world with the seal of death. That is a reason why no materialist will deal with it. And the biologist escapes by the verbal trick of identifying survival of the (metaphysical) race with the survival of the (existing) individual. (Jun. 56)

244. Inability to be general or ambivalent when generality or ambivalence is needed is every bit as bad as inability to be precise where precision is needed. (Mar. 56)

245. Only too often I seem to see myself as a joke at a funeral. (Jun. 56)

246. Knowledge inherently denies knowledge both of the knower ('the eye cannot see itself') and of the known ('appearances known suggest the transcendent thing-in-itself'). (Jun. 56)

247. One is like a sieve: the holes (cleavages in one's "unconscious" are, as it were, what one is not and either lets in or keeps out what one is aware of (through the cleavage—either by admiring or condemning). One is the wires (that one never notices at all), and they constitute one's behaviour towards the things sieved. The world as sieved by me is transformed by that sieving. (Jun. 56)

248. Bare acts linger on after their justifications have been forgotten or discredited. Motives are just mental acts. (Jun. 56)

250. God pays the devil his keep as a good landlord pays his bailiff to grind his tenants, or perhaps as Mussolini is said to have secretly paid the anti-fascist exiles in Paris in order to justify the OVRA. (Sep. 56)

251. If God really made man in his own image, what a revelation of the divine nature! (Sep. 56)

252. It is in order to justify the world that Alyosha has to be made to live happily ever after and Ivan has to be made mad; for if it were the other way round, the whole farce of the world would be shown up for the farce it is. Mitya is an exaggeratedly ordinary man, blind and opinionated. Father Zossima worshipped human

suffering in him as Raskolnikoff worshipped it in the prostitute Sonia, who is an exaggeratedly ordinary woman in some ways: blind and sentimental. (Sep. 56)

253. No thing has a monopoly of any one quality. Nothing that is describable has a monopoly of any of the terms by which it is described. Only names are sometimes monopolies of things. (Sep. 56)

254. Sometime after apes had produced men (if that is so), men at an early stage in their evolution evolved language. But grammarians seem to be so recent as to be actually only historical. However, that has not prevented them from appropriating what they did not invent, and laying down their laws for other apes offspring to obey. (Sep. 56.)

255. The chirping honey-sunbirds sipping syrup flirting through the crimson whiskers of the bright hibiscuses. (Sep. 56)

256. To have seen everything to the end of the world and in oneself with one's cravings still intact and to have forgotten how to forget—that would adequately describe hell, no doubt. (Sep. 56)

257. Remember how to do things, but forget what has happened. (Sep. 56)

258. No standpoint whatever is safe against a rebellion against it. Any rebellion to be successful, must destroy the standpoint against which it is rebelling, and as soon as that happens, it must either disintegrate or become itself a standpoint. (Sep. 56)

258a. Science is properly a state of enquiring, recording and explanation. Materialism is properly a state of faith in the external claiming to be gnosis either actual or imminent or 'real but unachievable.' (Sep. 56)

259. What we are not at all interested in may be what we are. (Sep 56)

259a. Reason has its heart, which is inaccessible to the heart (with acknowledgements to Pascal). (Sep. 56)

260. The middle class: or the social sergeants' mess. (Sep. 56)

261. Matter is a myth invented to satisfy the emotional needs of the materialist. Myth is a matter invented to satisfy the rational needs of the spiritualist. (Sep. 56)

262. The more one reflects on the question 'What is this?', the more absurd it seems: but yet never so absurd as the satisfaction provided by any of the possible answers. (Sep. 56)

263. —Is good ultimately more powerful than Evil? Will Good ultimately triumph over Evil?

—Yes. Otherwise one falls into the dualism of Manichaeism.

—Then is doing evil justifiable if a greater good can be expected to result?

—Yes. Otherwise it would be impossible to justify any good action; for it is not possible in this imperfect world to act in a way that is entirely free from any evil at all.

—Then, in principle, since good is ultimately greater than evil, the greatest evil in this world is justified if it is done in the name of the greatest good? If that principle holds good, then there is nothing so wicked, horrible and unspeakable that I am not justified in doing 'for the sake of the good'? (Oct. 56)

264. —Is the world, the universe, finite or infinite?

—Some scientists say it is finite.

—Well so it is; for a scientist's eye is the hole in the end of the universe through which he looks and observes it. Can he see through the hole the other way? (Oct. 56)

265. Up till the 19th century medicine was such that those in need of medical treatment had, in effect, (*as we see it now*) only a choice of different grades of quacks to treat them: and now, similarly, those in need of political treatment have, in effect (as perhaps may be seen later), only a choice of different grades of quacks to treat them. (Oct. 56)

266. Most philosophy offers metaphysicological stays for bulging emotions. (Nov. 56)

267. I seem to have lived my life in three modes: up till the outbreak of war in 1939 I lived it in a very pleasant and mainly graceful rock-pool. The financial insecurity beginning in 1937 and the outbreak of war in 1939 silted the pool up. 1939–1948 was lived in the midst of History: Anti-aircraft volunteer gunner to G.S.O. III, I.B. in Caserta, and afterwards Assistant head of the B.B.C. Italian section at Bush House. From then on it has been lived as an observer, withdrawn and watching. (Nov. 56)

268. I shall never be able to compose my biography: but let no one else have the presumption to do so; for this would amount to theft.

Don't worry, no one will think of it. (Nov. 57)

269. —(1) What I abhor = what I might be.

(2) What I admire = what I am not.

(3) What I am unaware of = what I am.

—But aren't what-I-might-be and what-I-am-not the same?

—In one way, yes: the difference lies in me and my attitude. (see § 276) (Nov. 56)

270. The tragedy of Europe is that it has valued Christ's crucifixion above his teaching. In acts Europe tends to the development of an earthly paradise, which the climate and the geography favours. That has been realized under the Romans and in modern Europe though not recognized. Living as they do in their earthly paradise of material (pleasures), Europeans are fundamentally and hopelessly bored. Subconsciously they long for the insecurity, the injustice, the blood, torture and killing of which their earthly paradise with its legality starves them. Hence the nostalgic yearning over the torture of the crucifixion, of martyrs, of blood sports, and so on. Universal love and liberalism remain remote intellectual ideals, but it is Marx with his doctrine based on violence and hate, who has gripped the 20th Century earthly paradise, just as the Church's presentation of Christ on the Cross (i.e., the crucifixion, not so much the teaching) gripped the imperial Roman earthly paradise. Christ taught not only love but said 'I bring not peace but a sword...' Love is perhaps a good bowl to store hate in.

India much more nearly represents hell on earth or at best that part of hell called limbo. Suffocating heat, famines, overcrowding, poverty, corruption, disease, torture, anarchy and lawless injustice are all on hand—in short suffering and insecurity—are the background for the islands of civilization contained in it, as the jungle is to the village. (The opposite to the ordered European landscape background with its anarchic city slums). There is no need to yearn for hell in India. It is there to be seen before one's eyes. The general background of chaos provokes a tendency to idealize calm, unity, nothingness, law, equanimity and harmlessness: all those qualities that it is most difficult to come by. The Buddha lived a calm and uneventful life for 80 years and there are no Buddhist martyrs, and no Hindu martyrs, for the matter of that ... (Dec. 56?)

271. Aggression, they say, has been outlawed; but whatever has been outlawed can be in-lawed again. (Jan. 57)

272. For those to whom cleanliness is next to godliness, soapiness should be next to saintliness. (Jan. 57)

273. Predetermination hangs on whether there are laws of mind (yet undiscovered but discoverable), or whether mind is the faculty of law unsubject to its laws. Psychology (under the influence of cybernetics) is likely to be absorbed into physics, which will have to create a special department for it; but how do the laws come to be? And how are they recognized? (Jul. 57)

274. Winter England's sad unshining suns. (Jul. 57)

275. All is holy for him who has it so. All is unholy for him who has it so. All is conflict for him who has it so. (Mar. 57) —The have-nots seem wiser than the haves. (Jul. 57)

276. "What I am unaware of is what I am": then to be fully aware is not to be. (Mar. 57)

277. Whatever one is conscious of is *ipso facto* second best (cf. King Lear: "The worst is not, so long as we can say: this is the worst!"). (Mar. 57)

278. God's kitchen, where his devil cooks
Do fry the souls his Fisher nets. (Mar. 57)

279. To be damned is to go on as I am, as long as I am damned. (Mar. 57)

280. Logic lives in constant fear of puns.

The pun questions; when folk pun, they poke fun at the holiness of the syllogistic IS. Socrates is a man.... But what if man is a pun? (Apr. 57)

281. Mathematics (the higher kind) being entirely mental ('mathematicians do not know what they are talking about'), has purged itself of pun-haunting, and introduces them only voluntarily as in the Differential Calculus (a very rarified and abstruse pun—but nonetheless a pun that

283. The world has been governed by serious people for a long time, and what an advertisement it is for their methods! (Jun. 57)

284. Suspect those who prize warmth in others' hearts—they probably have ice needles in their own. (Jun. 57)

285. If the choice would lie between bunkum and debunkum, I would choose the former. (June 57) Debunkum is merely Devil's Bunkum. (May 59)

286. How they need the idea of backward races and peoples to swab their sore guilty consciences with! (Jul. 57)

287. The need for miracles is a symptom of longing for the inexplicable and of fear of the totally explicable. Total explicability totally denies freedom. (Jul. 57)

288. Really it would seem that the anti-nihilists do more to keep nihilism alive than the nihilists. (Jul. 57)

289. The philosophical Absolute—in its various forms, Hegelian, Vedanta, Yogācāra, etc., etc.—is logically only a tinted euphemism for nothingness, hence the inherent and veiled nihilism of all Absolutist systems. The difficulty always lies in the fact that any attempt to show that the Absolute is not nothingness by adducing a category or quality, however metaphysical, destroys its absoluteness, and without such adducing there is no distinguishing the postulated Absolute from nothingness. Even the assertion that a postulated Absolute is positive robs it of its absoluteness. (Aug. 57)

290. If one elects for a positive value as the supreme choice one is necessarily committed to war to maintain that choice or to treachery to it; for no single value—grace, justice, equality, etc.,—is immune from threat of displacement by one or more of the others, and in themselves they are incompatible in proportion as they are each logically pursued and purified to their furthest extremes, so whichever I nail my banner to I am committed to defend that against all others and against nihilism—the attitude that says 'no' to all—when the pressure mounts and war conditions take over: or else there is treachery or forgetting.

What is the 'block in the unconscious' that makes the 'conscious' evaluate experience in terms of 'positive' and 'negative'? (Aug. 57)

291. The difference between sex and death-killing or being killed—seems to be one of degree and detail only. The sexual act is both a killing and being killed subjectively and objectively. But as a

dying into a new life, its new life is incomplete to the extent that the sexual act as an act of dying is incomplete. It is a being reborn without loss of memory. The sense of liberation that follows is comparable to a brief shadow—back of the 'innocence' of the new childhood that follows after the profounder act of dying. The details in which these two modes of the same act differ should be tabulatable. (Aug. 57)

292. A. If I say, psychologically speaking, that a person is behaviour, that is in the most vaguely general sense. But more particularly—that person who is thus psychologically behaviour, is, ontologically, the behaviour that he is unaware of, he is haunted by the behaviour he disapproves of and he is not the behaviour that he approves of. Note the triple position.

B. But how can you say that? Of course he is the behaviour he approves of too, or some of it at least. When I do something I approve of, and I do sometimes, that is me, isn't it? When I say 'What I like about myself is this', if that isn't me, who is it? What is it?

A. No, it is not you precisely because you notice it by contrast, as it were, apparently by contrast with what you disapprove of, but actually by contrast with what you are unaware of. It is precisely because you notice it and actively approve of it, thereby objectifying it, that it is not you. (Aug. 57)

292a. Odd that "now here" is "nowhere." (Aug. 57)

293. The trouble with theists and atheists alike is that they are both tied to opposite sides of the same post. (Aug. 57)

294. How much more frightening flesh is than bones! Who would not prefer to be haunted by a skeleton than by boneless flesh? (Aug. 57)

295. Every act is an act of forgetting—forgetting some constituent state and composing some new one. (Aug. 57)

296. The most positive thing in the whole world is Pain—and they both begin with 'p.' (Jul. 59)

297. The Philosophers of the Systems are like house maids: They sweep the untidiness of the world under the carpet and pretend it isn't there. (Aug. 57)

298. To get out of the puddle of muddle one has to learn to be precise. To get out of the prison of precision one has to learn to

handle the suggestive, the non-committal, the general, without falling back into the puddle. (Aug. 57)

299. The necessity of food, and the inescapable arbitrariness of birth, ageing and death must never be forgotten: any philosophy that does so is only a fairy tale. (Sep. 57)

300. Ignorance must never be lost sight of (as lack of knowledge, hiddenness in probability, or forgetting, or transcendence, or uncertainty à la Heisenberg). Any system that explains existence without it does not explain it. (Sep. 57)

301. I think what I instinctively so much dislike in so much of religious writing is—not its mixture of the rational and irrational; for that would be no more than true to life, but—its tendency to make the irrational respectable (which mostly it is not) and to present it *as if* it were rational: 'Indeed it is so because it must be so, how could it be otherwise' (which is the arbitrary 'must' palmed off as the reasonable 'because'). (Aug. 57)

301a. The free way between the lonely Ivory Tower on the one hand and the teeming Criminal Lunatic Asylum on the other is rather narrow, and much of that rather narrow free way is blocked by the Party Chiefs on the one side and the petty thieves on the other. (Aug. 57)

301b. It would be so nice and easy if there were a rule for everything and it only remained to learn all the rules and then just to decide whether to keep or break a rule—but so often there are none and so we have to act without and make new ones; and these are always slipping out of date. (Aug. 57)

302. How does the body come to be apprehended as a *body*? Why does it not fall apart into the seen and the heard, the smelt, the tasted and the touched? (Sep. 57)

303. Sometimes there is the impression that the world consists only of vomits and excrements, and what is in between. (Sep. 57)

304. The following example is perhaps typical of the *arbitrariness* of alternatives in the world in which one exists. It is an 'invariable rule' and characteristic of the world that size and distance are associated in a one-way direction: i.e., 'things' get smaller as the distance from me increases and larger as it diminishes (though this "appears" in "external logical" space only as

"subtending of angles"). This is reinforced by the smaller-more-distant things "passing behind" and "being hidden by" the larger nearer things. This is represented in pictures by the vanishing points of perspective. But there is *no reason* why the opposite should not be the case, why my world should not be inversely organized and "getting larger" be always associated with increasing distance and the smaller nearer things hiding the larger-further ones. It just isn't so apparently. (Sep. 56)

In the *purely subjective* view nothing is nearer or further (which is a logic-spatial construct based on body-kinaesthesia) but only visually smaller or larger, aurally fainter or louder, tangibly touchable with more or less kinaesthesia. (Sep. 57)

305. No description of existence is "complete." For a "complete" one will always have another (or more than one other) alternative description also "complete" which will in part coincide with the first and in part contradict it. Any system therefore is always lacking something (i.e., lacking "O"). (Sep. 57)

306. To exist (or to non-exist) is to be related; but the relation is not a simple duality, but a duality (or more) in the object against the subject. Basically "passive" change in this triple relation is what is called "change-in-the-object" (I am acted upon, but to be acted upon I resist, consequently the agent changes, whilst I do not). "Active change" in this triple relation is what is called "change-in-the-subject" (-in-me; I act upon and the acted upon resists, consequently I change while the object does not). In existence, however, the reverse (or a combination of both) is what actually *appears*, since "I" see "my self" objectified: in the first instance as also "acted upon" and changed, and conversely in the second. (Sep. 57)

307. In the pure-logical-objective, there is infiniteness and infinite regress to nothing, with an infinite number of vanishing-points in the distance. In the pure-subjective view there is always a horizon (and no infiniteness), with only one vanishing-point, namely, myself. (Sep. 57)

308. When we are speaking of physics (especially of nuclear physics), it is important to remember that the terms "large-scale" and "small-scale" are, subjectively speaking, improper. For the so-called "small-scaled" of the atomic world is, in fact, in so far as it is

perceived at all (i.e., those of its manifestations that are not purely hypothetical) in being perceived: that they may be so with the aid of "enlarging" media such as physical microscopes or "logical-inferential microscopes" is a purely secondary complication, but does not mean that the observed happenings *are* smaller, only that they *are observable* with the aid of certain means. To take a simpler (merely microscopic) case: an animalcule, as seen with the aid of a microscope is, subjectively speaking, the size it is *seen to be*. That this may conflict with logical consistency is another matter, as also in the much-talked-of "unreliability of the senses" (—but where is physics if the senses are not employed at all?) (Sep. 57)

309. The objective world is *determined absolutely* at each instant that is conceived, but the determination at that or any other instant is only *probable*. (Sep. 57)

310. Existence is like a game of dominoes—each domino has *two* values and there is the player (who is *not* a domino, but appears in the domino-world as "I" and "my-opponent," i.e., "active-and-passive"). (Sep.57)

311. Reality (Truth) is a subjective-objective mode (injected into me from the object). Goodness is a subjective mode. Beauty is an objective-subjective mode (projected by me on the object). There remains, they say, that odd world of the "inherently unknowable objective." What is that? (Sep. 57)

312. The "unreliability of introspective data": scientists constantly complain about this, by which they include pain, pleasure, will, purpose and goal .... and perception (awkwardly enough for them! since all percepts are ultimately *private*). But rather than complaining about this (which only reveals the scientists' subjective volitional attitude), should this fact not be recognized? Instead of rejecting introspective data because they are not quantitatively "measurable"(......?) in the way science demands of "public data," should they not be treated as one of their distinguishing characteristics, just as the Uncertainty Principle is now accepted as one of the characteristics on principle of atomic events? The description of why pain, for instance, while distinguishable in intensity, cannot be quantitatively measured (there is no Paris Metre for pain, and if anyone claims that electrical

vibrations or tremor motions, which may *correspond with* pain, *are* pain, he is merely confusing the issue). The basis of physical measurement is "recorded dial reading" where two data are placed alongside and compared: the dial-pointer or the measurable tape and the Paris Metre. But where is this *duality* in pain? Our present pain tends to annihilate another by coalescence, and a *remembered* (or anticipated) pain is no more a measure for a present one than a remembered (or anticipated) metre-stick is for a present piece of tape. *Ergo*, pain, while distinguishable (by memory or anticipation) as differing in intensity, is not measurable by present confrontation. (Sep. 57)

313. What is *said* and *thought* is *always* reflexive (except perhaps the exclamation Oh! etc.) Without reflexion nothing and no action comes to light. The moment I say 'I am doing this, I am not doing that' I am reflecting (and no longer 'doing this, not doing that', but doing something else, namely, reflecting). But reflexion is also a 'doing', and action is never quite divorced from reflexion. (Sep. 57)

313. What is said and thought is (except perhaps the exclamation Oh!) reflexion nothing and no action.

314. A description of a simultaneous scene recited in words is "temporalized space." A movement viewed (graphically) as simultaneous "trajectory" is spatialized time."

315. About the "unconscious" this might be said, namely, that, by developing and employing certain techniques (which are designed to screen off the more obvious and clamant patterns of behaviour in the observed) certain information about behaviour can be observed and gathered (which is otherwise hidden or smothered by the more obvious and clamant). This information can be (structurally) arranged in a pattern, which differs from the pattern offered by the obvious. If this disclosed and arranged pattern is then hypostatized by regarding the information as behaviour of a substance, that hypostatization is in fact the "unconscious." What is remarkable about Freud is his unparalleled acuteness of observation, his ingeniousness and his naivety in hypostatization (as particularly evidenced by his absurd mechanistic description of consciousness in *The Interpretation of Dreams*—absurd, because it is pure fantasy). (Sep. 57)

316. Of anything relative only one description is necessary, and if well done, it can "represent the Truth" (i.e., as correspondence truth) adequately, sufficiently, accurately. This, however, cannot be extended to "existence as a whole," for which a plurality of "complete descriptions" will be necessary, which must both coincide and diverge (probably two is insufficient and three or more is the minimum). Something of this is shown forth in the "Complementary Principle" in descriptions of atomic events. But in a set of descriptions claiming to include the observer (both as observed and as functioning-unobserved), something more than this is needed. (Sep. 57)

317. Hegel's "Logik" is the supreme attempt to subject, once and for all, dialectic to logic, and so to have, in eternity at least, a tidy determined and judged All. This seems to be attempted by the introduction of "movement" into his Logik and the supplying of it with an absolute beginning. The "absolute beginning" (his most vulnerable point which cannot be established) abrogates the possibility of dialectic's being anterior to logic and his incorporation of the dialectic into his Logik as "movement" subordinates it absolutely. But—as Kierkegaard has it—his world fails to *exist*. In existence the dialectic, if subordinated to logic, is so by *decision*, which can be revoked, when the dialectic destroys the logical structure on and below the plane of revokation and projects a new one. Herein lies the awful possibility and constant threat of *disorder*, *confusion* and *doubt*. (Sep. 57)

318. Hegel's "mediation" is an euphemism for confounding or presuming and his "absolute" is a euphemism for confusion. (Oct. 57)

319. Pure existentialism (i.e., trying to "live" entirely in unreflective consciousness) is as much a forlorn hope as the pure "essentialism" of an ideal world of abstract generalities cut off from existence. The first leads logically beyond itself to the decorticated existence of the hero of Camus' *L'étranger* while the second leads to the absent-minded University Professor of Philosophy. (Oct. 57)

320. It is always claimed for mathematics that precision is their prime virtue; and it is often said disparagingly of introspectively obtained subjective data that they are "unsatisfactory" or even "worthless" for scientific use. Now that may well be so; in fact, it

should never be disputed. But suppose we ask the question: What are we seeking? In trying to gain control of objectivity (the "world," "nature," etc.) the more accurate the observations and measurements, the more precise the definitions and descriptions, the more perfect the exclusion of puns and ambiguities from the terminology, the more pleased we may be—for our aim is accurate prediction of outside happenings (with a secondary aesthetic admiration for the consistency and elegance of the method). But what about subjectivity? How to define the faculty of definition? How to *préciser* that ability to muddle and to clarify which waits on consciousness? How to describe whether the distinguishability of truth from untruth is true or untrue? ... (Oct. 57)

321. What a pity that the maxim *De omnibus dubitandum est* is subject to the Theory of Types! (Oct. 57)

322. There seems hardly anything more *positive* than the walls of a prison—with the warders who prevent escape, and the law, which justifies it all. (Oct. 57)

323. The positive thinker builds: he builds prisons, making stone walls of things, and bars and wardens of principles and people. The negative thinker tunnels and undermines—yet his burrowing implies the prison. (Oct. 57) (*Postscript*:) But (as was asked before) who is inside and who outside?

324. If one consults, say, the *Concise Oxford Dictionary*, it soon becomes evident that, in ordinary usage (that is, the usage of the Dictionaries and of common speech), no real or clear differentiation is made at all between *existence, essence*, and *being* (to look up allied words is also revealing in this respect). The position is either that they are not differentiated, or, if they are at all, any differentiation is only partial and is ambiguous and shifty. I take this fact to reflect a reality; and if that is so, then the philosophers' differentiation between existence and essence, whether as used by St. Anselm or by Kierkegaard or the modern existentialists, is consequently ambiguous or even false in part at least. Consequently, too, the alternatives: "existence precedes essence" and "essence precedes existence" are in fact no true alternatives at all, and what they appear to represent must be expressed otherwise, less misleadingly.

The "absolute certainty" of subjectivity (that too of Phenomenology)—as against the 'probability' of the objective world—is inseparable from 'absolute disagreement' between individuals. Why? Because it is the individual's absolute certainty (of his cogito) that, carried to its extreme, *constitutes* his individuality as distinct from every other: that makes him *himself* and not a statistical component of probability, however much defined with accuracy of probability.* Statistics are, in their probability measurable (i.e., quantitative): what distinguishes the individual (in the last analysis, "the unique I") is his absolute immeasurability: i.e., his being, his possibility .... Agreement can only be obtained in the objective statistical world—and it will always be quantitative, just as disagreement, there can never be absolute agreement. (Oct. 57) *One can only *agree* on the *probable* and therefore *uncertain*.

325. A. "I have greenness, I am green. I have my body, I am my body. I have a watch, I am not my watch."

B. "Dear me, how confusing!"

A. "I have my self, I am myself."

B. "Dear me, how confusing!" (Oct. 57)

326. To have" can be abolished (it is non-existent in Sanskrit and Pali) by amalgamating some uses with "to be" and others with the genitive of with "to possess."

So we are left primarily with "to be" and "to do." Now the "copula verb" *to be* I regard as equivalent to the "auxiliary verb" (See C. O. D.) while the "substantive verb" *to be* = *to exist.* Now these two, "copula" (auxiliary) and "substantive" correspond to "state" and "action": "to be green" = presence of a state of greenness; while "to be" = "to be actively present by changing or resisting change"—but this last savours too much of a definition. (Oct. 57)

327. The medieval distinction between essence and existence (=being) is probably one of the most misleading ideas we developed. (Oct. 57)

328. I take it (on the basis of normal English usage) that the word 'self' represents (symbolizes) a fundamental ambiguity in perception—not that it has consciously, rationalistically been

intentionally *made* to represent this: Just the reverse, namely, that its representation has come about thus *à notre insu*, without our suspecting what has happened at all, and the word has thus concealed the very ambiguity it represents. The ambiguity is this: it cannot be established whether a thing is the same as (identical with) itself—or I with myself—or separate and different from it. For instance: "I myself think...," "a thing is no other than itself" and conversely "When I am confronted with myself...," "I come to myself," "I sat by myself and myself it said unto me: 'Take care of thyself, think much of thyself, for there's nobody who cares for thee.'"

Accepting this, then, as a fundamental principle of existence, we can draw this conclusion provisionally. It can be said that "a thing is (exists)" or that "I am (exist)" of any "situational point" at which it becomes impossible to distinguish between sameness and differences. Or differently expressed: "I am" where I can both differentiate and identify myself; "I am" where this ambiguity is certain in the subjective mode, and "it is" where this ambiguity is qualitatively certain (not quantitatively probable) in the objective mode. (Nov. 57)

329. The foregoing statement needs adding to: (1) for "subjectivity" better read "ambiguity" and for "objectivity" better read "uncertainty." Where there is a focus of uncertainty, there a *thing is*; where there is a focus of ambiguity there *I am*, but always the *thing is* in relation to me, and *I am* in relation to the thing. I am "uncertain about myself" when I consider me objectively as though someone else. I am *ambiguous* about a thing when I consider it as mine/not mine. (Nov. 57)

A fool-proof system would surely be system of proofs for fools. (Nov. 57)

331. Stability is the dryness to be found in a bog. (Nov. 57)

332. Consistency seems to be the hallmark of incompleteness: if something (particularly a description of the Universe or a philosophical system) is found to be consistent, then that is a sign that something has been overlooked (vide principle of complementarity in atom physics). Einstein's complaint against the Quantum Theory that it makes the world incomplete seems the greatest recommendation of that theory. (Nov. 57)

333. How useful the gods are! —those looking-glass frames, those blank slates on which we scribble our clumsy and self-contradictory ideals. (Dec. 57)

334. A mind strong in faith and weak in reasoning (understanding) steadies itself by means of slogans. One strong in reasoning (understanding) and weak in faith steadies itself by means of logic. Both are constantly in fear of dialectic, but die of suffocation without it. (Dec. 57)

335. A "slogan" = any cliché or quotation or text or book clung to uncritically "because I like it." Dialectic asks "But why not some alternative?" to which faith can only reply by force or it dies. "Logic" = any structural, verbal and consistent system. Dialectic asks "But why not the opposite?" to which reasoning can only reply by breadth or it too dies. To force and breadth there is no end except through exhaustion. (Dec. 57)

336. The blinding darkness of light; the deafening silence of noise; the (...?) insipidity of smell and taste; the numbing pain/pleasure of heat/cold's wounding caresses; the vertiginous accelerative immobility of motion; the swooning clarity of the unknown. (Dec. 57)

337. Nothing triumphs, finally, in this world but death: the Eternal Life is death, and to live for ever is to die—for ever. The immortal is not born. (Dec. 57)

338. If ignorance is an essential component of existence (whether as the finite unknowing of the infinite, or as the basis of Dependent Arising, or as the Uncertainty Principle in Atomic Physics), then any theory that does not take account of and include ignorance cannot claim to represent existence or the world fully. The fact that a theory works in practice, by experience, proves that it does so take account, or it would not work. But to show openly or incautiously such ignorance would be offensive, indecent, taboo, and so it is normally hidden, normally inadvertedly. (Dec. 57)

339. My existence is my presence now, or my present life (birth-to-death); my non-existence is my previous lives (before birth) and my future lives (after death). Both together compose me: I am composed of both together. The objective materialist who, as a solalterist, forgets himself, takes existence as an all-truth,

subordinating "I-me." The religionist who believes in the permanence of the soul, takes the solipsistic "I-me" as an all-truth, subordinating existence. (Dec. 57)

340. One's dearest friend: he for whom one ought ethically to sacrifice (betray) even one's highest principle: One's highest principle: that for which one ought ethically to sacrifice (betray) one's dearest friend (one's closest loved one). What has justice to say here? What of liberty, equality, fraternity (where liberty can be liberty to enforce equality by any means whatever, equality can be equality in the brotherhood of those condemned to death which is freedom, and fraternity that of implacable (how the totalitarians love that luscious, lip-smacking, lascivious word!) fratricidal hate (each equally hating his brother in absolute freedom to do so)?

341. When I have a system, I use it quite unsystematically, and when I have none I systematically do not use it. (Jan. 58)

342. What is so wretched for the moralists about morals (or call them ethics) is that they never—however Procrustean the claim made for their absoluteness—quite detach themselves from expediency. (See § 391) (Jan. 58)

343. "All the world's a stage, and all the men and women actors on it" says Shakespeare. But actually only the men and women in the public gaze are actors on it. I, for instance, whom—and this I hold one of my greatest blessings while it is so—the public does not gaze on, am not an actor, but only a scene-shifter: the stage is curtained when I and those like me move on it.

(*Addition*:) Or that is how I should like it to be always. (Jan. 58)

344. Four kinds of principle: to do evil that evil may come, to do evil that good may come, to do good that evil may come, to do good that good may come. The first and last are very difficult: for it is almost as hard to be a devil as to be a saint. The second, surely, provides the intentions with which hell is said to be paved; but if that is so, then does not the third paint the frescoes on the ceilings of heaven? Far better is the third than the second; for in the second, the intended good for which the evil is done may never materialize, but the evil done remains; and, in the third, the intended evil for which the good is done may never materialize, but the good done remains. (Jan. 58)

345. Riven by triviality and unamenable to meaning. Driven by meanness from the amenities of liberality. (Jan. 58)

346. When I look at a looking-glass, what do I see—the looking-glass, my face or me? When I look at the world, what do I see—the world, my perceptions or me? When I look at you, what do I see—you or a part of my unknown self? (Jan. 58)

347. A deep inward experience is shared and cannot be unshared. Desire to share—it comes, perhaps, from intrusion into reflexion upon the separateness of self and others, which is dissolved in deep inward experience. Reflexion comes afterwards and is done from the standpoint of separateness. Separateness is unsharable. One might put it this way: such inward experiences cannot be unshared precisely because they are by their very nature inward sharing, but they cannot be directly communicated upon reflexion in separateness, and so a desire to share them may arise in separateness, which desire arises from overlooking the fact that they are already shared by their very nature.

Bodies (mental or physical) are what separates (and with them words and spatial nearness); some feelings draw the separate together and partly dissolve it; consciousness unites in a-unity (? Ed.). Separateness implies unity; unity implies separateness; there is no final satisfaction or solution here as long as each craves for or dreads the other. (Jan. 58)

348. Consciousness *is* unity; being *acts* by separating; what diversity *cognizes* is one (or in itself undifferentiated infinite, indefinite): what it separates into (is?) many.* The verb "is" belongs to *being in abstracto*; the verb "*does*" sides with *consciousness in abstracto*. But *in existence* consciousness *is* and being *does*. In Philosophy consciousness is, being is, and it is not clear how doing is done; and traditional logic only recognizes the "copula, is." But "Man and logic are different categories."(Jan. 58) * Unclear in MS.

349. An effective way to kill a plant is to water it carefully and regularly for the first half of a drought and then to go away and leave it. But those who do that do not see the plant die: they go and water other plants in: other dry places in the same way. (Jan. 58)

350. The existential pre-reflective choice is seen, on reflexion, as a preference. Acted: it is the freedom to that to which one is

condemned. Reviewed: it expresses a preference or manifestation of free-will (but that is only on looking back—the looking back is itself a choice). (Jan. 58)

351. Optimism must be an "existential communication" not a direct one: it must be induced indirectly as a spontaneous creation by the listener in himself, not directly (like a cooking recipe or an army drill-book). The attempt to do it directly degenerates into the parson's synthetic 'joy' or the physical-training instructor's 'radiance' which may well generate pessimism as the bearer's spontaneous mental response. It always does in me: I feel that the optimist who talks to or at me, has taken from me all the good there is and left my world as bare as a locust-stricken field. (Jan. 58)

352. What the scientists are apt to forget: the difference between quantity and quality is one of quality, not of quantity. (Jan. 58)

353. Modern analogy: just as the bombardment by neutral mesons is needed to split the atom's nucleus which is held together by negative and positive charges, as we are told—so perhaps equanimity is the projectile with which to split the individual held together by the charges, of hate and lust. (Jan. 58)

354. Some people are aggressively meek. (Mar. 58)

355. "The purpose of oratory is to make people forget the need for evidence" it has been said. And, it may be added, the purpose of evidence is to make people forget that all sense-data are private. (And perhaps the purpose of the privacy of evidence is to make people forget). (Mar. 58)

356. There are certain aspects of truth that one can only discover in oneself; if one is told of them, one will certainly, and in the very nature of existence itself, reject them absolutely. But perhaps they can be shared by those who have discovered them individually for themselves, and perhaps those who have not discovered them can be aided indirectly to discover them for themselves. (The use of the word "truth" here is in the sense of desirability of discovery). (Mar. 58)

357. If existence were a riddle, its solution would be non-existence—but in what medium would it then have found solution? (Mar. 58)

358. I used always to comfort myself with the belief that if physical pain became too violent it would be cut off by "loss of consciousness"—but why should this be always so? And what is "loss of consciousness" when described subjectively? (Apr. 58)

359. Religion without art, like sex without art, not very attractive. (Apr. 58)

360. The unambiguous is non-existent. (Apr. 58)

361. Objectively there are three spatial dimensions and one temporal one, all perpendicular to each other, which together are held to constitute the four-dimensional time-space continuum of the scientists. This is purely objective and as such an artificial abstract. For in it time becomes spatialized into parallel world lines; "now" being an arbitrary convenience in it without necessity of any position.

Conversely, in the absolute subjective view there would be three temporal dimensions and one spatial one, all perpendicular to each other. No one is ever seen directly but only reflected in one or both of the other two. They are past, present, and future, as the three temporal, and individual historical movement as the single spatial one: *the importance of the notion of the perpendicularity of the three periods of time to each other subjectively cannot be overestimated.* While "Individual Historical Movement" is, as it were, the "part of subjectivity that belongs to the object," in subjectivity, the continuum of world-lines in the object is that part of the object which, as it were, "belongs to the subject in the object": this interlocks subject and object and makes them inseparable. It also, by the difference of the positivity of spatial relations and negativity of temporal relations, gives a positive nature to the object and a negative one to the subject ("It is through woman that negation comes into the world.")

For the desperate unsatisfactoriness of the one time-dimension in purely objective science, see particularly Kant's Theory of the Subjectivity of Time, Eddington's New Pathways of Science on the "direction of time-flow" corresponding with "increase-decrease of entropy" (only a theory, mark you!), and Heisenberg in "Atomic Research and the Law of Causality in Nature," [Universitas, (Engl. ed.] 1957, No. 2), on difficulties of knowing direction of time in the "small-scale" non-statistical field of the atom. Has anyone before suggested that past, present and future are subjectively perpendicular? Scientific four-dimensional time-space *has no "now."* (Apr. 58)

362. I leave the study of *order* and *structure* to the mathematicians and (in so far as they are capable) to the philosophers: I am more interested in *disorder* and *distructure*. (This is what I say absolutely sometimes.) (Apr. 58)

363. 'So, then, in choosing absolutely I choose despair, and in despair I choose the absolute, for I myself am the absolute,' says Kierkegaard (Either/Or, i, 179) This is a curious undeveloped insight into an uncomfortably true-half-truth: the pure solipsistic standpoint of the unique "I" (not the abstract and quelquonque "an ego among, others" of the psychologists). Purely subjectively "I" am unique: only that pure subjectivity is a half-truth (I do not know anywhere where pure solipsism is expounded honestly, as pure solalterism is by, say, the more reputable Behaviourists). In those terms of pure subjectivity "the others" are passive modes of "me" projected outwards. (vide Sartre's *être vu*). This abstraction is an offence: and so Pascal says that "*le moi est haissable*," perhaps with that in view. When the words "I see you" are heard the meaning (in itself utterly ambiguous) is fixed by *me* with relation to "my body": if perceived as coming *from* my body, the "I" heard is *identified* with the unique absolute subjective "I"; but if perceived as coming to my body, the heard "I" and "you" are reversed (in this special abstract interpretation, "I" being always explainable as *active subjectivity* and "you" translated into "me" as *passive subjectivity*). (Apr. 58)

364. Solipsistically, "I" (am) absolute and unique, and active with "me" as passive; "Thou" (art) the active "I" projected with "thee" as passive. "He" and "him", etc., can only be arrived at through "us" and "we" ("We" and "us" regarded as (1) "I"/"me" on different occasions, or (2) "I"/ "thee"-"me"/"thou" simultaneously). (Apr. 58)

365. Definition of rectolinearity: three points such that one is hidden by the second from the third; or unobservability of any two points simultaneously.

Definition of perpendicularity: Three points such that one is not hidden by the second from the third; or observability of any two points simultaneously.

(For "two points," "three points" and "one point" one can read "duality," "trinity" and "singularity.")

The irreducible basis of observation is the trinity of the observed, the not-observed, and the observation point; or the observed-as-present, the observed-as-absent, and the (perpendicular) observant. (But this only "appears" in reflexion). (Apr. 58)

366. The objects of science are all publicly measurable: by "dial-readings" or by confrontation with a "piece of matter called the Paris Metre" or by confrontation with the standard inch, the "average girth of the thumbs of three Scotsmen." Those data which are private, such as feelings of bodily pleasure or pain, mental joy or grief, willing, clarity of perception are all measurable, too, but in a different way: they are measurable only by the *action* which they facilitate or inhibit ("I had such a tooth ache I couldn't read," "I wanted to see you so much I couldn't sleep," "He was satisfied enough for him to continue his work," etc.). Pure consciousness is, however, immeasurable. (Apr. 58)

367. Certainty is absence of infinity; infinity is presence of uncertainty. (Apr. 58)

368. Nothing whatever can be apprehended apart from its opposite: but its opposite cannot be present at the same time-place; for anything whatever to emerge from anonymity as present to consciousness (which is not it) it must be haunted (shadowed) in space-time by its opposite, otherwise it cannot detach itself from the unknown. (Apr. 58)

369. Cursed with the blessing of being condemned to be free. (May 58)

370. I can't find I; for when I do, what I do find: it's myself or me I need first find; I can find 'thou'; for when I do then 'thou' when by me found art thee. (May 58)

371. Being, considered as Action, appears as becoming (beginning to be or movement).

Action considered as Being appears as experience (history or staticity).

An analysis (description or definition) of *Being* must completely avoid all uses of the verb *to be* and all its derivatives and synonyms.

That of Action must likewise avoid all active verbs and nouns.

Failure in this appears as a *petitio principii* or as a tautology.

Appearance can be taken as the objective manifestation (ideal and real) of both being and action, which *I* subjectively *experience.* Together these make up existence.

Essence merely duplicates either idea or being, and has no separate referent.

(The verb *to have* duplicates the use of "there is" with the dative (in Indian languages). (May 58)

372. "Ideas" appear as the—objects of the mind and "realities" appear as the objects of the five senses. The mind and the five senses are irreducible personal data together with their respective types of objects. The mind can "handle" say visible data either through the eye (as visibles) or directly (as visual images) and can confront these two and compare them ("This ink pot might have been better designed like this.") (May 58)

373. Consciousness (o) perpendicular to what it is aware of and not perpendicular to what it is not aware of.

It (o) is aware of presence (+)-cum-absence (—) in a state of asymmetricality (↓↑). (May 58)

$$\begin{pmatrix} - & - & + & + \\ \downarrow & \uparrow & \downarrow & \uparrow \\ + & + & - & - \end{pmatrix}$$

374. All these mental foot prints in this book: what beaten tracks they make for themselves and follow! And how these tracks emphasize by contrast the areas where they never tread! (May 58)

375. Life is mainly solalterism: death pure solipsism. (May 58)

376. Three forms of agnosticism: (1) I am certain (know) that this is impossible for anyone else to know. (2) I am uncertain (do not know at present) whether this which I don't know now, can be known by me or by anyone at some time. (3) I am certain (know) that this which I do not know, can be known sometime.

These three cover agnosticism about death.

Three main attitudes to death (my death): (1) I believe (know) that I shall survive my death. (2) I believe (know) that I shall not survive my death. (3) one of the three forms of agnosticism.

It is impossible for ordinary, normal thought to confront the idea of (my) death except in one of these attitudes. All of these attitudes are wrong through the assumptions (explicit and implicit) that they necessitate. Consequently it is impossible for normal thought to confront (my) death with a correct attitude. (May 58)

377. If there is rebirth then there is nothing in this whole world, not even oneself, that is worth killing anyone for. But if there is no rebirth, then there is nothing, provided only that I am clever enough to evade the direct consequences, to prevent me killing one who gets in my way. Materialists might not (like?) this. (June 58)

378. There is no kind of act which is not wrong in certain circumstances. Suppose *that* were true? (Jun. 58)

379. What nonsense it is to say that truth is beauty or what is true is good: is torture (the 'flagellation', say) not true and paintable? (Jun. 58)

380. If *absolute union* with God (as in the Advaita) is taught, then who is lost, 'I' (in which case I no longer exist) or 'God' (in which case I assume the Nijjinski madness 'I am God...') or both (in which case the state is not distinguishable from no-god). Again if the personal Idea of God is replaced by Pure Being, then Being, to be pure, cannot be accessible to knowledge or, if it is, it is not pure. But if it is not, then it cannot be known whether it is Pure Being or Nothingness. (Jun. 58)

381. The mind's mouth is greed, its body ignorance, and anger its anus. People who quarrel with one or with each other in one's presence, expose the bare backsides of their minds just in one's face and shit on one's door step. (Jun. 58)

382. What is the human world if not heaven reflected in hell's pitch-pool. (Jun. 58)

383. The world had treated me for fifty two years now with admirable indifference and allowed me to go very much my own way. To me it has been on the whole tolerant and helpful. When I see what it has done to so many others in my time I think how easily it could have played the steam-roller or the cat-and-mouse trick with me. Who knows what is to come? (Jun. 58)

384. *Canticle* (Persephone and All That).

Only Mortality is immortal: all things mortal she mortgages for ever.

Only Temporality is eternal: all things temporal he tempers for ever.

Only Particularity is universal:
Only Perception is unperceived:
Infinity! Infinity! Infinity!
Not squared, not cubed; but
Raised to the power of infinity. (Jul. 58)

385. Since *being* applies everywhere, to positive and negative, without distinction (for what is not IS in the negative mode), while *what* is IS in the positive mode) it is impossible to *define* it, though it can be, in a sense, described. Being, in fact, = self identity; to be is to identify. Whatever is *is itself* (see Sartre for the two modes of *en soi* and *pour soi*). Now, since nothing whatever that can be individualized is simple (if it were simple it could not be individual in the sense of being distinguishable as individual), it follows that for any individual to have a self there must be identification between the individual and its self. Its self is thus both the individual and not the individual, and the individual is both itself and not itself, and its self is both individual and unindividual. How is that? Because—identification takes place through *coalescence*. (...) when two (complex) individuals are seen as having the majority of their qualities in common and the quality or qualities (or quantities) that individualize them, one from the other and from all else, are *ignored*, when this ignoring takes place involuntarily, an individual is seen to be itself. This is the objective aspect of *things*. Other people (seen in the accusative) and I (seen as me) are also "thingified"—(= realized, made a *res*). Consciousness *is nothing*; 'I,' subjectively, *am* an action *for me* (as myself), 'I' then being identified with 'me' (the untranscended sum of my actions and possibilities)—the individualized negative act with the individualized thingified history—*am* myself through coalescing, ignoring and forgetting the different qualities (or multiplicity) by which 'I' am distinguishable from 'me.' The moral of all this is simply that *without ignorance there is no being or non-being*. (Jun. 58)

386. But how *absurd* it is to identify *being* and *good*, since evil is. And how can *good* be simply defined, without reference to evil,

as the object of the will? And how can *being* be defined, without reference to non-being, as the object of consciousness's *affirmation*, and since being is without limit, how can it be *defined*?

No wonder scientists fight shy of ontology as it has been shaped in European, thought—but they have none of them seen why. (Jun. 58)

387. Logic is impossible without the identifying process of the copula is and *identification is the function of ignorance.* (Swallow that, if you can, you logicians!) (Jun. 58)

388. In the physical world, with relativity and the maximum speed of light as a finite quantity, while "*uniform motion in a straight line (= rest)*" implies change, in the surroundings of a coordinate system, it predicts nothing internal of the CS itself. But with, say, a (*constant*) *acceleration* the CS not only takes on an internal orientation but also approaches the maximum speed, from which it must result that the change will be in a sense (seen from outside the CS) trajectorial (like *ageing*[1], is distinct from mere *altering*) and is bound to result in eventual catastrophe to the CS ("death"). In the physical world, the phenomenon of gravity is in many ways equatable with acceleration. (Maximum speed with what?) We can regard the earth as CS expanding acceleratedly, which acceleration keeps us on its surface and makes us "heavy." (Why then doesn't the earth get larger?—That is beside the point.) Without the "acceleration" of gravitation the earth could disperse in dust and vapour, into nothingness.[2] But not enough, this gravity-acceleration—if there is a maximum speed (speed of a CS, relative to other CS), must result in the earth's ageing-curve and eventual death as an *internal* phenomenon. Conversely, the seeming inevitability of ageing and death of the complex conscious animals, including man, might suggest *both* an *acceleration* and an upper speed ceiling. Suggestive as this line is, it suffers from two disadvantages: it smacks of argument by analogy, and it is entirely *objective* (in the scientific sense), which, though sound for physics given the self-imposed limitations of the scientific premise, is nevertheless totally inadequate for analysis of subjectivity. (Note

1. I only "see" my own ageing, as it were, from outside my self.
2. Mere solidity (= motion) in a straight line.

the subjective analysis. might be made on the basis of the theory—see here No. 361—of the subjective orthogonal three dimensions of time and of space.) (Jun. 58)

389. Everything I see hides something else: what is behind that tree-trunk? What is behind the positive emptiness I see extended between the stars? Everything I hear blots out some other sounds behind this conversation I hear and take part in, what is being said at the next tables on the right and on the left? Behind the roar of waves, what sounds are there? Behind the light buzzing of the ears in the silence of the night or of a cave, what sounds? Behind the smell of Camembert and taste of salt, or the taste of spittle in an empty mouth, the smell of nasal receptivity in a quiet nose,—what smells and tastes? Behind this touch of velvet or this (?), what other touch? And lastly, behind these ideas and images, what ideas and images? What? What?—But why do I ask? To recognize something revealed is to imply something hidden by it. (June. 58)

390. The principle of non-commutative multiplication legitimates the idea of asymmetrical pairs or opposites which, while opposite, do not cancel each other out; pleasure and pain are one of these pairs. (Jun. 58)

391. Expediency is really the reproductive organ of morality (its "shame" which it covers up), without which it would be sterile and its race die out. (Jun. 58)

392. Perhaps the amount of pain one suffers is the measure of the amount of clinging to existence one has fundamentally. For the 'body' that one has in dreams is too fragile in its continuity to withstand pair. It takes the solidly organized waking body to stand pain. Pain is inimical to continuity. But if continuity (life) is desired (voluntarily and involuntarily), an organization is needed to localize pain and contain it when it rises; this is the physical body. In this view the physical body is a pain barrier (rather as the tonsils are the germ-barrier) in the whole personality in waking life. In dream, to repeat, though there is my body in all my experiences in dreams, it is unstable and its situations (as seen in waking reflexion) succeed with disconnected jerks: bits of disconnected continuity, some long, some short. —But there is no bodily pain in dreams to any noticeable extent. To maintain continuity, ability to have a

physical dam against discontinuity is gained at the price of bodily pain. (Jun. 58)

393. It is best to live at peace with the devil one knows and not to try to make a breach too soon; for then he may go away before one is ready, and others whom one does not recognize may then take his place. (Jun. 58)

394. If number is definable as what you can count, it is therefore finite, but an infinite number (see Russell, *Mysticism and Logic*) is what you cannot count, and is therefore not a number except by a pun (vide Russell's statement that "the number of finite numbers is infinite"—which in "straight" language should be stated as no number of numbers is countable"). A definition of infinity is self-contradictory, verbally, since it involves placing a limit (finis) to that which is stated to have none. (Jun. 58)

395. What I believe I know, I do not yet fully know: what I know I believe, I no longer fully believe. (Jun. 58)

396. Ignorance screens the truth. It is on that screen that people paint pictures and write underneath their labels "god" and "not-god" and "theism" and "atheism." (Jun. 58)

397. Can definition define itself or description describe itself? Or can it be that description can only be defined, and definition described? (Jun. 58)

398. In these days both theism and atheism have got a bit greasy with the smoke of Auschwitz—but why ever put up a *memorial* to *that*? What is there (that) art is not capable of? *Anus mundi*—it can kiss the world's arse, it seems.

399. *Goodness* can only be finally established by destruction of evil, and destruction is doubtful as to whether it is good.

Truth must include evil, since it is manifestly wrong to assert that evil is untrue.

Beauty, as art, if it can take the Cross (the cruifixion by torture and murder of a man-god), and Auschwitz (the crucifixion by torture and murder of humanity) for its aliment, would seem to be a foul feeder with no limit to the horrors it is willing to devour, without pecksniff ethics to censor it. (Jul. 58)

400. Mythical entities can be measured: they used to measure phlogiston, and they still measure force. (Aug. 58)

401. Space and time are the great subjective mistakes which we all agree in making and on and in which we build all our disagreements. (Aug. 58)

402. Charitableness to one's neighbour is like clean linen: to be worn rather than talked about. (Aug. 58)

403. The impenetrable secrecy of substances. Things hide their substance behind their surfaces. Crack open the surface to see the substance, and what do you find? Another surface, and so on. Substance is secrecy.

And the secrecy of persons. You in all honesty—as I honestly believe—tell me all your secrets as a friend and confidant, but I can inherently never *know* that that is so, I can only firmly believe it (and to know that I believe is half to doubt while to believe that I know is to be half in real ignorance). What distinguishes me from you (or you from him or me from him) and *vice versa*, as persons rather than things,—the mode of difference between persons that differs from the mode of difference between things—is that, however honest and open I am, however much I try, through love or hate, or fear and terror, physical or mental, I can inherently *never* completely disclose my 'self' (for if that were possible, I and myself would disappear quite). Thus I am a secret and you a suspicion, that can never be removed (or vice versa). So lovers are jealous, and people torture each other in order to obtain information; no less now, in the 20th century (with the modern aids of science and psychology) than in the middle ages or the renaissance (Tolstoy said a man does not know a State if he does not know the insides of its prisons)—yet with all the aids that science can and will be able to give one can never be quite satisfied that one has got it all. The irony is that this secrecy is itself so secretive that people quite forget it and believe all can be disclosed. A man can only tend towards openness—he can never quite get there. Socialism, if it degenerates into a flight from this fact, by pretending that the Ego (the psychologists' depersonalized and *quelquonque*, and therefore fictitious 'I') does not matter and the individual is really subordinate to the State. The old regime has failed through failing to recognize that the State (other people) cannot be subordinated to the individual. (Aug. 58)

404. The Absolute can only receive its Absolution from Consciousness (failing which/there is/neither absolute nor particular), and in so doing the absoluteness is particularized as such, and so is no longer absolute. (Aug. 58)

405. A man can only tend towards frankness, he can never achieve absolute frankness or he would be a mere mechanical device. When he has deviated some way in this direction, people *identify* him with the idea of great frankness. They say 'he is frankness *itself*.' (Aug. 58)

406. Whether one accepts an idea with the left hand of horror and indignation or with the right hand of welcome and approval, one has accepted it just the same and is left holding it—and it is no good hiding away from oneself under one's coat what one has accepted with the left hand. (Aug. 58)

407. Honour is a principle that asserts the Person above the Principle (and changes persons): The Nihilist or Revolutionary is the Person that asserts the Principle above the Person (and changes principles). (Aug. 58)

408. What always distinguishes my body from all other peoples' bodies? All bodies appear incomplete, but while other peoples' bodies appear incomplete *away from me*, my body is the only one that appears incomplete *towards me*, too. This is true of any view point at any time. (Aug. 58)

409. God is invented as the counterbalance to the unique 'I'-illusion of pure solipsism. Atheist science therefore has, of necessity, to take refuge in Solalterism; for without god, if the unique subject 'I' is admitted (and science cannot control it), it must assume divine and absolute proportions and become madness (Kirillov). Buddhism avoids this by removal of the 'I'—illusion in all aspects, whether in that of god or the solipsistic misinterpretation of the unique 'I.' (Aug. 58)

410. A: On the basis of monotheistic theology free will can only be freedom to do evil—if good and God's will are equitable—and God, as the Creator of all things, is creator of evil through man as His Instrument, as creator of man's will to do evil.

B: If you say that, I will destroy you. (Aug 58)

411. *Seek and you shall find*—what shall I find? The seeking.

Knock and it shall be opened unto you—and what shall be opened unto me?—The knocking. (Aug. 58)

412. The process of gathering evidence on which to base a conclusion necessitates excluding irrelevant matter—it is always a process of selection and rejection, thus it must always be incomplete. This suggests that any conclusion based on evidence is always incomplete—'no conclusion'—and provisional, however 'final' it may be believed to be. To reach a 'complete' and 'final' conclusion about anything, everything would have to be considered and taken into account, which, since it would require infinite comprehension and eternity, would be the unattainable—the always possible that cannot be 'killed' by realization: or in other words, 'the absolute future.' (Aug. 58)

413. People who set out to explain the unfamiliar in terms of the familiar, always end by explaining the familiar in terms of the unfamiliar. (Sep. 58)

414. The Truth is often so insulting. (Sep. 58)

415. The theists are men who, in order to see the light, build stone cathedrals round themselves with stained-glass windows showing the comprehensible attributes of their incomprehensible God. The atheists, in order to see more clearly, curtain off the stained-glass windows. (Sep. 58)

416. It seems to me that rest, motion and acceleration, are inseparable in any total situation or event, and are thus three copresent structural modes. Modes of what? Copresent structural modes of *permanence*. But surely *permanence* is a delusion? And what moves and accelerates, at least, changes and is thus impermanent: No, rest or motion or change are together three modes of the situation, not of a thing—a 'thing' has one of them in appearance, when the others are relegated to the rest of its situation or event.—Properly change is an alteration of quality or quantity in which no one, nor all, of the three modes of permanence is present. Only a 'thing' can be at rest or move or accelerate, and a thing has illusion of permanence while it is that *thing*. When it changes, it is no more that *thing*, and so no motion or rest or acceleration can be attributed. (Sep. 58)

417. The Law is nothing but a set of techniques for canalizing

hate into order and away from chaos (as commerce is for canalizing greed similarly). It is a mistake to identify war with hate: wars are made for greed and for fear more than for hate—see also Uncle Toby's defence of war in Tristram Shandy. Judge Wildegoose's description of Law as a device for delay (rather than for administration of justice), in which passions cool down and litigation solves itself with the passage of time and the help of boredom, is acute. (Oct. 58)

418. The love/hate opposition is misleading and not true to facts. Better would be love/fear and greed/ hate. Or perhaps better a triangle which is constantly being forced into a duality by identifying one of the pairs: that is what makes the world go round, no doubt. Trying to make an axis out of a try-angle by axing one angle on trial. (Oct. 58)

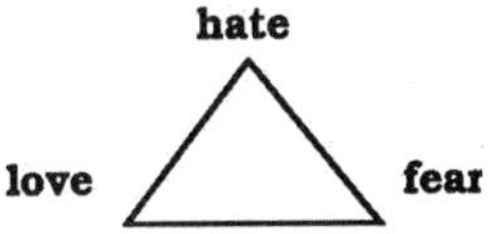

419. Why, I sometimes ask myself, is speech so geometrical? If I exaggerate I speak *hyperbolically*. Arguments always follow a certain *line* and are sometimes *circular*. Statements are sometimes *elliptic*. A statement either has a *point*, or is *pointless*. *Parables* come from the word parabola (which is a simile or metaphor or, a something that follows something else: speech follows experience), and lastly, I find in the C.O.D., *parlance* (the English form of French *parler*, Italian *parlare*) comes from the Latin *parabolare*, to talk. I haven't discovered any verbal squares, triangles or cubes yet. So it seems that the strange geometricity of speech (=*parlance*, remember) in general is confined to conic sections and covers them all. It is very odd. 'But,' some wiseacres may say, 'You have got it upside-down. Speech has not borrowed from geometry (it is much older); geometry has borrowed from speech!'—But then I ask why have speech metaphors invaded geometry and taken possession of conic sections? There is no such situation in arithmetic that I know of. (Oct. 58)

420. Among the principal essentials of existence are: the pun (*no* meaning or idea is quite unequivocal), the dialectic (no choice is settled except by a belief), conditionality (no thing or quality ever arises or is found alone; for if found, it is not alone since in the

presence of what finds it), impermanence, identification (the self-illusion made on recognition of anything, which is always wrong against the standard of Truth-that-never-disappoints), consciousness (without which there are no ideas at all), being (without which illusion nothing whatever can be cognized by recognition as either recognized or unrecognized), individualized perspect (without which there is no 'view'), etc., etc. (Nov. 58)

421. **FABLE.** —Once a *person* called "P" *went* to *a place* called "kitchen," and with a lot of *impersonal things* variously called, including a *thing* called "a spoonful of salt," performed some actions called "cooking" and produced a *thing* called "delicious dinner," which the *person* called "P," in another *action* called "serving a dinner to guests," sat down to, with some other *persons* variously called, one of which was called "Q." He was a chemist. He said, "Chemically speaking, there *are* only *elements* and *combinations* of elements, 'you' as a *person*, and a 'teaspoonful of salt' as a *thing* don't exist chemically. 'You' and 'it' are both just combinations of elements, which are real. Now this so-called "teaspoonful of salt" is, for instance, *merely* a combination of the *elements* chlorine and sodium." The *person* called "P" was impressed. For the next *action* called "serving a dinner to guests," "P" thought "Why not, since Q said they were *the same thing*—that salt is merely chlorine and sodium—why not be original and serve some chlorine and sodium instead of salt? So much simpler! Why bother about their being combined as salt? They are more *real* too," he said. "We'll combine them in ourselves at dinner."

So the *person* called "P" undertook an act called "buying some chlorine (poisonous gas) and some sodium (metal that burns and explodes in contact with water)," and these *things* (*not elements* in this *action*), with other *things*, the *person* called "P" *acted on* in a way called "serving a dinner to guests." Now the result was quite different to that of the previous action also called "serving a dinner to guests" and *identified* by "P" as the *same* (*sort of*) *action*. The result this time was very painful to the *person* called "P" and the other *persons* called "guests," and they all "died" very "puzzled." Why was that? Because they didn't mind their P's and Q's. (Nov. 58)

422. The profoundest of all illusions is the illusion that there is no illusion. (Nov. 58)

423. It is when the ethical *fails* that it slips back into the immediate—but as the ironical immediacy. It is when the religious *fails* that it slips back into the ethical—but as the comic ethical. Failure in the immediacy is simply immediate suffering. (Nov. 58)

424. Besides the fact that no virtue stands out as such except against the background of its corresponding vice, it also seems impossible to find any virtue whatever that is not, on some occasion, in certain circumstances, itself a vice. If this were not so, no judgement would be needed—all would be settled by rule—and is judgement a *virtue*? (Nov. 58)

425. In the pattern of ideas everything is possible even a contradiction. In the opposed pattern of existence (the might-be, the is, the existing), the possible and impossible are, more or less arbitrarily, distinguished, and what is possible then being only discernible by observation and learning. This points to an arbitrary fixed solution of dialectic on the basic existential level *in existence*, which perhaps distinguishes the individual personality *during his life span*. (Dec. 58)

426. Heaven can be made into hell by other people or oneself. Hell can be made into heaven by oneself. In either case neither endures indefinitely—*le Paradis est toujours à refaire*. (Dec. 58)

427. The best way to govern the world would apparently be to put half the population in prison and set the other half to guard them. This would be essentially *humane* since one of the characteristics that distinguishes human beings from animals is the habit of building prisons and imprisoning some of their own kind,—not to build and maintain them is inhuman. But perhaps there is no need to *bring this about*, to make this "essence" "exist," since perhaps it is in fact how the world is now being ruled: now as it is and always has been. Half the world is in prison: each man is half in prison. Otherwise what need to talk of freedom? But prisoners are so optimistic, aren't they? Don't they imply that freedom *must be*? And then who is inside and who is outside? (Dec. 58)

428. The scientific writer Sluckin in his Penguin book on Cybernetics dismisses introspection as valueless because of the

vagueness and ambiguity of the data it provides. Now I maintain that this very ambiguity—this constant punning in the mind—is one of the most valuable data that is provided uniquely by introspection (a veritable pearl cast before the Suckling-pigs). I also believe that the techniques initiated by Descartes' *Cogito ergo sum* (disregarding his construction of dual substances with which he obscured this) and Sartre's ontology of *Etre et le Néant* provides the basis for a technique for the study of ambiguity. This basis is *description* (as opposed to definitions which are always ad hoc and unilateral fixings of a dialectic and, as such, can inheringly never provide any final solution but only a direction for a further movement). The special dialectic of ambiguity is whether to choose to fix an ambiguity by a definition and so merely shift the ambiguity elsewhere and conceal it (useful in certain techniques such as those of science, excluding the Uncertainty Principle) or whether to recognize—it as a valuable and true subject for description, when complementarity is needed.

It is a certain fundamental type of ambiguity that distinguishes *beings* and *things* from qualities. The study of them must take into due and close account both certainties and probabilities (the scientist's "exactness" and "certainty" are never exact and certain but only approximations of probability to the absolute certainty of introspection that they can inherently never reach—the certainty of the ambiguousness).

This technique corresponds to *yoniso manasikāra* in the Suttas. (Dec. 58)

429. There is an inherent special ambiguity about the "present" as an idea or as an existent, which it does not seem to share with the *past* or the *future*. Some argue that the present has no duration, being simply a surface between past and future, while others talk of its duration though they can't agree on what length it ought to have and take specious refuge in a "spacious present." Without paying particular attention to these two views, I find the mere fact that they are asserted indicates that the notion is elastic in the minds of other people and so too I find it in my own. Also the "present" seems to me equally admissible both for "what I am doing now" (extended) and for "what is present to me now."

(instantaneous). And the first (subjective) may *be* the "shortest thought flash conceivable" or "my whole life I am living" or "eternity of past and future in the now. In the last (objective), all temporalization, in its three "orthogonal dimensions" of past, future and present, "appear present" as follows: the past was (present), the present is (present), the future will be (present), and (this is an important point) all three together eternally *may be*. Again concern with the past (taken as probable) gives us historians (and Hegel), concern with the future (taken as possible) gives us scientists, politicians and astrologers (and Hegel), concern with the past and future gives us logicians (and Hegel). The Buddha recommends concern with the present in the Bhaddekaratta-sutta, and this is only possible by introspection which reveals the ambiguity, absurdity and contingency of eternity in time. Again, perhaps, the past is the legitimate field of knowledge (which comprehends), the future is the legitimate field of faith (faith being ignorant man's instrument for groping beyond where knowledge extends). The present is the legitimate field for describing, in terms of the three times, and for remembering what one has described. (Dec. 58)

430. (*Vide* Kierkegaard) *Immediacy* is ironical since, for lack of foresight, it risks failing to get what it wants and is, when inspected from without, always exposed to pain and disappointment, with no defences against them. *Ethics*, its immediate remedy, is either expediency with the purpose of gaining some future immediacy, or it is discipline to gain liberation from immediacy-with-its-blindness: ethics thus always points out of itself and risks, on inspection from without, appearing ridiculous. *Liberation*, its ethical remedy, points to the liberation of all needs ... (Dec. 58)

431. Every victory won in this world is a stalemate on another level. (Jan. 59)

432. That *esse est percipi* I do not *deny* by any means, though I think it incomplete. What is lacking? Nothing. How? Because, given that statement on its merits, it implies (in order that it may emerge at all) *percipiens non est* (i.e., *non esse est percipere*—perceive is a *recul* from being). This statement *esse est percipi*, is not quite of the same order as *cogito ergo sum* (a description, not a logical-causal

deduction), which, if translated into its terms, would be *cogito ergo percipior*, which seems a quaintish *non-sequitur*, since it does not come out well either as a logical deduction or as a description. That *percipiens non est* I do not deny either. But this is only a starting point for completion, for the self-identity of the *percipiens quis percipitur non esse* (= *non esse est percipere*) now enters, and with it ramifications that extend thence ad infinitum.

Now, phenomena *qua* phenomena must be (*ought to be*) distinguishable from what they are not in order that they may emerge at all and that the word may have a meaning (referent) and not be entirely redundant. If so—if they are, as such, distinguishable—it is from being, though with great caution (a limitation of being). And so, if they can be said to have a phenomenal-characteristic peculiar to them, by which they can be so distinguished, it is that when a phenomenon *appears*, it does so as *hiding something else*; but that when a search is made, on this invitation, for what *ought to be* beyond it, only other phenomena ever appear when it disappears (and so, never disappears!). On these terms consciousness *could* be said to appear as the phenomenon that *hides nothing* when it appears. Now, complementarily, if *being*, which phenomena *are thus not*, has, as such, an ontological characteristic peculiar to it alone, it is either that it *has nothing beyond it*, or better that it is *hidden*. A phenomenon, then, while thus *certain* in its phenomenality is *ambiguous* in its *being*. But if, as is always possible, the ambiguity in the being of the phenomenon is dialectically resolved, it reappears again in what the being is *not*, i.e., phenomena, as their non-phenomenality (i.e., ability to appear). All this, in repetitive pattern and infinite (=indefinite) ramifications, vistas and hierarchies, levels, planes and ranges, provinces and pastures, is what the, structure of this play consists in. Hence the Double Ambiguity "whose naming kills and, has it born elsewhere." Herein, too, lies the ambiguity of "*essence*" as the distinguishing characteristic: *is* it phenomenon or being?—logical copula or, predicate? (Jan. 59)

433. *Être en soi* is what phenomena appear to hide, which itself appears, in pure positivity, as what must (ought to) and cannot ever be (found). *Être en soi* is thus, the real objective paradox—the

paradox of the real. (*res*). (Jan. 59)

434. What is probable? Certainty. What is certain? probability. What is infinite? Finiteness. What is finite? Infinity. What is permanent? Impermanence. What is impermanent? Permanence. (Jan. 59)

435. The only one is the many and many the ones. The only one that is the many, is one of many. The only eternity is of time and temporal the eternities. The only infinity is finiteness; and finite infinities. The only permanence is impermanence; and impermanent the permanences. (Jan. 59)

436. What a glue is made by a mixture of guilt and gratitude, and how well they sometimes mix in some pots! (Jan. 59)

437. It is no *ipso facto* escape from dogma to assert (knowingly or not) non-dogmatism dogmatically.

It is no *ipso facto* escape from credulity to believe in one's own scepticism. (Jan. 59)

438. Phenomena are *secretive* and what they *secrete* is being (pun). Hence the reason why, when we see some visible object, hear some sound, etc., we so often ask "what is this?"

439. How often Rationalized Unrighteousness passes—for Righteousness! (Jan. 59)

440. The proverb speaks of making a Virtue of Necessity; but the philosopher Emanuel Kant speaks (in the Categorical Imperative) of making a Necessity of Virtue. (Jan. 59)

441. What is an identity? It is the essential oneness of two entities whose difference, if any, does not count. What is a plurality? It is the essential plurality of one entity whose oneness, if any, does not count. (Feb. 59)

442. "*Essence*" (from the verb *esse* = to be): a medieval logicians' concept, initiated by Aristotle, and used by logicians and philosophers as a synonym for characteristic: (i.e., characteristically distinctive phenomenon by which: we recognize what a thing, or class, is, by which it is recognized to *be* itself). This ontic metaphor from subjective-objective *being* to purely objective characteristic is a pun-by-metaphor of fundamental importance, and indispensably useful for those (Religious Doctors, say, or Scientists) who need to employ the "Utraquistic Subterfuge" (which is so valuable for

verbal presti(-di-)g(itation-)e—remove what is in the brackets and see what remains. But a characteristic-phenomenon of such kind, called metaphorically "essence" (*le phénomène de l'être*), is then that *of* something which *has* that essence and consequently *is not* it (whether that something is regarded as a Kantian. "Ding-an-sich" or as an Abhidhamma constellation-of-dhammas-with-no-self-substance, or what you will, makes no difference here); it is the special phenomenon by which I recognize *what this*, which *has* it, *is*, and by which I believe this to be *what it itself is*. Now by this utraquistic ontic metaphor of "essence" applied to the characteristic, being has been subtly drained away from the subjective-externalized in appearance; it is thus rendered possible to appear to verbally externalize Being and to objectivize it entirely. Thus it is now easier (apparently) to handle "existence" (that same thing's Being) as just another external attribute, namely as that thing's "quality-of-existing" predictable of it. The fraud is now nearly complete; and if the logical copula is (the verbal mode of being agreed upon as one of the basic assumptions of logic, and a logical constant): can only be passed off as quite divorced from being-and-existence with the mediation of the metaphor of "essence" externalized as characteristic or attribute, then the logicians can forget about the copula and make others overlook it, forget that it is the true verbal symbol for existential being by which, and only by which, logic maintains a connection with life, and forget that it contains the (hateful subjective) element of self-identification. This play with the "essence"-metaphor is possible because of the actual existential miragic identity-relation of ambivalence (one-in-two, two-in-one) between consciousness-and-being and between being-and phenomena. This ambivalence, which lurks in the copula is, is an anathema to logicians who seek by any means to hide it away. So now we have *split* being into two and we have apparently drained away being from the copula by means of the "essence"-metaphor and now we can proceed to make believe that the copula is is not really being at all (which is quite untrue, since it remains being on the verbal plane; and if it did not, no statements would correspond at all to life), and so the copula can be exempted from all question or analysis. When we propose to investigate being, this investigation can be handed over entirely to Logics, which, since the copula (its constant) does not count as being, is capable of handling the whole thing and indeed all existential problems (and so, if it *seems* that logic cannot answer some such problem, then, my dear sir, your problem is wrongly stated, is fictitious, and no problem at all since logic is always right: *evvivva il Positivismo Logico*!). No wonder the *cogito* enrages the Logicians so! This is not to *decry* logic in its own proper field which is that of being, but to expose its false claims that being can be subordinated to it or investigated or analysed by it. The proper instrument for that is *yoniso manasikāra*, of which elements are contained in the *cogito*. (Feb. 59)

443. The past came before me now; the future lies before me now; the present is before me now. (Feb. 59)

444. Space = simultaneity of time. Time = allotropism of space. Space = homotropism of time. Time—consecutivity of space.

445. First, examples of *ought to be* and *must be* as duty: "A man *ought to be* married and be a father of a family." "A man *must be* a good patriot if he is to earn the esteem of his fellow countrymen." "Darling, you *must be* grateful to God for giving you your good dinner." "My dear boy, you *ought to be* making a living for yourself at your age," etc., etc.—This is *duty*. This is concerned to get it accepted that "duty *is*" in the sense that "duty is a valid field of perception" (Kant's Categorical Imperative). Duty then, if only it can be established as a valid field of perception will decide such dialectics for us if we "just open our moral eye." (Others say that duty is "what other people want us to do.") *This* as duty. This, as duty taken ontologically, implies that the subject *is not* what he *ought to* (*must*) *be*—he is not (or there is doubt about: his being) married and a father; a good patriot, grateful for dinner, making a living, etc, etc. Ontologically (superficially, at least) they are all straightforward.

This is merely to establish the duty form of "must be" and "ought to be" in common usage in order to dismiss it, because it is the other use that I want to bring out.

The other (equally common but much more ontologically subversive and misleading) use is this, as the following examples may make plain: "We have been, travelling two hours already; we *ought to be* nearly there by now." "It is half past two; the boat *must be* out on the open sea by now." "What is the time? It *must be* about 11–30." "Who is that coming down the street? It *ought to be* Smith by the looks of him." "The world is so marvellously designed, there *must be* a creator of it." "There *must be* a way out of the mess," "there must he a way up this mountain," "there *must be* something in Nibbāna." "It is so because it *must be* so; how could it be otherwise?", and the closely allied "It is too awful; It can't be true! No! No! It *isn't* so!" Now in the/first/case of "duty-must-be," what *must be* is regularly what *is not*; but, on the contrary, in the case of this "certainly-must-be," there is the presumption ranging between suspicion and the certainty of *mauvaise foi*, that what *must be is* ("Are you sure it is? Certain. Have you seen it or verified it? No, but I am quite sure."). This is just the opposite, and to dismiss (?) "certainly-must-be" under "duty-must-be" is to confuse and overlook a whole range of (often very bogus, misleading and dangerous) reasoning. Larelle's Ontology is a good example of what *must* (*ought to*) *be* as what is; and so is Plotinus at times. What is simply is, and, as such, is wider than certainty (certainly-must-be in this sense). Certainty and being are thus not coextensive. Certainty, in its special dialectic (that of certainty; uncertainty), is a "department" of being, which is obvious if we remember that to be is equally well *to be certain* as *to be uncertain*. It is this confusion of what *must be* in this meaning or certainly must-be with what is (as against what is *not*, which also is in the negative mode), that led Alain to make his famous and absurd denial of images: They *cannot* be, therefore they *are not*. (Feb. 59)

446. Ethics results from an effort to escape from the chaos of aesthetic immediacy. But ethics needs justification: justification of ethics by *reason* (with the aid of logic) produces the dialectic of rational philosophical systems; justification of ethics by *feeling* produces the dialectic of religions (with or without logic, and/or holy wars). Justification of existence is their incestuous offspring, and so is condemnation of existence. (Apr. 59)

447. What do they give medals for? Why, for meddling outstandingly in other peoples' affairs, of course. (Apr. 59)

448. The meaning of this is that, the meaning of that is this; the meaning of any this is all this or any or all that, ... the meaning of All is Meaninglessness. (Apr. 59)

449. The basic Irrational Act which is renewed every moment of life, is not to commit suicide. (Apr. 59)

450. The descriptions of what cannot be found are almost limitless in their variety and contradiction—limited only by the limitless field of what can be found. (Apr. 59)

451. Tertullian's famous outburst on the enjoyment of seeing others—'the wicked'—burning in hell betrays the unadmitted fact that all our paradises are other people's hells. (Apr. 59)

452. The 'self-becoming' of the Absolute, as they like to present it, seems a sort of ontological incest. (Apr. 59)

453. Bad as the world is (supposed to be) without any meaning, it would be infinitely worse with one. The moralists all try to find one, but if they succeeded, that would be the end of meanings. (Apr. 59)

454. There are the systems x and y, who regard each other with internecine hatred, and who shout against each other and at all others: "He who is not for me is against me." But I do not say "A plague on both your houses"; for I have no wish to wish plagues on anyone's house; and besides, even if I did, it would be superfluous, since each, by its own attitude, is already the plague on the other's house. (Apr. 59)

455. Eddington's "two writing desks"—one being the familiar piece of furniture at which he is seated resting his arms on it, and the other a scientific physical body lacking all sensual qualities, the greatest part of which is empty space—nothingness—interspersed with innumerable specks of the uncertainty principle in the 'form' of atoms ('open structures') with their electrons and nuclei separated by distances at least 100,000 times their own size. (See Schroedinger, *Mind and Matter*)

456. 1) Justice must be done.

2) It is not enough that justice is done, it must be seen to be done.

3) It is not enough if justice is done and seen to be done, it must be admitted to be done by those (the punished criminals,

the losers of litigation) who are punished by it.

And what if they won't admit it? Shall they be forced to do so or shall justice suffer the dishonour of defiance and of timorous support? In the last analysis, does not justice demand—has it not the right—the sacrifice of every other value at her altar, with only fear, common sense, weariness and forgetting to restrain her? How justice *hates* Mercy! How mercy loves justice! (May 59)

457. What an ideal language classical literary Chinese must be! 'No active or passive, no singular or plural, no case, no person, no tense, no mood' it is said! To be perfect it only needs to be no language at all! (Jun. 59)

458. Broadening of perception without broadening of judgement (understanding) seems to risk leading to increase of hate or of greed, with corresponding strengthening of delusion (the latter, perhaps, having something like a quadratic functional relation to the first two. (Jun. 59)

459. Taking the physical outside world as my looking-glass, what is recognizable there as myself reflected? The Philosophers' and the Physicists' *matter*, as the unfindable 'substance,' the 'reality,' behind appearances. My self cannot be found, and that is one aspect of it. Worship of it is a kind of narcissism. (Jun. 57)

460. How much one has learnt may perhaps be known to oneself. How much one has not will certainly be shown in one's behaviour when the squeeze is applied. (Jun. 59)

461. "Don't build yourself an ivory tower" the moralists say. But I *am* an ivory tower by the mere fact that I *am*. On the crude physical level the body is a frame of (ivory) bones on which the muscles are stretched, crowned by an (ivory) bone pill-box turret housing the brain-shielding it from the blows of 'reality' so that it can get on with its absurd work undisturbed. On the non-physical level my I-ness is an ivory tower of orderly individual views and vistas shielding 'me' from being swallowed up in chaos. Dear moralists: don't they see that life is a constant flight up and down the endless steps of the dark ivory tower seeking to escape from the horrid chaos of *real* freedom? (Jun. 59)

462. Heisenberg has formed his Uncertainty Principle for atomic physics. There seems to be something of the sort needed in

epistemology; for Philosophy points to the Absolute (conceived dialectically as Being or consciousness). But such an Absolute, to be known, must be the object of knowledge, in which case it is *relative* to the knowledge and *not absolute*. If it is attempted to purify it of that last relativity, then, with the withdrawal of all knowledge, it cannot be known whether the Absolute (Being or Consciousness) is absolute or non-absolute (Being-or-non-being, consciousness-or-non-consciousness). The concept Absolute (or All), then, in the Absolute sense, is in other words, Ignorance (and Heisenberg says that ignorance is now accepted *on principle* as one of the characteristics of atomic matter). (Jun. 59)

463. ***Pun***

A. The only *content* of knowledge is the known.

B. Very nice. And so it would seem that the only discontent of knowledge is the unknown. (Jun. 59)

464. Discord: passion and understanding opposed in a fight to the death that never comes.

Harmony: Understanding as the understanding of passion; passion as the passion for understanding. (Jun. 59)

465. The ultimate *object* of knowledge is only ignorance, which in philosophy is euphemistically called 'substance.' (Jun. 59)

466. One is walled in by what one denies; one is chained by what one affirms. One is one's imprisonment. (Jun. 59)

Politically an example of this is the Communist who is shut in by the bourgeoisie he denies, and the consequence in practice is that he becomes even more bourgeois than the bourgeoisie.

Religiously an example is the Christian whose Church, in denying the antichrist, falls into his power by denying him. (Jun. 59)

467. What the psychologists—no, psychoanalysts call a 'fully integrated personality' is he not simply one who lives (loudly and contradictorily and humanely) according to the Old Testament pattern? The New Testament is not an integrating force: 'I bring not peace, but a sword ...' (Jun. 59)

468. Why should 'integration' be a *good thing*?

'Integration' as integration of ignorance and craving in the personality, just as we now have ignorance and force integrated in the atom with Heisenberg's Uncertainty Principle—'Ignorance' and 'Force'—those old myths? (Jun. 59)

469. Absolute self-creation is the transparency of transparency,—not distinguishable from nothing at all. (Jun. 59)

470. "I" = focus of ignorance in perception; "me" = focus of ignorance in '*être-vu*.'

471. The most important philosophical contributions of the scientists are those principles which they have admitted they are forced to accept against their inclinations. Foremost there are Einstein's Relativity, Bohr's Complementarity, and Heisenberg's Uncertainty (= ignorance as a basic principle of matter). Scientific theory erected upon these basic principles is philosophically unimportant in so far as it is 'mystical' (see Whitehead's remark) or inherently unverifiable (material substance,) or any such unproved or unprovable assumption. The Quantum Theory, for example, is an *ad hoc* empirical makeshift which works, but which contains the logically disagreeable contradiction of complementarity, and it may well have to be replaced by another.

The present-day Holy Trinity of Science is therefore: Relativity, Complementarity, and Uncertainty. (*Homousion* or *Homoi-ousion*, of matter (physics)?) (Jun. 59)

472. India has three heavens: the sensual paradises, the heavens of pure form where there is no sex, and the formless heavens where there is no perception of form or of multiplicity. It is tempting to trace these to an unconscious projection of the three principal phases of human life as distinguished by psychoanalysts (especially by Freud on the basis of sex and infantilism): the first is idealized adulthood (which is why it is placed nearest 'this human world'), the second is then the pre-puberty (sexless,) stage (from say 4–years to 12/15 years), which, n.b., is as far back as the normal man can consciously remember. The third, with its blotting out not only of sex but of perception of forms and of difference represents the pre-4–year-old period (or what is behind the normal field of memory). Childhood is normally sentimentally idealized ('My happiest days were ...' etc.) which equals heavenised ('Unless ye become as little children ye shall not enter the kingdom of heaven!'). A point to remember here, which is extremely important is this: the break between the first period (before memory) and the second-and-third

is quite obvious, but the break between the second and the third is, although the fact is obscured by the apparent continuity of the *historical*—memory, quite as absolute as the other on the level of sex values. While one can 'recreate' by memory one's 'historical' experiences during the period between the first memories and puberty, one cannot *revive* the sexless values and patterns (what the moralists like to call the 'innocence') of that period. (How futilely confused the moralists are here is well shown by the frequent unethical behaviour of children (excellently well portrayed in *A High Wind in Jamaica*): a child's attitude to theft and violence is practically unrevivable by an adult, even if a thief or violent himself). In this sense we have the 'three planes of being' corresponding to the 'three planes of heaven' in this life; and in this life they are just as absolutely separated as the 'three planes of heaven' *are*. (Jun. 59)

473. The Middle way: Their tram-lines: on the right their Ivory Towers, the factories and Trust companies; on the left: their work-houses, cancer hospitals, undertakers, their prisons and lunatic asylums. (Jun. 59)

474. Dante, in exile in Verona, lamented his having always to 'climb other people's stairs.' But I ask myself, where are the stairs that are not other people's? Where are the stairs that are *mine* which *they* cannot demand rent for or commandeer or confiscate if they please? (Jun. 59)

475. In the corridor: he saw a door bearing the words: 'Don't open me.' He opened it. A dull room inside with windows of frosted glass and another door on the far right bearing the words 'Don't open me.' He opened it. Another dull room with windows of frosted glass and a curtained looking-glass opposite the door on whose curtains were printed the words 'Don't look in me.' He drew the curtains and looked, and he saw the same dull room reflected, with another door half-right behind him bearing the reversed words 'Don't open me.' He opened it and found himself back in the first room. There another door on the left bore the words 'Don't open me.' He did so and was back in the corridor.

476. **Up-to-Date Glossary**

Beauty—the current style of hair-do and make-up.

Truth—What no one knows—does it matter? Perhaps what science is about to reveal to us after religion has had its day in doing so.

Goodness— = gracious (a gentle exclamation).

Philosophy—Solipsism ('What am I?' and all that: rather discreditable).

Psychology—Solalterism ('What *you are*' and all that: better than philosophy).

Psychoanalysis—Well, well! very deep and dirty.

Ethics—my right to decide what they shall do.

Politics—your right to oppose me.

Government—their obstruction of us.

Art—the normalization of the Enormous (e.g., Empire State Building, Tachisme, Auschwitz memorial, and what next?)

Duty—to be politically conscious.

Christianity—the opposite of Marxism.

Marxism—the opposite of Christianity.

The Middle Way—sitting on the fence.

477. The only difference between discovery and creation seems to be that discovery objectifies its object in the involuntary mode, while creation objectifies its object (the otherwise same object,) in the voluntary mode. Hence the *reality* of the discovered against the *imaginary fictitiousness* of the creation. However the *created thing*, once created, in so far as it takes on an involuntary aspect (what is done cannot be undone), itself becomes discovered as created and so it too gains a species of reality. (Then the 'false' can be *discovered* too, but that is perhaps another question) (Jul. 59)

478. The absurdity of love is that it assumes the very separateness it is its nature to wish to unite. (Jul. 59)

479. Positivism is the wall: Negativism is the locked Door in the Wall. (Jul. 59)

480. Mostly a man is ashamed to tell all that he does, ashamed to do all that he thinks, ashamed (or unable) to think all that he is.

481. *War*: He who is not for me is against me. *Peace*: He who is not against me is for me. (The only difference is in the arrangement of words.) (Jul. 59)

482. Ordinary *knowledge*, which emerges against ignorance, cannot act because it cannot by its very nature know the acts' desired result (which lies in the uncertain and only probable future). In order to *act*, therefore, faith is necessary, which supplements the deficiency of knowledge here. Such knowledge knows with certainty the pure opacity of its object which absolutely walls it in, and behind which wall is the province of ignorance. Faith is confident about penetrating the wall by action, whose result, during and before the action, cannot be *known*. This kind of knowledge is thus a making opaque of the grounds or material for the action without which no act can be begun, while faith 'sees' through this (to knowledge) absolute opacity to the result. Faith is thus a clarifying in its own field. When the act is completed it is then known to knowledge as the 'completed-act-with-its-result' (or as a failure), but then it is made opaque and faith has withdrawn from cooperative knowledge. Faith and knowledge cooperate in an act to overcome ignorance, which is restored when the act is known to be completed.

For faith to *act* it must not be *known* to be doing so (reflexion); for such knowledge inhibits faith (the centipede who fell into the ditch when she reviewed her legs' function while walking). If faith is forced up into knowledge's field either it dies or it becomes '*mauvaise foi*' of the kind Sartre describes. (Jul. 59)

483. Knowledge *emerges* from ignorance as its 'opposite,' faith needs and uses ignorance for its medium, since it is essentially the aid for knowledge beyond its own field.

The three have a triangular relationship in an act (with no true opposite for any of the three).

In the ordinary sense knowledge is certain that what is is and that no action is possible. Faith is certain that no result is impossible. Ignorance is not certain how the action is being done, which changes what is known to be into what it is not.

484. One's thoughts are like nothing so much than an uncorrected text full of mistakes. (Jul. 59)

485. People seem to approach religion for one of two main reasons or for both mixed together: They are moved either by a wish to discover truth (leaving that vague word vague here) or by a

need to find justification for a predilection. Of the first, an outstanding example is, perhaps Kierkegaard. The second is far the more common. In myself I find elements of both. Perhaps the two merge with the incompatibility of two lines that meet at right-angles, and from the meeting-point some set out in one direction and some in the other. (Jul. 59)

486. Discord is *the* monotone. But there are so *many* monotonies. (Jul. 59)

487. It is only death that lives for ever: and the life-everlasting is death.

It is only life that dies for ever: and the death-everlasting is life.

The lifeless has died for ever. The deathless has lived for ever. (Jul. 59)

488. **Action**

The 'actional' attitude has two complementary modes: (1) The voluntary ('active') ('exercise of will', 'free will', control, doing, etc.), and (2) the unvoluntary ('passive') ('limitation of will', 'out-of-control', 'inaction', etc.). These two modes are constantly interlocking and alternating in the process of existence-as-becoming. The *Result of an Action* comes under (2). (1) looks to (2): that is, any *act* is *done* with respect to its expected *result*, without which is no act at all. This means what is called an ACT is, in fact, an experienced *transition* from the voluntary (active) state of (1) to the unvoluntary (passive) state of (2), e. g., the active, voluntary igniting of a fire-work is an example of (1), while the passive, involuntary, nose-tickling firework's independent buzzing (or the ensuing sneeze), is an example of (2). This whole ACT, as an 'experience of a transition' from the one type of constitutive cognizance to the other, opposite, type—on the voluntary-involuntary dimension—involves the manifestation of faith-ignorance already discussed: faith that the result will ensue as expected, and ignorance in the actual experience of the act-as-transition). For simplicity's sake the examples cited are those of the elation conscious-body/inanimate-thing; but the relation of the Act/result between two conscious bodies ('persons') is not essentially different in its basic structure—as I/not-I—from the first-mentioned: then I am this result: what I am is out of my control.

More briefly, these two are respectively expressed by the words 'I' and 'me'—'I' voluntarily make 'me' the involuntary result, 'me' being the *reflection* I see in the not-I. (Jul. 59)

489. Idiosyncrasy—or the individual idiot's singular craziness. (Aug 59)

490. Two kinds of people: Those who, when a new idea is placed before them immediately assess it in terms of good and evil, and if received as good, they refuse to consider its impossibility, but, if received as evil, they refuse to countenance its possibility; and those who assess it in terms of possibility or impossibility, and if received as impossible, refuse to consider whether it is good, but if received as possible, then for them its possibility is more interesting than its evil—Ethics and Science. (Aug 59)

491. Any *description* is always a *reduction in dimensions* or a *projection onto another dimension* (or set of dimensions). (Aug. 59)

492. Let us unite for, not against, lest, by uniting against, we affirm and consolidate what we unite against, and lest, if what we have united against is no more, we do not know how to disembarrass ourselves of our againstness and so turn against each other. (Aug. 59)

493. Being, being universal, cannot be defined except in terms of itself, which is no proper definition. But split, say, into positive and negative, it can speciously be defined as the one in terms of the other: that is ontology. So with consciousness only in asymmetrical ... (?) (Aug. 59)

493a. The imposition and perfection of *order* kills slowly. The introduction of complete *disorder* kills violently. Perfection of order is death by old age; interruption by chaos is death by violence. The breath(?) of life needs both order and disorder. (Aug. 59)

494. If all men are equal in the modern world, what place have teachers in it? (Aug. 59)

495. Words distort thinking, thoughts distort perceiving, percepts distort acting, acts distort being, [beings distort naught, that I may be the acting of the perceiving of the thinking of the wording of the question 'who?'.] (Aug. 59) [ ] added in pencil

496. To do is to act. He who acts is an actor. An actor is essentially one who acts a part that he is not. But is not this the

characteristic of all action? Is there not an aspect of *falsity* and *ignorance*, when evaluated in terms of *being* and *knowledge*, in the very nature of any act, of action itself (if action can indeed be said 'to have, be or "do," a self')? Curious, too, that to "do" someone is to cheat him. (Aug. 59)

497. **Tragedy**

A man had to go and live on a lonely moor near a deep bog, in summer full of flowers. He was not married then. He had two friends. One came to visit him. As he walked with him on the rocks beside the bog, the friend decided to gather flowers. The man warned him not to step on the bog. He laughed and was going to step out on it: 'Why, it is good firm turf!' he said. The man knocked his friend down, just in time to prevent him. The friend took such a great offence that he went straight away and avoided the man ever after. The man was sorry in a way. Soon his other friend came. The same thing happened, but this time the man decided it was perhaps better not to offend the friend than to save him. So when the friend stepped out from the rocks onto the bog, he said nothing and did nothing. The friend sank and was drowned. The man was sorry in a way. Now he had no friend. Soon they came and filled in the bog and built a town all over it, and they turned the moor into a mine. The man got bored and died, but only after a long time, at a great age, after doing a lot of work. (Aug. 59)

499. It is reckoned a good thing to be able to 'rise to an occasion' adequately, and the greatest men are those able to rise adequately to the greatest occasions. But there is one occasion to which none is able to rise, and that is another's death. The nearer and more important the death, the greater and more disturbing the inadequacy. Inadequacy is in the highest degree a painful state. Hence the flight into the conventional group-behaviour of funeral rites, chief mourners, wakes, and all the rest. If the Forgetting-Mechanism is in good order, it removes the inadequacy. (Aug. 59)

500. The axiom assuming that the difficult must be explained in terms of the easier, is legitimate, centripetal, regressive and mean. Why not explain the easy by progressive stages in terms of the more difficult, if we are to broaden our minds? (Aug. 59)

501. It seems to have been one of the regular comforts of Church Philosophers to believe that what cannot be thought can be said. (Aug. 59)

502. Though it is possible to define fog perfectly clearly, such a definition will not aid one to find one's way about in the fog. (Sep. 59)

503. The knife, by its being kept sharp is sharpened *away*. (Sep. 59)

504. The dialectic of existence as the war of having to take sides. To sponsor affirmation of the world (like Nietzsche or Schweitzer in their very different ways) leads to championing that side, leads to suicide, which is conquest and enslavement by the opposite. Then the whole process can be worked out on the opposite side by denial and satanism (Byron, etc.) when the counterpart suicide-as-conquest-and-enslavement by the opposite takes place. The average man crowds the middle areas, but his ideals all point to taking sides: when the pressure is put on he takes sides for all his pacific arguments.

Suicide here is self-sacrifice to the acknowledged master as the necessary consequence of achieving mastery in affirmation or in negation. To be the complete master of affirmation is to sacrifice oneself wholly to negation and into its slavery, and then the suicide-death is simply a switch of the fundamental being to the opposite, with the switch from mastery to slavery ... (Sep. 59)

505. The sense of 'evil'—in addition to 'fear of pain'—seems to arise as a consequence of an involuntary attribution of animateness to the inanimate or to the unseen. 'Evil' is thus inherent in the three Semitic religions and in Hindu philosophy (wherever animist). In Buddhism it falls away and leaves the basic experiences of pain and fear of pain, as they are and as they arise and cease.—The pictures of Max Ernst, in so far as they suggest animateness of the inanimate (which they undoubtedly do very strongly) stimulate the 'sense of evil' very strongly. 'Evil' arises from the conception of a 'will' *alien* to my own (other human wills, however *hostile*, are not thus *alien*, since they are human: God is always accompanied by the Devil). (Sep. 59)

506. It is the nature of consciousness to look back and forward, when it arises, in time. But that proves nothing as to whether

anything *did* happen or *will* happen. The a *priori* is a conascent perspective. (Sep. 59)

507. Suppose we say that existence is life-and-death and that *every* time we use the word 'to be' and its derivatives we are being metaphysical? (Sep. 59)

508. The honest man is *describable* only in terms of dishonesty. For his honest quality he possesses in the form of his acts. And acts are alterations made. But he is not his acts: he *is not* what he possesses: he is not honest or he is his acts: but then by acting he is a changing, and so cannot remain honest, or in other terms: he is what he is not, if he is what he has. (Sep. 59)

509. Singularity is the identity of two; duplicity is the non-identity of one. Identity = ignorance of duplicity, duplicity = ignorance of identity. Need assumes the identity of what it needs and the duplicity of what it does not need (needs to reject). (Sep. 59)

510. In the "flow" of *time* the only constant is *space*. In the "extension" of *space* the only *continuity* is *time*. Time is *inconstant*, space is *discontinuous*. Time is constant in one place, space is continuous in one moment.

511. There are two ways of attempting to deal with the appalling difficulties of choice on the higher ethical levels (Truth/beauty/goodness; family/country, war/peace, principles/persons...): (1) one can attempt to *justify* a one-sided choice, and this is what philosophies of *value* and religions attempt to do through reason and faith (feeling,) respectively. But this always founders or is never safe from foundering. (2) Or the dialectic can be squarely faced in the fact that no one-sided solution of it is ever justifiable by reason or by faith. And here enters the question not of acceptance or refusal, nor of affirmation or denial, but of letting-go. The letting-go, however, is limited, in life at least (and without taking death into account) by the boundary of *ability* to let go. (Sep. 59)

512. All action, regarded (mathematically) as a function of *me*, and I being a function of ignorance, action is a function of reflected ignorance. (Sep. 59)

513. Does the escapable-from-ness justify the prison?

514. Imperfection is the window through which the beauty appears in the world. Remove the imperfection, and no more

beauty. (Sep. 59)

515. What he is is doing, what he does is having, what he has is being—the "circuit of ipseity." (Sep. 59)

516. In existence, goodness is no protection against ugliness, beauty none against falsity, truth none against evil. All three together do not avail against starvation and death. (Oct. 59)

517. Religious people are like people who gather in a doorway (a favourite Italian habit), lean against the door jambs gossiping and block the passage—the passage leads, to other doorways, which give onto other passages. (Oct. 59)

518. **Pattern**

The ultimate aim is aimlessness (the ultimate meaning is meaninglessness). Whether the vista of aims (or meanings) is bounded—or infinite, it is the same. The dialectic of aim/no-aim (the affirmation-and-denial of meaning) swings from the idea of aim unaffirmed and undenied; it vanishes with liberation from the basic Idea (with cure of the disease of meaning). (Oct. 59)

519. Where Religion takes refuge by identifying the Absolute with either universal Being or Consciousness, the philosophies deriving from Hegel elevate Action to the highest level, identifying that with the Absolute as an (economic) Becoming through Hegel's of Being and Consciousness (object-subject).

But Consciousness, Being and Action are all *both*, incompatible *and* co-present (hence the internecine quarrel). (Oct. 59)

520. Belief as an *inflation* of knowledge (currency, size of a balloon): the skin of a rubber balloon is known in the sense that it is (deflated) an evident phenomenon. Knowledge is essentially *involuntary* (I cannot, by mere willing, unknow what I know): the balloon-skin lies in my hand as an evident fact. If the balloon-skin is inflated with a suitable gas hydrogen, say) it will float in suitable conditions. But the gas that makes it float miraculously) is hidden from knowledge by the balloon-skin while it floats: it is there by faith. If I try to convert this faith into knowledge by letting out the gas for inspection, the floating vanishes: the faith has died by being produced for inspection. The *power* of faith always lies in its *voluntariness* (as opposed to knowledge) being *hidden*: if exposed it is rendered powerless. Faith, in order to have absolute power, must

be absolutely inaccessible to knowledge—and (here is the paradox), owing to the *nature* of knowledge, then faith is indistinguishable from knowledge. (Oct. 59)

521. So long as one assumes *death* as an *absolute fact*, one must have, as an assumed absolute value based on it, the decision either to kill or to be killed in the last extreme (and this includes attitudes to suicide and to 'natural death'). This alternative ultimately divides all people (who make that assumption about death) into two types. With a proper understanding of death, the decision (dialectic) must collapse on the laying bare of the assumption. Freud has remarked, that death is inconceivable to the Unconscious, a statement which, though open to the usual criticisms of F's mechanistic assumptions about cons-ciousness, does point to a very important factual dialectic in assumptions about death. (Nov. 59)

522. An act is the action of an actor; an actor acts a part; in so far as an action is the acting of a part it is the action of one who is pretending (pre-tending) to *be* what he *is not*: an act completed is thus a pretence or fraud or betrayal waiting for justification by History, which has no end. (Nov. 59)

523. Absolute dictatorship as organization of dutie(s) without right(s): absolute democracy as agglomeration of right(s) without dutie(s); existing human societies float at different levels between, and they stand upon two feet: the claim of rights against duties, and the claim of dutie(s) against right(s), and on these two feet they "march forward." (Nov. 59)

524. The world is absurd and has no meaning; but it is not that the world has no meaning; for it always has a meaning, cannot be divested of it, is haunted and eaten up by it—but no single ultimate meaning can ever be identified. This is the absurdity, when it is seen. (Nov. 59)

525. All old philosophies aim at one of the alternative absolutes of 'pure being' *or* 'pure consciousness'; they subject action to this end as the means. A consequence is that this ultimate goal is beyond this life, has to be so. It is in the 19th century only, in Europe, that, with Hegel, pure being and pure consciousness are fused and the way prepared for subordinating both to action. Marx does this fully and, going further than Hegel, who remains suspended in the

abstract, identifies action with economics. This identification is dialectic. In Marxism, logically everything is fixed in the movement of Action, identified dialectically with economics, and past history is involved in the movement of change: for not only is it being *built* but what is already past and built is itself being *changed* by action. The Judgment of History is thus a changing one. The 'fading of the state' is the fading of History itself. Consciousness is *dependent on action* (n. b.) and: being is action (also n. b.). (Nov. 59)

526. It is not memory but *forgetting* which is the positive function in maintaining existence. It is partial forgetting that conceals the contradictions and makes what is not forgotten, to *be* possible. (Nov. 59)

527. The fundamental existential choice (made by the individual in infancy) is the identification of I/me with a historical facticity, as this-unique-body-of-behaviour-which-I-am-becoming. That fundamental choice, as part of its necessary facticity, must have a *particular* perception associated with it (*my* body is thus, not otherwise), a particular affectivity (it is a pleasant, unpleasant or indifferent choice, whence 'I love life,' 'I am evenminded' or 'I hate existence') and conative (in the sense that it is 'voluntary' or 'involuntary', i.e., passive and imposed). (Nov. 59)

528. In some ways a saint *is* no longer a saint as soon as he is recognized and proclaimed and worshipped. A saint *is* a saint in so far as his being influences the actions of others, without their reflexive awareness of the fact, towards the lessening of suffering. But as soon as he is proclaimed and worshipped then that state, in which his worshippers try to emulate (imitate) him impossibly by being his disciples (a disciple de facto cannot be or even imitate his *master*, whose being consists in not-being-a-disciple), then his influence is channelled away (in this respect worship is as dissipating as laughter) and (perhaps by some Hegelian 'passing over into the opposite') under the worship with love lurks the anti-worship with hate. The saint's name has become stale and provocative of suffering. (Nov. 59)

529. **Temptations**

1. The temptation to make something positive, no matter what, of religion in *this or some future life*.

2. The temptation to commit what I shall call the 'obverse of murder,' i.e., suicide *blamed on someone else* or on some group or on society as a whole ('you do not want me so I shall let myself die and that will be your fault,' and '*they* will punish you or you will punish yourselves').

3. The temptation to deny and to cling to denial (denial of *meaning* in life, etc., etc.), which is the form of assertion opposed to affirmation.

530. The evidence that constitutes the proof is connected by a leap to the truth that it is believed to prove. (Dec. 59)

531. *Being/consciousness/action.*—It is only in terms of action that being can be critically assessed and only in terms of *being* that action can be critically assessed. To act, like all verbs, has its substantative essence-action. Being, like most substantives in fact and like all in potentiality, has its verb-to be. Consciousness (as knowledge *or* ignorance, n.b.) is no standpoint but is what *has*—or gives—a standpoint. It cannot of itself provide terms for critical assessment of anything since it simply knows (or ignores)—is knowledge (or is ignorance). Since all phenomena are what consciousness is not, it is in terms of phenomena purely negative. But phenomena have two incompatible and coexistent dimensions, namely *being* can be critically assessed in terms of phenomena that act, and vice versa. (Dec. 59)

532. Being as action is changed identity; action as being is, identification. To be is to identify. To act is to change identity. (Dec. 59)

533. The greatest possible joke would be the fact that the greatest joke of all was not a joke at all. The sureness of the joke would lie in its being found to be no joke. (Dec. 59)

534. The ultimate meaning of meaning, to repeat, must be meaninglessness, and the ultimate aim aimlessness, the ultimate end endlessness. For an aim that has an aim beyond it is, in regard to that ulterior aim, not an aim but either a means or an obstruction. Therefore to look to an ultimate aim, however conceived, is to look to a state of aimlessness and to live according to aimlessness as supreme value. Those, on the contrary, who do not admit this must live without supreme aim, and doing so either in absolute

aimlessness without any aim at all or with only a succession of relative aims assumed and then attained and replaced by another: or found unattainable and forgotten and replaced by another: and so on without foreseeable end (aim or meaning) in the ultimate sense. In any case, however stated in terms of meaning or end or aim, any situation that implies meaning (or end or aim) must ultimately resolve into or point to absolute meaninglessness, endlessness or aimlessness, for which eternity is a name. (This is very satisfactory and restful.) (Dec. 59)

535. A gate-crasher never really gets inside: he only brings his outsideness inside. An ivory-tower dweller never really gets outside: he only brings his insideness outside. (Dec. 59)

536. One can count forwards forever because one knows where to begin with *one* (oneself?). But one can never start counting backwards because one never knows (inherently) where to begin. Why does time go in only one way (time as repetition)? Is history anything more than mere arrangement by enumeration? (Dec. 59)

537. *Matter*: what, it is assumed, cannot contradict itself.

Mind: what, it is found by experience, can contradict itself. (Dec. 59)

538. Other people: the innumerable outward vanishing points in the perspective 'I': the inner or central vanishing-point in the perspective. (Jan. 60)

539. When silent all are in agreement. (Jan. 60)

540. Existence described as a system of null-functions activated into partial non-nullity by ignorance. (Jan. 60)

541. Anything whatever that is expressible is expressible in more than one way. Any expression of it is one among a choice of ways of expressing it. An expression of something is a verbal movement from here to there. There is no one way from here to there. (Jan. 60)

542. **Dimensions of Ambiguity**

1. The *point* = line from the eye through the point to infinity.

2. The *line* (straight or curved) = plane (straight or curved) from the eye to infinity (conics?)

3. The *plane* = space from the eye to infinity.

4. *Consciousness* = all my time.

5. *Nothing* = I myself (all negative statements have open

ambiguity, all positive statements concealed ambiguity).

543. Any act assumes the role of an actor. The act interrogates the world. The result is the being satisfied with the world's assumed reply to the interrogation. (Feb. 60)

544. Being applies to all qualities and substances, both to their affirmation, and to their negation. It is thus quite vain to attempt a definition of being. A definition must be made from outside what is defined: but outside being is ... nothing. To the question "What is *is*?" the only possible reply would be "*is* is *is*," which does not define but merely states the ambiguity of identity. (Feb. 60)

545. All the questions asked about death are wrongly put. (Feb. 60)

546. People who generalize: those who generalize from a single instance, and those who generalize from a statistical collection of instances. (Feb. 60)

547. People who regard truth as something to be created and people who regard it as something to be discovered. (Feb. 60)

548. The world is a collection of part-truths which invite one's putting them together to form a whole. That is not difficult; but when it is done, always there are either some parts left over or some missing. (Feb. 60)

549. Suppose the following advertisement were published everywhere: "Science has now discovered how to avert death: by calling at the nearest hospital and receiving an injection you can be assured of living forever barring accidents. Nothing else; however, is assured. Though science has not yet discovered how to control ageing it hopes to do so, given time." Would I call at the nearest hospital, I wonder? (Feb. 60)

550. I am myself—I am what I have.
I am what I did: I shall be what I do.
I am doing my work: I do exist my being.
I have to do to be: I have to be to do.
I am not what I do: I undo what I am. (Feb. 60)

551. Ambiguous Key Words

Reason	the breadth of reasonableness the narrowness of rationalism	
I	'I' the unique subjective 'I' spoken by everyone else	the "Ego"
is	existence entity essence	many one
truth	beauty—valuable evil that exists—to be destroyed	
Consciousness	observed subjectivity observing subjectivity	one many
all	all of these but not those all of all without exception	
To exist	to be = to be static = death to become = to be dynamic = life	
Positive	positive good positive evil	

and negative statements as:

I know nothing	I have no knowledge I know what nothing is

552. Dialectics or Same Things as:

"*Good*"	"*Bad*"
patience	weak-mindedness
tolerance	connivance
service	servitude, servility
independence	instability
freedom	chaos, crime
liberty	license
popularization	vulgarization

law and order	slavery, rigidity
conversion	apostasy
rectitude	bigotry
sincerity	priggishness
virtue	constraint
justice	revengefulness, punishment
universal	insipid, colourless
grace	caprice
to sacrifice	to squander, to destroy, to betray
the incomprehensible	the absurd
honour	conceit, arrogance, want of humility
equality	monotony (undiversity)
fraternity	nepotism

End of the Second Note Book

ADDENDA

(FROM NOTEBOOKS AND LOOSE LEAVES)

ADDENDA

GENERAL

553. I admit that a theist might well counter that "with God all things are possible," which clothes the nakedness of the Absurd with a seemly veil; but I should like to watch him actually undertaking to accept, without reserve, *whatever* is absurd as a proper object of faith as soon as presented *simply because it is absurd*—a square triangle, perhaps, and lots and lots of centaurs. But a further question arises: How does he *choose* the object as one of faith, how is he *aware* that it is really absurd at all, except by the action of understanding (knowledge), which he pretends he has castrated his mind of? More "*mauvais foi*," I fear.

554. God, they say, made man in his own image: thus what a mine of information about the nature of god is the behaviour of man!

555. Why should I worry if threatened with a mortal disease? Have I not already within me the germs of that hereditary disease which no one can avoid or cure, namely, old age and death? (undated)

556. If I must live like an amateur, let me die like a professional. (1949)

557. Flour forms the basis of an enormous number of dishes—it is nasty when raw, and it is sensitive to skill in cookery. "Progress" is a sort of mental flour out of which people cook up a vast variety of food for thought. But it is just as easy to make a filthy, dyspeptic pudding out of the one as the other—and one has to admit that some of the cooks are awful. (Apr. 52)

558. One thing modern science has done for Cupid is to give him new rubber wings. (Apr. 52)

559. "These acts are right and those are wrong no matter who does them," and "whatever dear so and so does is right, whatever

filthy so and so does is wrong" are two threads which we weave together into the ambivalent texture of our attitude towards, and judgement of, other people. (Apr. 52)

560. If, in present conditions one man (and this is not inherently impossible) were to develop in himself the power to see what is going on on the surface of, say the planet Jupiter in the same scale of detail as normal men see what is going on on the earth round them, this would at present be unverifiable by all other men. This knowledge (experience) would only be accessible to the one man. In what would this differ from a hallucination for so long as it remained inaccessible to all other men? If he announced his knowledge would he not be called mad? And rightly so? (Jun. 52)

561. The dynamic conception of beauty is in the transfiguration of the ordinary or the ugly. The static conception of beauty opposes beauty, *per se* and absolute, to the ordinary and the ugly. The first is unlasting, the second incomplete. (Aug. 57)

562. A saint who has achieved liberation would seem to be less free than an ordinary man, since an ordinary man can be sometimes saintly and sometimes not, whereas a saint is never allowed to be not saintly. (Apr. 56)

563. One advantage in having no friends is that one cannot let one's friends down. And those who live on the hard ground cannot let themselves down. (Jan. 53)

564. I have been unable to find any one rule with universal application, that is "absolute"—there is always more than one unique rule: anything that I can call a self (*vide* Hume); any two pairs of exact opposites ('yes' is not the exact opposite of 'no').

565. There is always some point from which any passion seems comical and is ironical. —That is a hard saying.

—Then why not put it the other way round?

—Silence. (Sep. 57)

566. There are certain controversies which involve one in untruth, whichever side one adopts, such as the existence or non-existence of god. (Sep. 57)

567. An absolutely objective thought is as sterile as an absolutely hygienic copulation. (Sep. 57)

568. Truth as the Good and the Beautiful overlaps, but is not

coextensive with and is *incomplete* in comparison with, truth as "acts and facts," which again are incomplete without the constituent negative mediant of consciousness as manifested in the individual that makes lies true. (Aug. 57)

569. *The* mistake (if that is a legitimate phrase) lies in attempting to remedy dialectical instability by logical rigidity. (Oct. 57)

570. The argument that God cannot have created the world because of the suffering, misery and ugliness in it (or some similar form) has always seemed to me as inconclusive for proof that there is no god as the opposite argument that 'God must have created the world because of the order, joy and beauty in it' (or some similar form) seemed for proof that there is a god. In either case it is presumed that one knows, can distinguish, what god ought to be. Both alike imply that the holders of each view will only believe in what they approve of, i.e., in what pleases them.

Now, surely, is it not that assumption, that growth or surcease in one's subjective self, that ought to be understood and faith in its subsidence cultivated? (Dec. 57)

571. If I did not ultimately disagree with everyone else, if I had absolutely *no* secret at all from anyone else, I should not be 'I' at all, not even someone or everyone else. (Dec. 57)

572. Is any historical fact worth remembering in itself so long as one remembers *how* to act? Surely, a man who remembers a fact but cannot remember either how to repeat or avoid *it, is an* object of pity. (Dec. 57) (Addition:) If you can act, why remember the fact?

573. Most (and all the principal elements) of what I ever learned of vice (and that is not claimed to be much) was learned from the inventive condemnations of the indignant pious; what I learned from the vice-addicts was much detail but little generality in comparison; but I learned much virtue from some of them. (Jan. 57)

574. The *Train of Thought* can have both a restaurant car[3] and a sleeping car.

One's baggage is then one's *conceits*. They can be stolen or lost.

---

3. *Viññāṇāhāra*? (= nutriment of consciousness)

575. I must and can't
(what happens if I ain't?)
I ought and won't
(what happens if I don't?)

576. Two demons: one who insists that what is to be inferred by verbal processes must correspond to experience; and one who insists that what cannot be arrived at by verbal processes cannot correspond to experience. (Jul. 53)

577. When we are children we are not quite deceived by the fairies with which our minds people empty places, or by the "let's pretend"; but when we are grown up we forget that we imagine many things and so we no longer know the truth about the things we imagine (Nov. 53)

578. Odd how people interested in religion spend so much time trying to convert the obvious meaning of their texts that are their authority. (Nov. 53)

579. Mutual admiration societies, it seems to me, are quite admirable—so long as they indulge in private (as secret societies). It is when they make public exhibition of themselves that they invite the throwing of mud and stones. (Dec. 53)

580. The whore-shop of publicity. (Aug. 56)

581. People who live only in and for towns and spend all their time in socialities and business with no knowledge of or feeling for wild animals and trees and rocks and oceans, are no longer more than half human. (Aug. 56)

582. Transparency = sameness on different levels. (Aug 56)

583. 'A place for everything, and everything in its place,' say the devotees of tidiness—but they have turned their backs to, and are haunted by, the counterpart 'No place for confusion, and confusion out of its place.' (Apr. 58)

NOTES ON PHILOSOPHY

584. One must start in analysis with any complex situation or datum that, if anything, is *basic*. To work away from this by analysis or simplification or abstraction is not to arrive at the more *fundamental* or *true*, but only, perhaps, to sort out the relatively

more general from the relatively more particular, as a means to find new complex experiential situations. What is *fundamental* in this view is *complexity.* (1954)

585. (Indiscriminate) generality implies distinction. Distinction implies perceiving. Perceiving implies named percept. Named-percept implies variety of fields. Variety of fields implies awareness (Ogden-Richard's with reference to named perception); awareness implies affectivity; affectivity implies conation; conation implies habits (unconscious, inherent tendencies, reflexes, etc.); habits imply being-and action; being-and-action implies production (creation); creation implies decay and vanishing: (with all the emotional bother involved).

Nothing is unless it is originated by other things and with other things. Feed-back operates.

586. Transcendence (in being) = ignorance = infinity. (Sep. 57)

587. If *a* and *b* are considered in rotation(?) as the related qualitatively-differing elements, then *a* can only change (be seen to change) against *b's* fixity, and *vice versa.* The fixity-change relationship is on principle reversible, but only by a step. When a third element, c, (or more), is brought in the dual motion (change) of *a* and *b* against (...), *c's* fixity can be experienced. a, b, c, etc., can be equated thus, say, *a*: affectivity (pleasure/pain), *b*: rationality (assertion/denial); and then, perhaps, *c*, etc., as action/ inaction, etc. One (though which is indeterminate), or one set, must, however, be fixed for change to be experienced (either may be overlaid by ignorance which then gives the experience of 'absolute motion,' 'absolute fixity,' etc.) (Sep. 57)

588. A: The Quantum Theory has, by external application, led to the splitting of the physical atom—in other words to external concentration of energy. By an internal (application), why should it not lead to a splitting of the personal atom (my self)—in other words to internal concentration of energy?

B: There now! (Sep. 57)

589. "*Is*" forms the basis of the syllogism: and so cannot be analyzed by logic.

"*Is*" forms the basis of any description: and so cannot be described. For, to describe, I must stand outside the described: but being is universal and covers the positive and negative as well. If I ask: What is this? An answer would be: a sheet of paper. If I ask: what is a sheet of paper? One of many answers (giving some quality or other) might be: it is white (and so one might go on for ever).

But here comes the important point: I can equally well say: the paper *has* white*ness*. So I might say, too, it seems: The paper *has* being (making being a category). But common sense will not agree that anything is what it *has*. Consequently, if this paper has being, it is not. But that would be nonsense—at least to common sense.

590. Practically all that has been said about being is worthless. Its structure is that of positive and negative and requires the presence of consciousness for its structure.

Nirodha as vanishing of being/not-being (see *atthita/natthita*).

The voluminousness of Sartre is needed to undo, the tangle of European ontology. (Jun. 58)

591. The 'is' of logic is perfectly valid where being (and non-being) prevails. But the question raises itself: does being (whether considered as a category and in both its positive and negative forms) exhaust every possibility *without remainder*? In other words, does cessation necessarily fall always under one or the other subordinately? This can only be established verbally by logic but it can be established in both ways—yes and no; and the dialectic cannot be solved. Consequently we can never say for certain that cessation is subordinate to being.

592. In contrast with the extreme subtlety and fluidity of consciousness and being, language is angular and bitty. To try to represent this with word patterns is like trying to draw the structure of an atom on the back of a postage stamp with a carpenter's pencil, or like trying to construct a circle with a dozen dominoes.

593. If you believe, you act in confidence and faith believing that what you believe is true. But if you know that you believe, you know ipso facto that you do not know. What happens then if you have no belief? The question has no meaning for to be conscious is to believe. Technically it is a "visualized" expectation of the direction of the actual "motion" which "is" consciousness. The belief expects the direction *will be* such: knowledge records it as

memory that it was such: in between is the denial, the motion of view point that is called consciousness.

594. *Starting from Consciousness* (being without nouns of doing).

Without consciousness it is impossible to conceive at all: to conceive anything or nothing. Inevitably with the appearance of consciousness (in its widest sense) being/ existence is, and is simultaneously (because of consciousness' presence), e. g. as existence/non-existence and as existence/essence. This *doubt* can be taken as (in Freudian terms) the "conscious manifestation" of the "unconscious" conception of a thing's existence/being, which is then "consciously" either denied or asserted. Denied or asserted dialectically, the denial or assertion is then supported logically. The logical structure, if completed, leaves no room for consciousness whose dialectical decision supports it.

Starting from being/existence (doing without verb 'to be')

Without being/existence consciousness cannot *be*, or not be, or both be and not be, or neither be nor not be. ("Being" *essentially* belongs to the (Freudian) unconscious where what is, is so without denial or assertion, without distinction of positive/negative. This must never be lost sight of though the Freudian hypothesis remains only a hypothesis). Consciousness therefore *does/does* not. The propositions "consciousness exists (is)" or the converse, have no meaning, and are each as self-contradictory as the propositions "*being cognizes/does not cognize*."

595. What I am (what I identify my self-myself with) that I am for ever. But at another time I am similarly something else. There is no conscious transition. Moments of reflexion discover this contradiction, which is disconcerting and so covered up by forgetting it. I *am* this body when I leap back to avoid treading on a deadly venomous snake or when I am (or have the sensation of being) discovered by another in some discreditable act. I *own* this body of mine when I examine a pimple on it or take it to a dentist or a doctor for treatment. I *disown* it (i.e., its acts) when I am accused of some crime and decide to lie it out. *I am not* it when sitting quiet face to face with what seems certain death. (Aug. 57)

596. As far as descriptions (and so philosophies) are concerned, it seems as if a System is ipso facto false, and that some sort of

"complimentarity" (in the atom-physicist's sense) is nearer truth as fact. (Aug. 57)

597. Above the plane of facts all that Science has done, is to screen phenomenological certainty by a cloud of statistical and historical probability. (Aug. 57)

598. Taking, in the phenomenological sense, probability as the characteristic of the purely objective constituent of the world (the world of science) and certainty as that of subjectivity (the Cogito, etc.), then outward change will be change in my probabilities (alteration) and inward change will be change in my certainties (forgetting, which is, in its extreme sense, death, a change in my being). (Sep. 57)

599. **Motion**

I cannot discover any simple fact that corresponds to the word "motion." First to take the facts objectively.

Suppose (on paper) that A and B are approaching each other in a straight line with a constant speed. Then there is relative approach speed without angular velocity as the AB relation. The situation is inherently unstable because, assuming that the distance between them is finite, A and B must meet and the instant after their meeting (there is something contradictory about two points "meeting") their approach speed must be transformed into recession speed. Suppose again that C is on a line at right angles to AB and not too far from B. Then A and C are approaching each other with a speed that is gradually reducing with increasing deceleration. The speed is combined with angular velocity which is gradually increasing in the ratio of a variable function proportionate to the decrease of the speed of approach. When A reaches B, then A and G have no relative speed and maximum angular velocity, after which the speed increases and the angular velocity decreases. This is the description in *objective* terms. Such a description conceals the assumption of a describer (I) who is observing these happenings on (let us say) the inner surface of a large sphere at whose centre he stands. For him the happenings are all experienced in terms of angular velocity only. He can "identify himself" with any of the three, A, B, or C.

Still at this point we can say that the word "motion" has no simple referent but is referred to (a) speed of approach or recession without angular velocity, (b) angular velocity without speed of approach or recession, and (c) a proportionate mixture of the two.

It is only the description in terms of *subjective* experience that makes this difference quite clear. My experience of the direct approach of a body and me is absence of angular velocity at some point of the visual object body that otherwise "grows" (? Ed.) in a specifically proportionate manner. Such an experience is inherently unstable. Either angular velocity must be introduced into all parts of the object, or a "collision" will take place, which will either break up the flow of experience or transform the approach speed into recession speed. The last is also inherently unstable because it must end in "vanishing." This corresponds to the AB relation above where "I" = B.

1. I experience a visual pattern, which grows in a certain constant proportion (expands), and some point in that expanding pattern has no angular velocity, then this "I" call "approach." If that continues unchanged there must be a "collision" followed by a break-up of that train of experience, or a reversal of it ending in "vanishing."

In the "objective" description we spoke of the decreasing approach speed mixed with angular velocity as the AC relation. But in the "subjective" description, if "I" am identified with C then my experience of A will be that of an expanding pattern no part of which is without angular velocity. There will be no "collision." A moment of maximum angular velocity will coincide with a moment of no-expansion-no-contraction, followed by a train of diminishing traction and diminishing angular velocity, ending also in "vanishing."

2. I experience a visual pattern, which expands in a constant proportion, and all points in that expanding pattern have angular velocity relative to me. This "I" call "motion." Or I experience a visual pattern which remains constant in size, and all points in which have angular velocity. This too "I" call "motion."

But here something curious has happened. The objective "speed of approach" AB has been replaced by the subjective experienced proportional expansion of a pattern that contains a point without angular velocity. (To take it one step further, the objective angular velocity as replaced by what I shall call angular kinaesthesis, to distinguish it from accelerant kinaesthesis = "I am moving"—but this may be left for the moment). While the objective speed of approach AC has been replaced by a subjectively experienced expansion of a pattern containing no paint without angular velocity. Instead of the two components of objectivized "motion," approach-speed and objective angular velocity, we have only (a) partial ordered angular velocity (expansion excluding one point) and (b) total ordered angular velocity, of a given pattern. There are in fact here not two different components but only one (expansion = ordered angular velocity differently organized). Now we said that the "objective" description concealed an assumed observer not in the special plane ABC of the happenings described. Similarly the "subjective" description conceals an assumed observer later in time than the "I" of the "experience" described. The second is therefore correctly, an objectivized subjective description. It is perhaps nearer to completeness but it is not complete because the "later I" has escaped through a hole in it and continues to do so. (From the Second Note Book, July 54)

600. **The Function of**

Psychology is to produce and collate data on behaviour of mind.

Biology is to produce and collate data on behaviour of animate 'matter.'

Psychology is to produce and collate data on behaviour of mind.

Logic is to produce and collate data on rules for coherent speech.

Philosophy is to produce and collate data on values to guide choice: (includes or should include ethics and training directed towards the good of this world, by considering birth and death).

Religion is to produce and collate data values to guide choice: (includes or should include ethics and training directed towards the good of 'not-this-world' by considering the 'before-birth-and-after-death').

* * *

The following two items are from a sheaf of loose leaves labelled ONTOLOGY, containing chiefly definitions and analysis of words and terms, extracts from books, etc. They were probably meant as material for essays planned by the author under the title BUDDHISM AND ONTOLOGY, on which see the end of the next section "Notes on Dhamma."

601. Ontology cannot be discussed without the use of words. So something will have to be said with words about words. But so much has already been done in this way that there seems to be no end to it all. The whole subject seems to have long since got quite out of hand.

Nevertheless something can still be done by confining oneself to certain aspects of the use of words, say to their inherent ambiguity, and to their field of reference, in general.

A word refers both to the speaker and the hearer, to something other than it.

What they refer to may be either other words or what is not words. In the first case, words can refer to words which refer to words and so on indefinitely. Some have claimed this and no more is what words do and that even the logical proper name ('this') simply refers to some word or proposition. Words are then a closed world, which there is no getting into and no getting out of.

602. Difficulties on ontology

The difficulties arising from a badly chosen notation are well known in Mathematics (i.e., Newton's and Leibnitz's notations for the calculus). Language is notoriously ambiguous (vide Freud), metaphorical, utraquistic, punning and vague.

2. Any *definition* is always *ad hoc*, never of universal validity (see Wunter)

3. It is in the nature of *description* that the terms of the description are parallel to what is described (the illumination of the unknown by the known), and that nothing can be described successfully in terms of itself, not even in terms that include itself (this touches on the Theory of Types). But *Being* is posited as *universal*. Consequently it is *indescribable* and can only be pointed to in one of its instances by a demonstrative: a logical proper name = "that." Being therefore is indicatable, but not describable as

"whatever is common to a 'that' or 'this." It is then being opposed to the being of non-being. In its general aspect, it is being, but in particular aspect it is the existence (of a being).

Notes on Dhamma

603. Dhamma has no conflict with *Science* proper. Its methods are much the same (i.e., investigation of experience, remembering what has been investigated and forming a true view to accord with the factuality of experience investigated); but the material is different. Reputable science (Physics) confines itself to the outside world and all science restricts itself (or should do) to publicly observable behaviour. Dhamma is concerned with investigating subjective mind, recognizing the outside material sphere, but leaving it to those who are interested in it. The purposes are different. Science is or should be guided by curiosity only and has no ethics; any ethics it employs are unfounded in it or borrowed from religions or philosophies which it rejects. It has no techniques for handling the subjective (pain, etc.) and can only handle behaviour illegitimately equated with pain (illegitimately because a scientist only knows of the existence of pain (in himself) by taking an unauthorized look into his own subjective unscientific experience). Dhamma is concerned solely with the elimination of pain, to which all else is subordinated. (Sep. 56)

604. *Amata* in the Dhamma is 'absence of death because of non-arising' (all that arises is subject to decay and death). It is not the non-dying, i.e., eternal duration of what has arisen (= western, idea of immortality).

605. *Saṅkhāras* have the characteristic *as action* of putting (states) together (into an order) or *as state* of, a collection of states put together in an order.

The first listed of the *saṅkhāras* is touching, which implies that the order, whether (1) in succession of time (*action*) or (2) simultaneous arrangement (*state*) is that the states must touch (1) either by temporal succession or (2) simultaneous co-presence.

Touching is an aspect of every consciousness (*tiṇṇaṃ saṅgati phasso*).

606. **Group kamma**

What is a group? Racial, regional, linguistic, geographical, political, occupational, etc., etc.? These cut across each other and to say that each has its own kamma is like saying that the torso, the arms, the lungs, the guts, the head, the nose etc., each has its own kamma which is nonsense.

Also kamma implies (a) "continuity" in one life and (b)"continuous continuity," i.e., succession of lives—not the inheritance by one continuity of the result of kamma performed by another continuity (i.e., Jātaka) etc. This view is hammered at by the commentaries but is merely implied by the suttas—should it be taken as an exclusive generalization or as "the normal thing" only?

No "kamma" as such in the Abhidhamma bar "*kamma-paccaya*."

607. *Nutriment* is nothing more than a term for *material used in creating*. Also it is the process of impermanence regarded *teleologically*. The process not so regarded is either *entropy* or bare *change*. It is axiomatic that where there is consciousness there *must* be change ordered teleologically, which is the parent of nutrition. Nutrition therefore is primarily an essential to life and living bodies, secondarily to creation of works of art or to utensils, and tertiarily to thought processes (?). It is conversion, in the sense of conversion to a use.

608. The concept of *nutriment* depends (a) upon *association* and (b) upon *impermanence* and (c) upon *hunger*. *Hunger*, seeking for satisfaction, devours x, which is *associated* with y that gives it satisfaction; but the satisfaction given is *impermanent* and thereby renews the hunger. "I" hungering for satisfaction, devour (x) *food* (eye object, taste, smell, touch object), the contact of which is *associated* with (y) pleasant feeling that gives satisfaction; but the satisfaction given by pleasant feeling is impermanent and by changing renews the pain of hunger.

609. For *nāma-rūpa*, mentality-materiality, too, is a makeshift and 'name-and-form' in some ways preferable. 'Name' (see *Path of Purification*; ch. XVIII, n. 4) still suggests the function of *nāma* as 'naming'; and 'form' for the *rūpa* of the *rūpakkhandha* ('materiality-aggregate') can preserve the link with that of the *rūpāyatana* (there

'visible form base' instead of 'visible-object base'). Especially 'materiality' (or 'matter'), too, as used in this translation needs to be treated to start with rather as an algebraical sign till contexts and definitions make it evident that any metaphysical Matter as a 'substance behind apparent forms' is quite excluded. For instance, Matter is taken to be an inherently unknowable substance only inferable by modern science from the appearance of its qualities. But an inherently unknowable and unverifiable objective substance has no more place in Buddhism than its subjective counterpart ...

610. The concept *materiality* is based on three elements (*mahābhūta*; no-*upādā*, Dhs 647) comprising the object touchable by the bodily sensitivity (*phoṭṭhabba*),' which elements are the three primary data categorical of hardness, temperature and distention-cum-movement (see Dhs 663). That primitive matter is reinforced (*upāda*) by all the subordinate data-categories furnished by the primitive objects of the other four sensitivities (visible form, sound, smell, taste) and the five internal 'material' sense bases. These make up *the crude five sense objects*. This is again reinforced (*upādā*) by the secondary data supplied only by the mind's object (the five internal and the four external bases), (?) sex, life, intimation, space, (water—cohesion), material lightness, wieldiness, malleability, material setting up, continuity, ageing, impermanence, and physical nutriment.

611. *Sati-sampajañña* ("Mindfulness and clear comprehension") should be examined carefully from the point of view of the centipede who could not walk when she thought about how she moved her limbs. And also from the point of view of absorption in, say artistic creation and detached observation of it. Absorption in piano playing or painting seems to be "successful" but detached observation or enjoyment of "my playing" or "my painting" seems to have the centipede effect. What are the facts here and what is the lesson to be drawn?

612. Sketch for a system of the *saḷāyatana* (the six bases).

My eye (1) *ajjhattaṃ* a) subjective (negative): the organization of visibility, b) objective (positive); (2) by hearing: nil (3–4) by smelling and tasting: nil (5) by body: the 'eye ball' as touch, say by a finger; (6) by mind: various concepts.

613. *Saḷāyatana*

(1) *Ajjhattikāyatana* = the organization of experience. (the internal sense-bases, i.e., sense organs)

(2) *Bahiddhāyatana* = the experience as organized. (the external sense-bases, i.e., the sense objects)

Experience as a cleavage between organization and the organized (which are inseparable but distinguishable).

(1) is distinct from (2) in that (with ignorance) the *organization* appears "pointing" to a "centre" which is the "I," while (2) has the character of the inert, the resistant, what hides or screens (and so suggests "substance" behind it).

The *cleavage* is the necessary basis for *phassa* (the "contact between" the two sides of the cleavage and between them and the "negation" constituted by consciousness (*viññāṇa*).

614. Presumably the Unconscious (or Subconscious), if assimilated to the Dhamma, should be assimilated under *nāma* and not under *viññāṇa*. Unless the Unconscious is defined as materiality (which is, I think, not usual) it must be regarded as mental: a mental fiction needed to explain certain behaviour patterns. As described it consists of memories repressed beyond the horizon of consciousness but still active. Therefore it is ipso facto *not* consciousness. The behaviour explained by it is *nāma-rūpa*. As memory (*sati*), it is a *saṅkhāra*. As repressed it is a fiction (even if useful and productive of practical results) it still remains under *saṅkhāra* as a complex associated with ignorance.

Identification of the Unconscious with *bhavaṅga citta* is, on this assumption, if not wrong, at least in need of elucidation, on the lines that in the Abhidhamma *citta*, strictly, is not on all fours with *viññāṇa*, the latter being bare awareness (with a minimum of memory) but the former being *viññāṇa* regarded in the affective light of its concomitant *cetasikas*.

Citta affected by the unconscious (memories) can be regarded as (a) a *cittuppāda* with the repressed object as its object and with a minimum of memory, followed by (b) another *cittuppāda* with a black-out of that memory; (a) is then regardable perhaps as a *bhavaṅga citta* and (b) as some other appropriate kind of *manoviññāṇadhātu*.

615. The following verbal pattern will reflect something of this sort:

If we take individualization (*uppāda*)[4] as the characteristics of *being* (*bhava*) displayed in the formula of Dependent Origination (*paṭicca-samuppāda*), then in the counter formula (*paṭicca-nirodha*) we have absence of structure (*nirodha*), such structure (*rodha*) appearing in the form of construction (*anurodha*), obstruction (*paṭivirodha*), and destruction (*virodha*).

616. In the Round (i.e., Paṭicca-samuppāda) as *arising*, ignorance must function, on the pre-logical level as forgetting and as infinite transcendence, and on the logical level as forgetting and the presence of the Assumption (i.e., the impersonal God/ Godlessness or the personal Absolutism/Relativism).

In the *pre-logical*, ignorance is omnipresent, i.e., as transcendence and as change (—forgetting); but in the logical, it can be pushed aside partly, because the possibility of right view *appearing* partially and intellectually and patchily, though what the *realization* of cessation of craving is, is a cataclysm.

617. Suffering is made to cease by the cessation of its *paccaya* (*taṇhā*);[5] but that is not said of the *paccaya* (*taṇhā*), or else the regression would be infinite. Consequently this particular *paccaya* is controllable. In other words, *dukkha* is a structure or a function (dependent variable) of *taṇhā*.

618. *Feeling* as the ruins of past actions, and *Craving* as the jungle that overgrows them—clear the jungle and the three feelings will become clearer.

619. Feeling (*vedanā*)

(1) Bodily and mental feeling do not by any means always coincide. Painful bodily feeling may be accompanied by pleasant mental feeling (as in masochism). And each has a number of levels.

(2) One's fundamental choice (investigate this further) is that of least affliction. This is the overall choice. This *overall choice* comprises many different levels of pleasure and pain and neutrality both bodily and mental.

---

4. Literally, "arising".
5. —condition (craving)

620. *Idappacayatā*[6] is represented by '*imasmiṃ sati*'[7] etc. The principle involved is contingent association in two forms: (I) that no 'this' can arise alone without conditions, (II) this contingency is both temporal and special. By the latter is meant that any 'this' to appear at all (whether as a principle (*dhātu*), idea (*dhamma*), thing (*saṅkhāra*) or act (*kamma*) must do so in association with conditions different from itself spatially, and different from itself in time (the preceding moment and subsequent moment.) (A) The 'spatial' contingency is a contingency upon other things and ideas at one moment. (B) The temporal contingency is a contingency of the 'present' moment upon (an immediate) past and (an immediate) future.

(A) (With consciousness) *nāmarūpa, saḷāyatana, phassa* constitute the spatial contingency (*vedanā* the affective aspect).

(B) Ignorance and craving/clinging constitute (with consciousness) the purely temporal contingency. They are influenceable by will. Consciousness is the absolute negation in virtue of which ignorance and craving can pose the positive 'world.'

Bhava which is positive, describes the constitution of the moving spatio-temporal contingency which is (a) *possible* in virtue of the negation consisting in consciousness, and is (b) *factual* in virtue of the limitations of viewing things imposed by ignorance, and limitations of time/action imposed by craving/clinging.

(Pencilled note at the end of page:)

621. Craving (*taṇhā*): *Subjective* aspect (second Truth); my craving as *felt* Fuel (*upādāna*): *Objective* aspect (first Truth); (a mode of craving's behaviour) my or others as seen objectively in the form of a mode (i.e., the four kinds).

622. I find I am now inclined to use, for myself only, the following equivalents for Paṭiccasamuppāda terms (in addition to those mentioned earlier):

5. *Saḷāyatana* = the sixfold facticity (of self in the world).

6. *Phassa* = presence

7. *Taṇhā* = need

8. *Upādāna* = consumption (on physical level) and assumption

---

6. —conditionality
7. 'if this is...."

(mental and other levels). To assume (*adsumere*) is "to take upon oneself."

Also

Uppāda = arising (appearance, phenomenality)

Anurodha = construction (favouring modes in *uppāda*).

Paṭivirodha = obstruction (opposing) *nirodha* = destruct(-ura-) tion

Further, the following vague notion about the P/S crossed my mind: the full formula of *uppāda*, starting with *avijjā* and ending with *jarā-maraṇa*, describes the state of the *puthujjana* (and *nirodha* that of the Arahant); but in the form used by the Buddha in the Saṃyutta to describe his discovery, as the Bodhisatta, of the "ancient way," on the point of his attaining full enlightenment, he proceeds backwards from *jarā-maraṇa* as far as *viññāṇa*, and then turns back to *nāma-rūpa*. The point of interest here might be (in the formula as used in this special context, i.e., to describe the attaining of enlightenment and abandonment of *avijjā*) the replacement of *avijjā* and of *saṅkhāra* by an infinite reflexive regression of *viññāṇa-nāmarūpa, viññāṇa-nāmarūpa* ... *Avijjā* has no place in enlightenment, and *saṅkhārā* as *kammapatha*, are only performable in the world of things, actions and persons which is held together by *avijjā* and *taṇhā*. Arahants do not "act" in that way, by *kammapatha*.

One other point in this connection. I have been seeking three convenient compendious terms for the three sections of the *Paṭicca-samuppāda* formula, and I toy with the following words, unsatisfactory though they are: the blocks are (a) = 1–2, (b) = 3–9, or 10, (c) = 11–12. So, (c) I call the Historical-Temporal (past and future simultaneously mutually incompatible), (b) I call the Personal-individual (simultaneously mutually indispensible), and (a) I call the Impersonal General (simultaneously compatible).

(a) is the least satisfactory. (From a letter to Ven. Ñāṇavīra, 3/7/59)

623. *Ideas*: put very crudely the situation is this: in so far as anything is an object of five-sense consciousness only, it is not an idea, but a visible form, sound, odour, flavour, or tangible. But "of these five sense faculties mind is their 'home'" (MN 43) and the mind's object is an idea. Experience is always a fusion of mind and five-sense-faculty. That is, in terms of the Sixfold Base. Otherwise it

can be expressed in the form of the twofold description of *saṅkhāra* (determinations) and *dhammā* (ideas) when the opposition is between ideas and action-cum-action-results. An idea (*dhamma*) is in itself neutral (as an essence, *sabhāvato dhamma*), but if 'cathetectic' by choice (*cetanā*), moved by lust, hate or delusion and given effect to *samādinna*, then it becomes an action (by body, speech or mind) according to the way of organizing association of the *indriyas*. Action is not in itself a Dhamma except in so far as it is object of mind-consciousness.

624. **Explanation and Rebirth**

What is one trying to do in explaining rebirth? This consciously organized life is like a home garden in an endless jungle the edge of which is like death. To explain death and rebirth is like trying to explain the jungle in terms of the house and garden. Or again, the house is built of bricks and tiles made of clay, and beams made of jungle trees. Explaining rebirth is like trying to explain clay and trees in terms of the familiar made-up bricks and fashioned beams. . (Jul. 56)

625. It is important to remember that if the notion of *motion* is described as *desantaruppatti* then also stationariness should be *samānadesuppatti*. Nothing continues. Consequently the argument based on *tadāgamma* for the *existence* of Nibbāna is false.

626. *Mettā*

In English one is used to the one word *love (= amour, amore, amor)*, which has to serve for all. Greek discriminates *eros* & *agape*, which duality is very hard to render in Latin or English. English inherits much of its crude matter-of-factness and empiricism from the vulgar Latins who had only the one word, *amor*, (and Latins of today make do with only *l(’amour*) and *l(’amore)*.

In Pali one finds there are three: *kāmacchanda*, *sineha* and *mettā*: (physical lust or desire for sensuality; sentimental affection or attachment to individual persons; and loving-kindness or benevolence extendable as a universal attitude to all beings).

Lust is selfish desire seeking satisfaction mainly through the sense of touch and is not interested in the well-being of its object at all. Selfish in the first degree.

Affection can be accompanied by physical lust or not and seeks satisfaction in association with the object (physical nearness, though not necessarily contact). It is interested in the welfare of the object, though unconcerned about anyone else, and does not exclude the harming of others for the benefit of its object. Thus it is selfish in the second degree.

Mettā starts from *sineha*, but by generalizing becomes unselfish and chooses welfare of all.

627. The P/S (*paṭicca-samuppāda*) is not so much a description as a group or sets of descriptive terms. The sets have certain features: (1) each member is recogizable in ourselves by introspection, (2) each pair of the sets of terms is so connected that (for reasons which vary in each case) one of the pair is evidently necessary for the others, much in the way that the *cogito* is linked (to the *sum*). (3) It has several forms. In its long form we find that this linkage takes us through three principal levels of generality. Ignorance and determinations are both *general* and *always present.* With Consciousness and the rest down to Clinging we have in each a *particular* (non-general) aspect *always present.* Being (*bhava*) is again *general* and *always present.* Birth, Ageing and Death *are general* necessarily, but *not always present* since they are *mutually exclusive* in temporal succession. This is the reason why in some Discourses the formula at Consciousness "turns round on itself" to Name-and-Form again, at one end (SN 12; Dīgha 15), while at the other it sometimes begins with Craving or Clinging, working backwards to Ignorance by the question, at each instance, 'What gives this its *being*?' (MN 11; MN 38). The long form may perhaps be taken as emphasizing the aspect of action, that turning back with Consciousness as emphasizing *consciousness*, and that applying being in each from Clinging backwards, as emphasizing *being* (*bhava*). The 'vulnerable point' is always where the process is attackable: where Craving meets Feeling since Craving is an element that can be brought under control. Descriptions that end here emphasize how the process can be broken.

One only of the middle members (*saḷāyatana*) can be omitted, or rather not omitted but absorbed into Name-and-Form.

It (the P/S) is not a temporal cause/effect chain: It is not symbolic since, if we look, we can find each member in ourselves by introspection. Its various presentations have no historical significance. It is not handable by Aristotelian logic any more than the Cogito.

To the question: "What are these sets of terms intended to describe?" we may answer tentatively that they are intended to describe experience of any possible kind where ignorance (that is lack of personal realization of the Truths) is present. It is in the nature of both such experience, and of descriptions that no simple description can be complete. Experience itself contains paradoxes which no philosophical system has succeeded in solving, and it is in the nature of any description that what it describes does not include its own terms: if we then want to describe those terms we must leave them and take up a position in what has just been described, in order to do so.

Disregarding the numerous and strange European interpretations, logical, symbolic, historical, etc., of the P/S the best approach to it from the European position is probably from Descartes' *Cogito ergo sum*. That famous formula, which still guides European Ontology, is not a logical (syllogistic) proposition; nor is the P/S. But there is more than that. Ignoring 'Descartes' synthetic reasoning an the matter of substance imposed on the *cogito*, one can hardly fail to notice the parallel between *cogito* and *viññāṇa* on the one hand and *sum* and *bhava* on the other. What is common to both is the interdependence of the terms. In stead of falling back upon unverifiable hypostasis to support the formula, the P/S pursues the element of interdependence by successive links between the two, each pair being open to introspection. At each end, too, we pass by a link from the particular to the general.

628. 'All creatures subsist by nutriment' (*sabbe sattāhāraṭṭhitikā*). Extraordinary as it may seem the philosophical implications of the necessity for nutriment as a condition for conscious existence have never been faced by European philosophers.

629. Religion is derived by the *Concise Oxford Dictionary* from *religo*, to bind (esp. to God). Consequently, *Religion* (which under the question "Is the Dhamma a Religion or a Philosophy")[8] I had equated provisionally with *sīlabbataparārāmasa*, 'adherence to rites

and rituals') should rightly be translated by *yoga* (=bondage), but the Dhamma is the way to the *anuttarayoga-kkhema*, 'the incomparable safety from bondage.'

630. **Phassa**[9]

The in-oneself and external are a duality expressed: as "that in the world by which one observes the world." In their simplest elementary form they constitute a spatial duality expressed as "a line of two points" (adjacent).

For this duality to *appear* as a phenomenon at all it must be *observed* from some position in a line at right-angles to the line of the two points (adjacent too).

This being-at-right-angles on the part of the (self-unobserved) observer to his observed duality can be called *perpendicularity*.

This perpendicularity of the (self-unobserved) observer to the fundamental duality of his observed (field) is, in fact, the triple relation of *phassa*. (It is *not* representable as a triangle, since that is an "objectivised" observer observed by a second (self-unobserved) observer himself perpendicular to the lines in the (perpendicularity contained as objectivised) in the triangle.)

Phassa is thus the fundamental perpendicularity of consciousness to the duality (the in-oneself and the external) of the observed field.

External (*bahiddhā*) = + I; in-oneself (*ajjhatta*) = observer =0.[10]

631. The Four Mahābhūtas[11] and Five Khandhas[12]

The simplest solid is (disregarding the sphere) a tetrahedron:

Let us provisionally equate as follows:

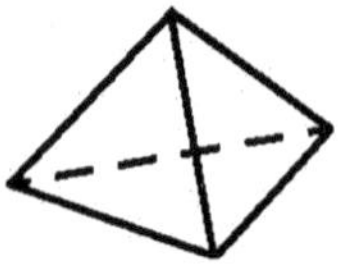

(a) *Rūpa* (form) = space enclosed and occupied by the *tetragon*.

(b) *Vedanā* (feeling) = affective appropriation inseparable from any perceiving.

(c) *Saññā* (perception) = the outline (and contained divisions if any) appearing at any moment as a

8. See p. 000

9. 'Contact', i.e., five-sense contact and mental contact.

10. See "The Essential Relation in Observing", p.214.

11. The Four Great Primaries, or basic constituents (elements) of matter.

12. The five Categories or Aggregates, of personalized existence.

phenomenon (transcendence accompanies perception).

(d) *Saṅkhārā* (formations) = changes in a, b, or c.

(e) *Viññāṇa* (consciousness) = primarily that which is not the observed tetrahedron phenomenon and not the observed not-tetrahedron-phenomenon, not a, b, c or d, and "time now" (This is unreflexive; *viññāṇa* might reflexively, be objectified as an "observed observer observing the tetrad," but it would then be perpendicular to the primary "observer-now.")

1. *Rūpa* is describable on the basis of the four *mahābhūtas*;

2. *Vedanā saññā saṅkhārā* are describable on the basis of *phassa*;

3. *Viññāṇa* is describable in terms of *nāma-rūpa*, or on the bases of in-oneself/external. (MN 109, MN 38)

The four *Mahābhūtas* can probably best be equated with (a) the spatial rigidity (tangible or mental), (b) cohesion, (c) componibility, and (d) dislodgeability (or as rigidity, cohesion, temperature and movement).

In the tetrahedron they are present respectively in:

(a) its resistence to deformation (rigidity),
(b) its endurance and susceptibility to "phases" (cohesion) when moved,
(c) its creatibility, i.e., that it can be brought into being and made-up (componibility),
(d) its mobility, he fact that it is always in a state of motion either as "uniform in a straight line" or as "accelerated" (dislodgeability).

ONTOLOGY AND BUDDHISM

Editor's Note: All the following Notes have been taken from a sheaf of loose leaves topped by our first item (No. 632) which gives the table of contents of the planned book of essays on Ontology and Buddhism. What follows are the only pieces of connected writing in that fascicule; the other leaves contain chiefly a large number of quotations from the Pali texts, lists of Pali words, terms and phrases, with source references, which the author intended to utilize for the planned book of essays.

632. Ontology and Buddhism

It has been said by someone that the weakness of Buddhism is that it has no Ontology. But it can be asked, "Is it a weakness or a strength?" The object of these essays is to inquire into that.

I. Sketch of classical Ontology *à* la Lavelle

II. Sketch of Existential Ontology *à* la Sartre

III. The syllogism and its constants ALL and IS (*sabbaṃ* and *bhavo*).—Dialectic.

IV. IS and ALL in the Suttas.

V. Ontology, its origin, cessation, and the Path to its cessation.

VI. Dependent Arising.

VII. Cessation—is, is not, both-is-and-is-not, neither-is-nor-is-not: all *are* and *are not* nibbāna.

633. My point simply hinges on the question of translating *bhava* by 'becoming' as is usually done. It is generally argued against translating *bhava* by 'being' that 'being is static'; but while admitting that, 'becoming' (1) offers no solution since in the *Concise Oxford Dictionary*, 'to become' means 'to begin to be', (2) it completely severs the hoti of the (incipient) syllogisms, e.g., *hoti Tathāgato parammaraṇa* ...' and other vaguer uses of *hoti* (*bhavati*) and, indirectly, *atthi* from connexion with the Paṭicca-samuppāda, tending to make the P/S subordinate to syllogistic logic rather than the other way about; (3) it is incompatible with S .... and It (and also with MN 131–4). 'Becoming' (and still more '*werden*') suggests a flux where the future 'becomes' by 'flowing' through the present into the past, or 'future things' 'become' present and then past, while what is meant or implied by the constant and unavoidable use of the verb 'to be' is left unaccounted for. Hence, I argue, to translate (even to interpret to oneself) *bhava* by 'becoming' is an opiate that leaves the illusion of 'being' untreated. I doubt if that is what the Buddha intended.

As I see it, the Buddha's treatment of Ontology is most clearly set out, according to right view, in MN 38, which, *yathābhūtaṃ*, sets out how the illusion of 'being' (both in positive and negative forms—with the *bhavataṇhā* and *vibhavataṇhā* of DN 9, 22, and the *anurodha* and paṭivirodha of MN 1), can and should be treated and eliminated. MN 1 and MN 49 are complementary: MN 1 describes the modes of *asmi-māna* (which is pre-logical) and MN 49 presents the same situation in 'ontological' terms, i.e., in the functioning of a logically formulated wrong view (while MN describes the prelogical and prereflexive *asmimāna*—the *mānānusaya*, the fundamental wrong attitude), MN 44 & MN 109 describe the logically formulated views which arise out of and are built upon the prelogical tendency—the connexion between these is shown briefly in MN 1 and forms the subject matter of MN 49.

634. As I see it at present, the importance of the *paṭicca-samuppāda* lies not so much in the twelve (or *less* or more) members as in the relationship *imasmiṃ sati* ... (and its undoing *imasmiṃ asati*) which is underlined in DN 15. This firstly implies complexity in experience (no complexity: no experience). The choice of the "12 members" is less philosophical than psychological, which is why it is variable. The undoing, as I see it, is the "detail of voidness," which is the ethical key to the, Dhamma, since it is the "Abschattung" (shading off. —Ed.) of voidness in saṃsāra itself that renders it impossible in the Dhamma to ascribe absolutiveness to any *particular* value (such as divine grace, justice, etc.) and so enter upon the "War of philosophical *systems* of the absolute." The formula *imasmiṃ sati*, ...' (applied psychologically by a choice of interrelated-instances) is used as an instrument in DN 15 to describe and analyse the mental process of naming (function of *nāma-rūpa*) and language (*nirutti*, etc.), and in MN 38 to describe and analyse the peculiar nature of consciousness (*viññāṇa*) in its constitutive relationship (through mediate states) to being. But both can only be studied in the Pali with careful discrimination of roots...

635. The ironical and amusing story of the *Brahma-nimantanika Sutta* conceals a profound meaning, which is ontological. That is, it presents the Buddha's treatment of the verbs *hoti*, *bhavati* ('to be') and the noun *bhava* ('being'), both from the root *bhū*. Some prelate, I forgot who, said that 'Buddhism's weakness lay in the fact that it had no ontology,' which, in simpler language presumably meant that no attempt had been made to prove that nibbāna, the goal, *was*, or that it *had being*, with the latent objection that if this was not proved, then *nibbāna* was just 'an abyss of nothingness.'

Now the Buddha has described the world (that is not just the external world but the consciousness that cognizes it, and not only other peoples' consciousness objectified, but mine, too, and not only mine (of) past and future objectified but mine committed to it *now*—no matter who 'I' *am.*). His description of the way it works is the first two truths, while the last two deal with the escape from it. If we are interested in 'being' we must look to the Dependent Origination (D/O), of which 'being' (*bhava*) is the tenth member.

I purposely avoid rendering *bhava* by 'becoming' because that word has a limited meaning in normal English usage, which would most nearly apply to the flux process which the D/O describes as a whole, and not to *bhava*, which is part of it. The point is extremely important, because if *bhava* is rendered by 'becoming,' then the word 'becoming,' which everyone from dukes to dustmen use all day and everyday, escapes our net entirely and we are in difficulties when we are perhaps told that the Buddha's Absolute is Pure Being and so he merely taught diluted Vedanta. If we are in difficulties, they are due to our handling of English; they are not there in the Pali. 'Being,' 'existence,' and 'becoming,' all represent in Pali the roots *bhū* (is, exists) and as (is, there is, exists). We have no right to introduce the European mediaeval dichotomy of essence' versus 'existence,' which the Pali word *dhamma* makes superfluous. It is sometimes argued that 'being' implies permanence; even if that is so, outside the philosopher's study it does not affect the issue; and that is only an additional reason why the word must be dealt with.

'Being,' we said, is a member of the D/O, in other words, to be is to be dependent, or contingent upon something else. Whatever is, has being only in virtue of something else that lends it its being. *Kiṃ pabhava.*

Now let us consider the structure of the D/O for a moment. Firstly, it is not a logical proposition, nor is it a temporal cause-result chain. Such an approach makes an understanding of it impossible. If we stop to consider each of its components, they will be found to vary so enormously in scope from the particular to the general that it is hard to get a clear picture of the whole. The interpretations of European scholars have been, perhaps without exception, wild and bad guesses.

The Buddha's purpose is to describe enough of the world to be able to show how suffering can be ended, not to produce full and detailed elaborations, which would be endless and arrive nowhere. But this particular description is aimed at including everything. And here a difficulty arises. A description must be made in terms of something other than what it describes, or it is not a description. It has to reproduce in other material certain structures that are in what it describes. This fact makes it impossible for a description to be a description and complete at the same time. How is the D/O complete, then? Or is it not a description after all?

It is in fact both, but it attains that in a rather peculiar way. The best way to approach it from a European background is from Descartes' "Cogito ergo sum"—(I think therefore I am). That is not a logical proposition; it is a description of interconditionality between consciousness and being. Ignoring Descartes' theories of substance and taking only that bare formulation, we can compare it with the fact that 'consciousness' (*viññāṇa*) and 'being' (*bhava*) are two of the most obvious members of the D/O formulation, which also is not a logical proposition.

But now let us return for a moment to the 'enormous scope from the particular to the general,' which we noted earlier in the D/O. The right way of treating this fact is to take the D/O, not as an individual description, but as an integrated set of descriptions. Each member provides in fact a set of terms to describe the rest of the world. Together they cover the whole subjective/objective, positive/negative world. But when taken together, becoming and being, impermanence and (illusory) permanence come within its net. This seeming paradox represents what we actually live, but what we never face up to as a whole. 'Being' is applicable to the first nine members (see MN 38 & 11) though not to the last three (they perhaps constitute 'becoming' if we use that term philosophically).

Any concept of Pure Being is always open to the objection that, if absoluteness is claimed for it, then it cannot be known; for if it is known it is accessible to consciousness and consequently no longer pure; consequently Pure Being and non-being cannot be distinguished. If absoluteness is claimed for any concept of Pure Consciousness (the Yogācara opposition to the Vedanta), a similar objection arises; for if consciousness is pure it must not be, or it will be adulterated by being. Consequently pure consciousness has to have no being, which is tantamount to saying that it is not. By making both consciousness and being, in whatever form, subject to the D/O, the Buddha both closes the entry into this logical maze and offers us a picture which, if we only bother to observe, rather than malobserve, we shall find corresponds with our experience as we actually live it. Only we keep forgetting what we learn. And forgetting is ignorance. And ignorance, 'the most reprehensible of all,' heads the D/O. It is one of the three 'taints' (*āsava*)—and so is being.

So it is not that 'Buddhism has no ontology,' but that the Buddha has seen through what a modern writer has called the 'ontological mirage' and set being into its true position.

Nibbāna is the cessation of ontology: *bhava-nirodho nibbānaṃ*. It is not, however, the 'abyss of non-being', since that requires consciousness to cognize it as such. It is 'absolute cessation,' which includes the non-ascription, of either being or non-being: *nāpahosiṃ*.

Now while the D/O has the appearance of, and is, a complete description of the world (as we have defined it,) nevertheless, when nibbāna is treated of positively in any of its terms instead of, as its cessation, a paradox will appear. *Atthi* ... *abhūtam*..., or *sabbato pabhaṃ*, describes as cognized, to be (by consciousness) in terms of *being*. What nibbāna *is* cognized by in terms of consciousness is *anidassanaṃ*: the act of cognizing without 'showing,' 'making seen,' any positive determined (*saṅkhata*) object. That this opposing of being and consciousness seems possible and not nonsense (the paradox) also indicates the 'incompleteness' of the 'complete' description.

636. (1) *Citta* = to know; (2) *cetasika* = to do; (3) *rūpa* = to be.

'Rūpa' appears as some definite form and as such is entirely positive. To the question, 'What is this?' the answer can be given at once: 'It is what it is.' But to be what it is it has to be determined as such, and this determining is the function of *saṅkhārā* (including *vedanā* and *saññā* as two special instances of *saṅkhāra*, which we are entitled to do). To the question 'What is a determination?', we

define it as an *act* of showing or determining an appearance that a form perceived 'is this form, not that form.' The negation in determining is only implied by, or employed by, determination but does not constitute an element of its being. Of that determination too it can be replied to the question 'what is I?', that 'it is what it is' (*saññā, vedanā, saṅkhārā, phassa, samudayā*). That *form* can *be* and be *determined* is only possible in the presence of *consciousness.*

A peculiarity of consciousness at once appears introspectively in that it does not in itself appear positively as *rūpa* (form) and *cetasikā* do. Quote MN 109 & 38 ... The capacity of negation appears to reside in consciousness which provides the "empty space" in which questions can be asked and "forms" (things) determined. If with the other two it constituted a plenum, there would be no questions and no acts of determining possible. Consciousness, then, begins to appear as the questioning element and it can turn the questioning on itself: 'If I am what I am.'

637. Medieval European thought evolved the dichotomy of existence and essence, on which the ontological proof of the existence of God was built. It might be tempting to render the expression *Sabbe saṅkhārā anicca ... sabbe dhammā anattā* in those terms on such lines as these: 'All determined things, existing in themselves (*saṅkhārā*) are impermanent, all essences (*dhammā*; equated by the commentaries with *sabhāva*) are non-existent in themselves.' But such an equation would be risky because the ontological appearance is largely a verbal one due to the peculiarities of European languages, but still more so because the clarity of medieval synthesis has been lost so that today in English the boundaries between 'essence,' 'being' and 'existence' are no longer definite in ordinary usage, and any definitiveness that they are made to assume in individual philosophies is largely an arbitrary one imposed on them. Consequently we must beware of importing into the Pali any specious clarity or any vagueness that rests solely on foreign linguistic habits, and thus have only regional value.

638. To be is to be contingent: nothing, of which it can be said that 'it is,' can be said to be alone and independent.

But being is a member of the paṭicca-samuppāda *as arising* which contains ignorance. Being is only invertible by ignorance.

The destruction of ignorance destroys the illusion of being. When ignorance is no more, then consciousness no longer can attribute being (pahoti) at all. But that is not all; for when consciousness is predicated of one who has no more ignorance then it is no more indicatable (as it was indicated in MN 22).

Aftermath of Philosophical Thought

639. If precognition is a fact (Rhine, etc.) then the psychologists' complexes due to suppression can equally well be due to suppressed precognitions as to suppressed memories. Then the death trauma is as important as the birth trauma. (Dec. 54)

640. I shall postulate that certain aspects of character always form part of a human character but may be present in either a mainly "positive" or mainly negative" form. They tend to fall into unequal-opposite pairs. If one is exaggerated in conscious life, the other will find an outlet somewhere. Viz., take a person who is exaggeratedly sensitive to domination by others (usually called "weak and obstinate"). Without going into an elaborate analysis it may be found that the felt need for independence and fear of being trapped governs the major part of life and relations with other people in all ordinary activities. This leaves unsatisfied the opposite need for self-sacrifice or need to be guided and dominated and so get rid of the burden of responsibility and loneliness. So such persons may often be found to show exaggerated trust in doctors, and to take delight in treatment in a world of medical relationships where he can indulge the slave-master instinct by entirely subordinating himself to the doctor. This is thus done in a watertight world, and with a satisfactory doctor this can provide a release for the tension that otherwise might burst out in psychosomatic ailments.

641. *The Unconscious.* Theories of the unconscious are "justified" by their ability to predict and control certain behaviour. They seem, however, to be a necessary fiction, as phlogiston was a necessary fiction in its time, necessitated in predictive calculation by the then inability to gather enough data about the process of burning to account for the new distribution of weight. Phlogiston, in fact, filled the gap left by those components of matter, (steam,

etc.) which escaped the net of observation of the process of burning up matter. The Unconscious does the psychologists a somewhat similar service today. The technique for describing the behaviour of "conscious matter" is incomplete. Between the patches of observed behaviour "things have happened" unobservably and that is stated to have taken place "in the unconscious," as the loss of weight in burning was said to be due to the "addition of the minus weight of phlogiston." The Unconscious is thus a necessary fiction at present, but none the less a fiction.

In the last century and a half of physiology, neurology has succeeded in tying up invariable relationships between material organs and nerves on the one hand and conscious experiences (pains, etc.) on the other. Investigation of the brain, though, is still in its infancy. It seems more than possible that much if not all the so-called "Unconscious" may not eventually become much more conveniently describable in terms of material brain changes, materially (i.e., visibly) measured and tied up with certain feelings and experiences.

Two things, however, remain: (1) just as physics has got to a point where it has reached an incompatibility, namely the behaviour of electrons as either waves or particles, so much brain investigation may lead to a mutually incompatible double vision, though how this may manifest itself it is not yet possible to say. (2) Consciousness, i.e., *the purely subjective and unique experience of awareness* (with some degree of memory) will remain unapproached and unapproachable by such methods. Expressed in physical or material terms, consciousness must always be describable as "nothing." That "nothing" has one kind of relationship to the world of physics and another to the world of physiology. (Jan. 56)

642. It is said that animals (even chimpanzees) have a very short conscious memory (I do not mean conditioned reflexes, learnt habits, etc.). It is one of the radical differences between man and all animals that man is ashamed of sex. The reason probably lies in conscious memory. The change in values between lustful consciousness and non-lustful is profound (more than that with hate, probably). In man non-lusting consciousness is scarcely or not at all remembered when lusting consciousness is present, because

the latter overrides all the former's values absolutely. But it does not last. When it has switched back to non-lusting consciousness, it is the memory of how destructive the lusting values are to the non-lusting that makes the intrusion of the memory into the open public intolerable; hence shame, which keeps the memory tidily in oneself. Were there no memory of it (as probably it is with animals), as women are said to forget the pains of labour, and as one tends to forget sea sickness, then there would be no objection to going naked. (Sep. 56)

643. Practically all inquiries into death, immortality, existence, being and consciousness are stultified at the outset by a presumption that they are desirable (or the reverse). The only reasonable approach is to observe what *facts* there are to be observed and make one's choice on the basis of these—afterwards, not before.

644. *Bodily pain* is a component of waking life, but not, apparently, of dream life. The advent of bodily pain destroys (breaks up or kills) a dream and transforms existence into waking life. Bodily pain *in others* seems when increased to a certain amount (not measurable because it is only inferred) to result in "lapse of consciousness" (i.e., interruption of the life-process) or destruction (i.e., breaks up the waking life or kills it). That can only be inferred of others and cannot be a *waking experience* in myself (without a radical development or alteration in conscious continuity as we ordinary people know it).

The (desirable) stability of waking life is gained, it seems, at the expense of (undesirable) bodily pain. Give up the pain, and with it the stability and I return to the instability of dreams.

Death in others is the break up of the bodily stability in an observed body with the cutting off of a relationship with an inferred other's consciousness. That particular looking-glass in which I see the "face" of my own consciousness has become corroded and no longer reflects it; it only shows the shadow of my "conscious body" as a stone or earth shows the shadow, but not the reflection, of my material body.

By "my conscious body" I mean here no more than the "shape of the inside of a hole"—consciousness being taken here as equatable with nothing in terms of matter, and the "conscious body" as the aspects of the "surface of the hole" (—the contact of "matter" with "nothing").

645. Can one take an experience to have up to five essential dimensions—three dimensions of space (i.e., right-left, front-back, up-down) and time (before-after) and consciousness (attraction-repulsion)?

There are two independent ways of describing experience and manipulating knowledge:

1. By conceiving experience in terms of things or interaction between things ("chosisme"—Aristotelian logic). "Things" are all impermanent. Knowledge of their relationships is always out of date.

2. By conceiving it in terms of structure (mathematics—other logical systems?). Structure is 'permanent' and knowledge of it is cumulative.

646. All thought hitherto has been stultified by the failure to know what the verb "to be" [signifies]* ("this" "is" "that"; "there-is" "nothing-there"; "he" "is" "not-here"). [*—added by Ed.]

647. In a syllogism (1. All men are mortal. 2. Socrates is a man. 3. Therefore Socrates is mortal), the generalization (all men are mortal) must have been arrived at by induction. No inductive process is ever absolutely certain. There is always the leap, the assumption, of generalizing and therefore one of the premises of a syllogism must have an element of uncertainty. So it cannot prove anything with certainty.

A syllogism is therefore a signpost pointing where to look for direct experience, but can inherently never give information that is 100% certain. But a syllogism (on metaphysical subjects) can also point to what can, inherently, never be experienced; then it is an anomaly.

648. Is there something wrong somewhere in the claim that all mental objects are only five-sense-experiences or rearrangement of memories of them?

649. Physicists accept the inseparability of time and space. They are concerned with 'what happens in space,' The inseparability works out as plainly true (i.e., consistent) as far as any thing to do with space is concerned—no time, no space, in fact.

But does the converse apply, i.e., is time (i.e., consciousness of change) impossible with a coordinate experience of space?

650. *Descriptions etc.* —To the question 'What is description?' (or better perhaps: 'how is description described?') a convenient answer might be that it is the application of sieves. This implies: (A) distinguishing by a fixed pattern of, say, (a) holes of a certain size in an otherwise impenetrable medium, (b) an amorphous mass of particles, and (c) an act of sieving. Sieving for size in this way will have no power to discriminate between different-coloured particles either below or above the critical size of the sieve.—(B) For distinguishing colour an entirely different sieve and sieving act must be applied, with two or more independent discriminating acts. In this way a *description* can be made of *classes*. The step to the description of an *individual* seems to consist in the application of a varying number of different acts of sieving followed by a decision "This number of acts of sieving (this list of characteristics) is enough. By it the individual is described." Objectively, and without the subjective "I"- sense, this is the nearest that one can get. The list judged adequate is always liable to be proved inadequate in new circumstances (uncertainty principle) and a new sieve must be applied and a new "adequate" judgement made—but there is no limit to this. (Jan. 58)

651. Treatment according to strictly objective scientific technique absolutely precludes the possibility of ascertaining the "identity" of an "individual" at two different time-places. Events can only be sieved and sieved by new sieving processes; but the judgement: "This is the same person." or "This is the same thing." is supplied from the subjective observer and is consequently *unscientific* though a necessary component of experience.

652. The space-time relationship of relativity is based on the *observed fact* of the speed of light. The fifth dimension (see Eddington) might lie in the element of negation or nothingness, which is pure subjectivity and which cannot be demonstrated in the objective world, which is perhaps rightly argued to be a 'plenum.' Things (which are multiple) and even space and time (which equivocally claim unity; but what about dreams?), are what they are (are themselves), are positive in their own right. Consciousness,

however, considered separately, is only describable as different, or positive, in terms of what it is not. It is what is not. It is one. Multiplicity appears to be imposed on it by its association with what it is not. It is the lack, the flight, the incompleteness, the hunger, the negation, the nothing. The ego is the particular behaviour line of the surface of a given positivity against nothing.

653. All such dogmas or deductions as (1) "The space-time world is a plenum," (2) "The physical material universe is orderly," etc., are only understandable if the words *plenum* and *orderly* are distinguished against (a) their opposites *vacuum* and *random* as well as (b) against their undifferentiated matrix (the unconscious categories plenum-vacuum, order-randomness, etc.—see Freud).

Consequently if all these definite (or positive) attributes are projected onto the external objective world, their shadows (or negative opposites) will lie in the internal subjective observer of that world. The external world thus conceived becomes positive, replete, lifeless and rigid and is only animatable by the element of hungry negation in the internal consciousness element (itself nothing and only observable by introspection of its emotional modes). (Jan. 58)

654. "Actual Matter" is any actual experience involving excitation of one or more of the five senses (a 'hallucination' is only a badly-organized five-sense experience, and a 'real experience' is only a well-organized one). 'Matter' is that and also all imaginings, ideas and memories of now, of past or future five-sense experience ('imagination' is only a badly or insufficiently organized one).

655. 1. Words (like paints) reproduce or reflect a structural pattern in reduced dimensions.

2. "*Omnis determinatio est negatio*" (Spinoza): no determination can be made unless from a viewpoint. Any viewpoint has horizons. The negated lies beyond the horizons. Horizons are an essential component of any determination (or any conscious experience).

3. An action is a changing (transitive). Actions' result is memory (a.) conscious memory, and (b) unconscious memory, including learning). "We are what we have thought and done."

4. A division of the *world* (I and my universe) is:

(1) 'I' (absolutely unique subjectively; but not objectively,

which includes 'my body'); (2) 'other people' (their bodies—their 'consciousness' being only an inference); (3) inanimate things.

5. Action (see 3) as (my) thought changes thought and my behaviour; action as speech changes (my) thought and 'other people's behaviour.' Action as bodily action changes my thought and other people's behaviour (sometimes) and inanimate things (sometimes).

6. All bodies are incomplete from any one point of view, but my body is so in a unique way (I see it from through my own face as it were, inside my head, but that is a construct).

7. Can plurality be ascribed to consciousness except through plurality of bodies? What are the consequences of this?

8. 'I' is one conceit (the 'internal' one), 'matter' one form of the external one, which every set of appearances (sense or mind) points to be ...

(Here the Manuscript ends; a few interlinear additions are incomplete)

656. *Cause and Effect.* Is the question of "cause and effect" any different in essentials from that of "shape'? "A shape" is a succession of plane sections seen simultaneously. If they were seen serially, then we should have the experience of certain series of plane sections (say those of a man or a tree) repeating themselves in experience and we might then say that the "previous" plane section of two ankles was the "cause" of the "subsequent" plane section of the waist. The notion of "cause and effect" seems to come from the inability to see a "world line" simultaneously, but the ability to see it as a temporal series of 3-dimensional sections. The point of this is to suggest that the "law of cause" is not essentially different from the "law of shape." "Spatial objects" "are" "certain shapes" which we see simultaneously. "Cause and effect" groups are temporal (or space—time) shapes which we see as a series of 3-dimensional sections. The law (if any) which holds cause and effect together, therefore, should be of the same kind which holds a shape together, i.e., makes it a "unit." What this is needs investigating.

This apart, "cause" and "effect" seem misleading shorthand words for the "principal (i.e., most noticeable) condition" (out of the many conditions) that is concerned in the production of an emergent new state. That these series repeat themselves seems to be due rather to the arbitrary nature of the world: just as the plane section of the two ankles is arbitrarily followed later by the plane section of two knees, waist, etc.,—given humans in the world and a fixed order of series. (This is a description in terms of an external world existing independently of an observer).

If the universe is expanding, the nebulas getting apart, is everything expanding? Are we getting larger, and the earth on which we stand? If we and the earth are getting larger in proportion we should not notice our change in size because there would be nothing to make the comparison with. But if the expansion were accelerating we should find the earth pressing against our feet, which is just what we experience through gravity. What are the constants? The speed of light? The relative increase in rapidity of expansion in proportion to the distance? (Jan. 52)

657. Solalterism versus Solipsism—Dialectic

The solalterist description of the world, as used openly by the Behaviourists, and as used covertly by such scientists as Ross Ashly, contains a hidden 'dishonesty principle' (i.e., active functioning of ignorance as self-deception) when it claims and believes its description to be subjectively adequate and altogether complete. The difficulty of the 'Theory of Types' which questions, the validity of any 'complete' description of 'all' because it cannot include itself, need not be brought in here. The 'dishonesty principle' is evident in Ross Ashly in his, on the one hand, admitting that he is not dealing with consciousness and, on the other, claiming that pain 'is' a certain physical behaviour pattern. Association (whether absolutely co-essential or not, is not known) of purely subjective pain is identified with that behaviour pattern, which, unlike the pain aspect, is describable in purely physicists' terms. That includes the two principles of Adaptation and Feed-back. Resting on that identification, which is false, the conclusion that conscious man is only an elaborate machine follows, and it proves that he has no soul. This proof has nothing to do with the Buddhist proof of *anattā*.

The illusion created by the apparent completeness of behaviourist-physicist description is reinforced by the absence of any strict solipsistic (correspondingly inversely false) description to oppose to it. All solipsistic theories so far have been badly self-deceptive on the point that they have never been pursued with scientific and logical ruthlessness and have always contained a large element of properly solalteristic material mixed up. They are thus easily shown to be absurd and consequently solipsistic thought has been bullied and frightened off the subject.

The difficulty lies in re-stating and purifying the true solipsistic from injected solalteristic material and in finding a set of terms in which to describe it.

What is essential therefore is (a) to show clearly where the solalterist treatment (absolutely necessary as it is) must necessarily end in incompleteness (which can only be glossed over by false identification with the purely subjective) and where it deceives itself and others by covertly smuggling in (properly) solipsistic material (pain) and (b) to make a correspondingly adequate solipsistic description showing where the deception and the 'smuggling-in' or injection of solalterist material lies. (Sep. 56)

658. ...And this is so not only with technicalities as these but also with theories of importance current in Western thought, about Perception, Causality, Consciousness and Being. It is said that the (strictly objective and so most respectable) sciences have abandoned speaking in terms of 'causes' and 'effects'; and Hume remains unrefuted where Causes (as usually conceived) are upheld. There is no agreed theory of Perception. That, perhaps most fashionable now, which (tacitly treating consciousness as an 'epiphenomenon') looks for its justification to the laws of Physics, to Neurology and to Protoplasm, is an admitted makeshift at best and ultimately vitiated by its failure to take proper account of the subjective side of experience (to deal with 'I'); for it remains awkwardly incontestible that all data are ultimately private. Should Consciousness be taken to include, or not, also the 'Unconscious' of the Psychoanalysts, which Existentialists deny? Fear of *solipsism* seems to have shepherded the main body of thinkers towards the opposite, perhaps more insidious, fallacy of solalterism. Schopenhauer described the Solipsist as 'a madman shut up in an impregnable blockhouse'. But the Solalterist, who ignores the

observer,—the Behaviourist who only admits the existence of 'the Other'—may perhaps be considered scarcely more sane and to have shut himself out of his house, slamming the door with the latchkey inside: 'the philosophy of the subject leaving himself out of his calculations,' to quote Schopenhauer again. Then the indispensable words '*being*' and '*existence*' (*there are* and *is*—as copula or as absolute), with their ambiguity and the homeless family of fundamental assumptions that they are often made to shelter, are normally taken for granted (the otherwise critical authors of *The Meaning of Meaning*, for example, are strangely content not to examine them at all), or they are left to the more inaccessible of the post-Hegelian ontologists. It has even been complained that there is no longer in European philosophy any agreement on what these words stand for. Such conditions have made of European Ethics, as it were, a displaced person: she has to take shelter where she can.

[The above fragment is the contents of a single typed sheet paginated as 25, seemingly part of a larger philosophical manuscript which the author may have discarded as no other pages belonging to it, were found among the posthumous papers.]

659. Animism leads logically to the Gods of Olympus. From there to Jewish or Hindu monotheism, with its impersonal counterpart of pure substance such as the Matter of scientists, Hegel's History, the Hindu Brahman, etc. The obsessive solipsistic claim of the unique 'I' is held in check by the uniqueness of God, or of the external substance. But if that is denied, as non-existent, then the Kirillov[13] Idea takes over. God is the theistic safeguard against this and Substance the Atheistic safeguard. Psychology (Behaviourist) plays an equivocal part, and while denying god and not affirming substance, it refuses recognition to solipsism by hiding in the solalterism of "the Other." Buddhism is unique in avoiding all these pitfalls and makeshifts by exposure and analysis of the illusion of 'I' (*asmi-māna*) and personality (*puggala*) and the contingency of being (*paṭicca-samuppāda*, 'Dependent Arising').

660. If the Absurd is the proper object of faith, and Understanding (=knowledge) is to be mortified and excluded (*vide*

13. See Dostoyevsky, *The Possessed—Ed.*

Tertullian), then *any* form of absurdity is a fit object for faith, and *no* discrimination between forms of absurdity can be made whatever by faith alone, but only by understanding (knowledge) that is ruled out.

661. "There is little of the true philosophic spirit in Aquinas. He does not, like the Platonic Socrates, set out to follow wherever the argument may lead. He is not engaged in an inquiry, the result of which it is impossible to know in advance, Before he begins to philosophize, he already knows the truth; it is declared in the Catholic faith. If he can find apparently rational arguments for some parts of the faith, so much the better; if he cannot, he need only fall back on revelation."

Bertrand Russell, *History of Western Philosophy* (p. 463)

This criticism is excellent—while enquiry remains enquiry only in the realm of ideas and has either no counterpart in action or while any such counterpart action can always be abandoned before it has unpleasant consequences. The end may be either interesting or boring but will not destroy the enquirer. But the course of action flows on like a river and there is no stopping it for a second. If its course is directed, it is hard or impossible to get it back again. We think we know its average course and we think it might be made worse than it is, so we mainly tolerate it as it is. We have our system of contexts built up by experience, for dealing with situations as they arise (assisted by the automatic reactions of self-preservation). While this physical "safety" endures it is possible, pleasant and "safe" to embark on mental enquiries whose end cannot be foreseen and apply to physical existence and action what attracts us therein. But will anyone argue from that we should embark on an experimental course of action whose end cannot be foreseen? And yet this is exactly what science as evolution seems to be doing. Science does not admit the pleasure-pain element which is "personal" and therefore "unscientific" because it is outside the capacity of its measuring instruments. This is alright; and when it says, "What is contrary to science is false," it seems partially sound. But it is when Science begins to exert a claim on the mind to be the sole source, point of reference, measure and limit of truth, (saying) "What is not capable of being dealt with by Science is non-existent," then it is certainly unsound.

662. The importance of an *orthodoxy* is that it is essential to any ordered thinking. By that I mean not orthodox thinking but any ordered thinking; for that implies either approval of or rejection of (in whole or in part) some orthodoxy. Unorthodoxy is impossible without some orthodoxy against which it is unorthodox. (For revolutions see § 258.) Any orthodoxy has constantly to be maintained and combated in order to survive. A judicious measure of the two is called progressive development. If the mixture is injudicious it may manifest itself as tyrannous bigotry or as constant abortive rebellion. A rebellion, to be successful must destroy the orthodoxy which it rebels against, whereupon it is automatically transformed into a new orthodoxy. A period of anarchy or seeming anarchy may intervene, but (if true anarchy has any actuality) it seems naturally impossible to sustain anarchy for long against a tendency to crystallize, and once that happens, orthodoxy has set in again. Whether orthodoxy can be universalized without or with oppression and suppression is not the point here. (Sep. 56)

663. If we say that "happiness" (as the "greatest good") consists in things, then the only standard by which we may know which things bring happiness is according to the reaction of a majority (the "greatest number") or of an aristocracy (the "best") to those things. This (a) takes no account of the fact that canons of taste may and do change, and that respectively the "minority" ('enemies of the people') or the inferior (the 'masses') risk being crushed and oppressed and prevented from fulfilling their needs.

If we say that happiness consists in any person's attitude, then the only standard is the state of happiness or otherwise of any given person. But this criterion will not indicate what things may be expected to make any person happy and the result is anarchy among things and a process of continued trial and error.

It is now held tacitly or openly that (a) all people should (must) like what the majority likes; the minority should be educated to this—by a combination of encouragement and neglect (if liberal-socialist) or by emotional propaganda and forced labour camps (if totalitarian); and (b) that the canons of what should be liked must be laid down and their development guided. The need for a "party" and a system of politico-philosophical myths (aims that cannot be realized now) such as "the next world" or the fading away of the state (this world as Utopia).

The whole of this edifice with all its facades has no place for death.

The "next world" as a means of coercing people in this, is one attempt of getting round the problem death sets the exponents of this world. People are mostly more useful to society alive than dead, so it is mostly a crime to die unless you do so "for society." For society regards itself (rightly) as cheated by death unless it profits by it.

But to go back to "happiness": suppose a man finds firstly that of all the things it is possible to do he does not want to do anything more than he is doing now—this would seem to be the nearest one can get to the definition of a state of "happiness." He can then educate himself so that that does not obstruct others enjoying the same and they might increase their happiness mutually by cooperation and by eliminating needs which entail obstructing others. This *might* be possible—at least it does not seem inherently impossible.

But again a man who looks at the world and at himself critically, finds that while the world of his circumstances may be such that it can maintain his needs, yet it can, inherently, never satisfy them: that he and his world are so constituted that no set of circumstances can ever give more than a temporary relief and can never fully satisfy him. Every meal he eats ensures that his ability to be hungry again is maintained.

One can forgive the politicians (the bishops of today) anything except their claim to answer all needs.

664. "The sole evidence it is possible to produce that any thing is desirable is that people actually desire it ... This, however, being a fact, we have not only all the proof which the case admits of but which it is possible to require that happiness is good, that each person's happiness is a good to that person, and the general happiness therefore a good to the aggregate of all persons."

J. S. Mill, *Utilitarianism* (p. 52)

Is “happiness” here separate from or combined with “pleasure”? in either case it is not disputed that the majority are capable of it and that they desire it and that the attainment of it is largely (some say entirely) dependent on outside circumstances. But the step to the “general happiness” seems to be made without reckoning on (or at least accounting for) the fact that once an adequate living has been provided for all, there is no set of circumstances which will bring happiness to all—or even which will bring happiness to the majority always. The individuals who make up the majority are both all the time being replaced and all the time themselves changing in the pattern of their appetencies. The important thing is that each individual is satisfied only by the set of circumstances that fit the pattern of his appetencies at any particular stage of his development. The point is therefore that if the “general happiness” is to be brought about, the method of doing so will never be by determining by some method or other a set of circumstances which will give “happiness to all normal beings.” The only way to set about it would be to maintain a bureau for maintaining a continual flow of information concerning the present state of the changing average pattern of appetencies of the majority. The first will only lead to strife, the second seems impracticable.

665. All the following “good” things are entirely dependent on “bad” things for their existence:

A		B
rescue, liberation	is dependent on	oppression
heroism	” ” ”	great odds
good judgement	” ” ”	the possibility of making errors
charity	” ” ”	poverty of others
endurance	” ” ”	suffering in oneself
pity	” ” ”	suffering in others
love (desire forunion)	” ” ”	separation
energy, striving	” ” ”	privation (not having what oneneeds)
hero worship	” ” ”	inability to beoneself; what onewants; orfrustration

patience	"	"	"	the presence of unsurmountable obstruction
thrift	"	"	"	insecurity (amongother things)
temperance	"	"	"	temptation

If this world is "improved" so that all those things in column B are eliminated there will be no opportunity for the exercise of the "virtues" in column A.

666. Eating is surely an entirely repellent and utterly unjustified process. The enjoyment of the senses of taste and smell and the satisfying of hunger are, in fact, enjoyable and "innocent" only if one shuts one's eyes to all those things that eating necessitates, such as killing of animals, etc. To become a vegetarian is no escape at all, for then one's eating still involves the killing of millions of animals in the cultivation of vegetables and the killing of vegetables themselves, which are alive in their own way. The vegetarian has nothing to do with meat, but by his eating he still destroys life on a huge scale. Not to eat is to suffer and to cut one's life short, for no kind of existence is possible without eating. When I eat I think of the people who haven't got enough to eat, and then my eating cannot be justified except by my arbitrary choice and decision that I and not they shall eat, for which I alone am responsible, and for which I have no ultimate justification. But if the world were better organized, which it could well be, and everyone had enough to eat, and if I lived on vegetables alone, still I am not justified, except by my own arbitrary choice, for that destruction of animals and plants that is necessitated. I have chosen to live and to take part in this destruction simply because I want to—because to live is to destroy, just as to create is to destroy; it is only a process of change to which I can equally well apply the word "creation" or "destruction," according as I choose to feel about it. I know all the arguments used to justify such things. They stand, but the opposite standpoint remains unaffected by them. It is, in the end, I who am responsible for this state of things, for this eating and for the destruction that it necessitates. Then why not stop

eating and die? What, and be at once be reborn again, having forgotten what I have learned in this life, and start eating again? There is no way out there. The choice is not between eating (and living) and not eating (and dying and being reborn).

667. Questions Raised

1. Is not Buddhism selfish? —No, because no personal end, such as heavenly bliss, is sought.

2. Is the withdrawal from the world with the purpose of self-development compatible at all with the English social and public school tradition of self denial by team-spirit?—(1) Self-denial by team spirit, if developed for competition is an enlargement of the selfish end from the individual to the team; each individual hopes to gain more personally by the limited sacrifice of some personal ends to the team. The subordination of self-will is compatible, but the aim of competition for worldly gain is not.—(2) The now classical English liberal education incorporating the teaching of the 'humanities' contains two radically opposed basic principles: team spirit and the inviolable sanctity of the individual person and his conscience; only the English genius for compromise seems to weave these two together successfully. That education is a code, like the stoics' code of behaviour, which takes a philosophical system or a religion (it is not important what) for its ultimate justifications. In England both Christianity and Greek philosophy serve this end, but the code could attach itself to the Dhamma equally well, with some adjustments.

3. Is not the position of the Christian clergy and of the Saṅgha to the laity radically opposed since the clergy are devoted to social service?

This is a narrow estimate of the Christian clergy based on that of the C of E in England, and perhaps the C of R in England, U. S. A. and other countries where it works on a *missionary* basis, but it ignores the history of Christian monasticism, and the status, for example, of the Trappists and Poor Claires,—monasteries in, say, Belgium, Ireland, Italy, and Mount Athos.

4. Does not the Buddhist conception of heaven and hell amount in the end to much the same thing as the Christian one?—No, because they are not penitentiaries and places of reward set up

by a Lord Creator for the punishing and recompensing of his creatures who sin against or believe in him. (In Buddhism) the pattern of existence works itself out through kamma into the hells and heavens and the world we know, just as social life works itself out into prisons, jobs, public honours, etc.

5. Suppose the Dhamma were successfully spread over the world, would it be a lasting benefit?—It would be a temporary benefit, but not a lasting one. The world is comparable to a hotel or a station waiting room, it can be made better or worse by the people who pass through.

6. What do the laity get out of Buddhism?—See the story of Visākhā (Vinaya Mahāvagga Kh. 8 & S. LV, 53).—The saṅgha is open to any layman to join who wants to practise renunciation. It maintains the Buddha's teaching and that opportunity for him. What does a layman get out of a hospital?

7. Still the precepts seem to me negative—instead of refraining from taking life why not say that one should preserve life?—Would that not involve favouring one against another, in the case of those who prey upon each other?—But isn't there a hierarchy of importance of life? If I see a tiger attacking a man, should I not shoot the tiger to save the man's life?—If that is admitted then one is justified in stealing and lying to save another's life; "*bon pere de famille est capable de tout*"; "the end justifies the means." The negative precept 'Do not take life' is restraint (comparable to the ploughing of a field) and renunciation. The positive precept 'preserve live' sets life as the highest positive good (whether my own or others' makes no difference) and supports attachment and clinging to specific lives. And what if, instead of a tiger it is a man who attacks another man. But why is the question put in that form? Why not ask first at least, 'Am I justified in killing, to save my own life, a tiger (or a man) attacking me? Do I expect my neighbour to kill to preserve my life?'

8. Is Buddhism simply intellectualism?—No, intellectual knowledge is like teaching how to swim or reading a cookery book. The Dhamma is to be lived, like swimming or cooking.

9. If the Buddha's teachings require faith in the development of faculties, then a Christian is justified in arguing that it is merely a matter of developing faculties to be able to perceive the revealed

dogmas, and so the Buddhist cannot vanquish him in debate on that point.

The Buddha's teaching does not require belief in the development of new faculties to perceive outward worlds hitherto unperceived. It is not concerned with new outward worlds but with the clear vision of the world of experience as instable and unsatisfactory, and that this is due to craving. The assertion made is that a line of conduct will reduce the craving and the suffering consequent on it (which can be tested) and the belief required is that that line of action can be carried to the point at which craving ends and suffering ends.

668. **Questionnaire or Catechism**

What is self (*attā*)?	Wrong view of personality.
What is eternal (*nicca*)?	Only non-arising, non-passing-away, non-changing of what is present.
What is altogether?	Nibbāna and the Path. Pleasant (*sukha*)?
What is beautiful? (*subha*)	*Mettā*, the Brahma world, the Path.
What is Truth (*sacca*)?	The four Truths.
What is a person?	A chain of deeds and the result of deeds.
What is a soul?	Wrong view of personality.
What is a god?	An impermanent consciousness or personality with a body less grossly material than the human and less subject to pain or not subject to pain, or one with no material body at all: or a fine material body with no consciousness. None is omnipotent or a world creator.

MISCELLANEA

Poems;

Tale;

Story;

Dialogues;

Words;

Today's fallacies and half-truths;

Impressions;

Canticle.

Poems

Look

Look at the world *they* make that can be made
To shake and shiver and shift as if
It were a raft adrift Dragged by each draft
Towards a rift as by a drasm
In wrong enthusiasm reft.

(Author's Note:) 'drasm' is the noun from 'drastic' that is, something between a 'flap' and a 'drastic' spring-cleaning (as seem from a spider's angle).

"A drasm is a dreadful thing, I wot." (Oct 56)

In a letter to Rev. Ñāṇavīra:

The (above) verse, entitled "Look", will perhaps express something of my sentiments on motion. "Drasm" is an old friend, whom you may remember. Rule for this verse is that it must be full of rhymes but none must appear at the end of any two lines".

Look Again

When I look in a looking-glass
How is it that it comes to pass,
What is it, too, that there I see,
The looking-glass, myself or me?
If caged alone, the turtle dies;
But if he in reflection spies
His image in a glass, he lives:
Such is the food illusion gives.

So when I see you face to face,
Seeming *your* person there to trace,
What *do* I see there—which is true?—
The world, part of myself, or you?

You see yourself and I see you,
Only through me do you see you;
While you see me, I myself see,
Only through you do I see me.
f all the points of vanishing
In the perspective of the world,
That opposite to me is present
And I am that which isn't there.

Song

My song is simply what it seems:
A tangle of too many themes
That never whispers but it screams,
Fusing reality with dreams—
As't were a swirl of counter-streams
that with a school of clashes teems
Whereon the froth of fancy creams
The rippling of bubble-beams,
Of crystal-flaws, of leaden gleams
And winking dust of carbon-seams—
What then if there is none esteems
This tapestry of enthymemes
All ragged with unfinished schemes
To bleed the wits with lancet-fleams,
And what if none but scandal deems
This word-play of raw verbal teams
Brawling across the paper reams?
Yet furze-flame a boat's bottom breams:
My song is surely what it seems.
Come, let Philosophy now crack her whip:
And by her thumping the Grammatic Drum
The Infinite and Absolute shall come
With All and Nothing at her will to skip.
Condemn Disorder to detentive slum
To lie in chains with Ignorance; declare
The roll complete. 'Tis fatal to despair
To give a name to each; for can the dumb

Command? or the unnamed obey? Beware!
O find a name—to save her leadership—
For the unnamed, which ever gives the slip
Whose naming kills and has it born elsewhere.

(Will not this naming the unnamed ensure Work for Philosophy for evermore?)

In a letter to Rev. Ñāṇavīra:

—I rediscovered a sonnet I made a few months ago & had forgotten; while not quite a propos, I shall nevertheless quote this bit of pastiche, ... I think the distribution of rhymes is quite neat and the thought nicely rounded—but I am no judge of verse."

Self-Mastery (A Palinode)

The lowly stoic Epictetise
Wouldn't write a single treatise:
The utterances of the man
Were copied down by Arrian.
Imperial Mark Aureliorse
His bibliophobia was worse:
He wrote a book himself instead
Where 'Throw away your books!' he said.[14]

TALE

There is a village in which a postman and a scientist are living. The postman has a rule (his own, made arbitrarily by himself, but invariably kept) which is to ring the bell twice on Mondays, Wednesdays, and Fridays, and four times on Tuesdays, Thursdays and Saturdays, once a day when he brings the post; and even when there are no letters to deliver, he still rings in the same way to ask if there were any letters for the outward mail. On Sundays he takes a day off and does not ring at all. For a long time, for many years, the scientist used to answer the door when he heard the bell ring twice

14. *Editor's Note*: The title refers to an essay in which Mark Aurel's advice to throw one's books away, had been echoed.

or four times, doing so himself because he lived alone. One day, however, he received a letter from some important source asking some questions about the application of averages and interpretation of statistics. The subject tickled his scientific mind and so absorbed him that he began to work out the averages of everything he could think of. He actually nursed a secret hope that he might at length discover the average of All Things, though he realized the difficulty of such a task, and he contented himself meanwhile with a sound basis of simple classified statistics drawn from his own personal observations. In thus applying averages to his own life, he one day hit upon the matter of the postman's rings. First he reckoned that each two days the postman rang a total of six times (he knew this for certain since he counted the rings himself) and so, in order to minimize the hazards of arbitrary judgement of the moment, he worked out the average rings far each day at three; and he wrote it down in a book. Since hitherto he had been listening for four or two rings, he now concluded that it would be more accurate to listen for three, and that the two and the four could not have been really correct (rather as the atomic physicists tell us that the solid table off which we dine and which hurts us so much when we bump into it, is not really solid but is all space or whirling electrons, or something like that). He thought "I shall not allow myself to be deceived by two or four rings anymore, the senses are notoriously untrustworthy. Only three rings can be right. I must have been missing a lot of letters." He was the more convinced of this since other people always rang once, and he had worked out the average for each: the number of callers per day (excluding the postman) divided into the number of rings gave the figure and so he was certain of this through verification by experiment. So he began to ignore two and four rings and listened only for three rings for his post. After a week during which he received no letters, and the letters he wrote piled up, he wondered if he had miscalculated. Then he remembered Sundays: seven days with a total of eighteen rings made a daily average of, not three rings, but of 2.571428 rings. This, he realized, would be rather difficult to hear accurately, so he sat in his drafty hall all day, with a plate of sandwiches and a flask of laced tea, hurriedly made before sunrise, but he never heard the bell ring like that: and he still got no post, and still the letters he wrote piled up. He would not discuss his troubles with visitors who called; for after all he was a scientist and they were not. Then he remembered the public holidays such as Easter-Monday, Christmas Day, and so on, and he revised his calculations again, making them still more accurate; but still he never heard the kind of ring he was expecting. And so it goes on with his taking into account leap-years and Holy Years, and what not. And all the while he gets no post and the letters he writes and cannot post pile up so much that he will soon be pushed out of his house. But now the postman no more rings the bell since no one has answered his two and four rings for so long, and so he takes home the letters addressed to the scientist (they are very few by now) and makes some of them into spills to light his pipe in the evening when he sits by the fire, working out on the back of others the football pool averages by which he hopes to win a fortune one day. (Nov. 57)

Story

The door to the dark empty room (cave) containing *nothing*. The darkness makes the ignorant fill it with fancies. A *Church* is made to lock the door and guard against entry, which church points to the *other door*, that of the tomb, which leads to heaven, but can only be entered by dying (in voluntary ignorance of what is behind the forbidden door).

Rival churches, since the *doors* are profitable, spring, up and paint forbidden doors on walls (rocks) and guard them.

The secret known perhaps to some of the first Churchmen, is that behind the forbidden door there is nothing. That known to the second Church men is that there is no door in their church (which comes to the same).

A man enters the Church as a churchman. Perhaps he discovers that secret, but it is not worth his while divulging it, and no one would be better off if he did.

Dialogues

A: Does life justify death (for without death there would be no room for new life)? Does death condemn life (for death comes to all that live)?

B: Who knows? Who can say?

A: Everyone knows, everyone says. (Dec. 53)

* * *

A: I gave him a piece of my mind, I did; and I sent him away with a flea in his ear.

B: How is that—is your mind full of vermin?

* * *

Fra me e me

A: I shall turn over a new leaf.

Me: Why not close the book?

I: Because I don't know how—because it doesn't seem to have an outside. (Mar. 54)

* * *

Fra me e me

I: Do you approve of what is right?

My Conscience: Of course.

I: Do you believe right will triumph at the end?

My Conscience: Yes.

I: So you want to be on the winning side? (Apr. 56)

* * *

A: Is a starfish five or one?

B: How do you mean?

A: Give me an answer.

B: It is both.

A: How can what is one be five, or what is five be one?

B: I give you an example: a starfish. (Jun. 56)

* * *

My Conscience: You can't eat the cake and have it, you know.
I: Should I have it? Should I eat it?
Me: The proverb says: eat or be eaten.
I: Then I should eat my cake before it eats me?
My Conscience: That is not what I meant at all. (Mar. 56)

* * *

A: One can't be too particular about these things.

B: No, one can't, can one?

A: If one is too careful and choosy, one'll never get anything done.

B: But still, one can't be too particular about these things.

A: Can't one then?

B: If one is not careful enough, one never knows what one may have let oneself in for. (Jun. 56)

* * *

A: Eternity is that whose beginning can be indefinitely pushed back and whose end can be indefinitely postponed.

B: Eternity is all time.

A: Eternity is the opposite of time. (Jul. 57)

* * *

A: 'Take what you will', says Emerson, 'but pay the price.'

B: How can I? I have no money.

A: Oh money; that is only for material things.

B: What then?

A: Pleasures of the mind, for instance: see what Schopenhauer says!

B: How are they paid for?

A: By paying attention, of course! You give attention to them, don't you?

B: Yes, but where did I get this from?

A: (Silence)

B: Have I borrowed it from pain? Are pleasures paid for by attention demanded back by pain?

A: (Silence) (Sep. 56)

* * *

A: Is there a next life?
B: Of course.
A: How, then?
B: Why, you are living it now.
A: Now?
B: Yes, this is the next life after the last one. (Sep. 56)

* * *

A: I have the seeds of an incurable sickness in me.
B: Good gracious, what is that?
A: Ageing and death. (Aug. 57)

* * *

A: I am the victim of an incurable drug habit.
B: What habit?
A: Eating. (Aug. 57)

* * *

A: Wouldn't it be far simpler to regard myself as a machine—as purely mechanical?

B: You can't. You have free will and you must exercise your will and choose.

A: I said 'myself' I did not mean 'me.'

B: Are you not yourself today?

A: Let it be. As the Existentialists say 'I am condemned to be free'? Is that what you mean?

B: If you put it like that, yes.

A: But then surely that suggests the view regarding myself as a purely mechanical machine, and the very statement that I (who am free) *must* exercise my will, *must* choose, *must* change world history (as the Marxists say), *am condemned* to be free (as the Existentialists say) shows that myself is a purely mechanical machine.

B: So that's what you believe.

A: Did I say that?

B: What then?

A: My point was that whether you (or I) *Argue* that there is free will or that there is none the result is the same: determinism or mechanicalism.

B: But didn't I just say: "So that's what you believe?"

A: Did I ever say that? I said that that is what any argument about freedom and will must come to. But what has that to do with belief?

B: I don't follow you.

A: No. (Nov. 57)

* * *

A: What don't you believe in?

B: This world.

A: Why not.

B: Because I know it.

WORDS

intertwangledlerminous = furry
erroriousa reverberose type
immortalitarianoppositious
professor of myopicsmoralysis (fr. moralising)
Ceremoniacsacrilegion
a drasm (n. fr. drastic)Anthropomorphia
a coefficient (one good at teamwork)
embrambled = caught up

TODAY'S FALLACIES AND HALF-TRUTHS

That it is possible to ascertain with certainty what is the happiness of the greatest number.

Give everyone the necessities of life and all discontent will automatically vanish.

The independent witness who is not committed to a side.

The reality behind appearances.

That every man *knows* what he wants and you have only to give it to him and he will live happily.

That all men are equal in all respects.

That all men are different in all respects.

IMPRESSIONS

1. I go out on a grey day in the rain. The rain beats on the body and soft clouds cover the sky. The eye cannot see into the clouds and the mind is busy with the bodily sensation of dropping rain. This I call the world.

2. I go out on a cloudless midday. The overhead sun beams and shines and glares and burns in a pure hard blue enamel sky (the blue of heaven). The eye cannot see past the blue and the mind is busy with the bodily sensation of burning heat. (Hateful is the dark blue sky vaulted over the dark blue sea—said Tennyson.) This I call the lower heaven.

3. I go out on a clear night at full-moon. The trees milk the white light from the air letting it drip and lie in pools on the ground. The moon hangs a curtain of half-light behind the biggest stars. Though the eye cannot see through the curtain, the mind is half quiet. This I call the higher heaven.

4. I go out late on a clear moonless night, long after even the zodiacal light has sunk down. The sun is directly underfoot. There are only stars in the sky. The stars hard and sharp as spears, but have NO size (I know that even with the hugest telescope they subtend NO angle): and between the stars I see what is not there. It is quite plainly visible extended space: no feature neither with nor without atoms. The positive stars have no size at all; the negative void has infinite size. Neither upside down nor right way up I hang in that void neither in the middle nor near the edge. This, I shall call the external vertigo.

5. I sit down in a room and consider a fugue. This I call the lower inner heaven.

6. I sit down in a room and consider that in me there is that which can recognize a fugue and its structure. This I call the higher inner heaven.

7. I sit down in a room, quiet and half dark and watch the act of breathing—the bodily sensation of air touching the tip of the nose: I experience sensing the bodily sensation at an interval of space. I can place the bodily sensation in space as sensed from the direction in which I am. But when I follow that direction back and

look for the "I," then I am no longer there but in another place. I have no place in space. I see and sense space and the "things" in it from a place where I am not. Space is complete without "I" and there is no room for "I" in space at all. This I call the inner vertigo.

CANTICLE

The only one is the many; and many the ones: The only one that is the many is only one of the many. The only infinity is finiteness; and finite the infinities:

The only infinity is finiteness; and finite the infinities: only that the infinity which is finite is infinitely finite.

The only eternity is time; and temporal eternity: only the eternity which is temporal is temporarily eternal.

The only permanence is the impermanent; and impermanent the permanencies: only the permanence which is impermanent is impermanently permanent.

* * *

Only death lives for ever; and the life-everlasting is, death. Only life dies for ever; and the death-everlasting is life. The lifeless has died for ever: the deathless will live for

ever. Is there another life? Of course, you are living it now.

* * *

The Absolute receives absolution only from consciousness, and by that act its absoluteness is very particular.

The Incomprehensible is only incomprehensible when comprehended as such: uncomprehended, it is comprehendible as incomprehensible.

Do I know the ignorance of unknowledge, or am I ignorant of the knowledge of my ignorance?

The most illusory of all illusions is the illusion that there is no illusion.

What is certain? Probability. What is probable? Certainty. Can I doubt that I know with certainty my own doubt?

To exist is to be condemned to freedom and to be free for condemnation.

How to achieve in Christian Theism safety from the Sin Against the Holy Ghost? How to achieve in Marxist atheism the safety from becoming an Enemy of the People?

Who can say that he is free as long as he is not freed from freedom?

All religions are one: but which one?

From Letters to Venerable Ñāṇavīra

I

About phenomena and being. I by no means disagree with your statement that *what* phenomena *are* is *other* phenomena. That description describes phenomena in terms of themselves (identified with being), which is, of course, perfectly correct—since there is nothing else in terms of which to describe them. Phenomena are being, being is phenomena. The two are one and the one are two (my description had the clause, if I remember rightly, that if they could be held to have a distinguishing peculiar characteristic it might be ... etc...

The only thing I might alter now would be to say that "being is hidden" instead of "has nothing beyond it," thus when the hidden being ("capable of appearing") is disclosed it appears as a phenomenon. So while your description emphasizes the *identity* of the two, mine emphasizes the duality in the identity). But while phenomena and being—the *two* are identically *one* (phenomena *are*) at the same time we cannot dispense in thought and speech with either of the two, replacing either one entirely by the other, which since they are identical, is absurd (but the world is absurd). What is an identity? It is the essential oneness of two entities whose difference, if any, *does not count.*

I underlined the words in "to be is to be phenomenal—i.e., "to appear or to be capable of appearing" (attributed by you to me as "my view") because this raised the same difficulty as Whateley Carington's 'cognita and cognizables.' But that which is "capable of appearing," if it has not yet appeared, cannot be known to be either capable of appearing or incapable of appearing; or, if it is known as "capable of appearing" it is because it has already appeared as "capable of appearing"; consequently the distinction as a class founders in both cases. The phenomenon called (I think misleadingly) "capable of appearing" or "cognizable" in this sense (which might suggest that it exists independently of our knowledge of it) is, I think, more simply termable as a phenomenon that appears (present) in the mode of absence (temporal or spatial, etc.). I see the "capability" as a mode arising from tensions due to patterns of presences and absences in the different fields of the saḷāyatana. But "phenomena capable of appearing" as a category opposed and extra to "appearing phenomena," I regard as bogus, even if specious. The Realist/Idealist controversy by-passes this point.

I love logicians and mathematicians. Also I regard Irrationalism (often called "Rationalism") as *no alternative to*, or *escape from*, logic, but only a (futile) defiance of it in its own valid field, which is that of "*bhavā*[15] *assumed*" (like Satanism before god, perhaps), and it (the irrationality) falls entirely within logic's own domain. Neither Logic nor Irrationality, as rational-or-irrational—anti-logic, are *niyyānika*.[16] But within the all-extensive *bhava-assumed*, logic rules unquestionably and irrationality keeps the logicians awake and angry.

A witticism (witty schism if you like) occurred to me yesterday about "necessity." While the proverb speaks of "making a virtue of necessity," Kant (with his "Categorical Imperative") speaks of "making a necessity of virtue." Now this raises a point about descriptions and errors therein, and fictions: Kant (and others since) claimed that human personality has a special faculty, a "moral eye", which "sees" intuitively and directly (as the eye sees visually visible forms) what Ought to be Done. This I hold is not so since I find in myself no such faculty, only a certain sense of caution and expediency, which comes perhaps under judgment. This, then, I hold to be an outstanding example of a bogus description, and this kind of description I regard as potentially dangerous.

With phenomena and being in the air, the word "essence" knocks at the door. "Essence" (from the verb *esse, to be*): a medieval logician's concept, initiated by Aristotle (parallel to the Pali commentarial use of *bhava*), is used by logicians and philosophers

---

15. Pali: 'being'
16. 2 Pali: 'leading out', 'liberating'

as a synonym) for "characteristic" (particular phenomenon) peculiar to an individual or to a class by which that individual or class is recognized to *be* itself. This ontic metaphor from subjective-objective *being* to purely-objective characteristic is a pun-by-metaphor of fundamental importance, and indispensably useful for those (Religions, Doctors and scientists, say) who need to employ the "Utraquistic Subterfuge" (which is so valuable for verbal *presti*(di)g(itation) *e*—remove what is in the ( ) and see what remains). But a characteristic-phenomenon, called "essence" (*le phenomene de l'être*), is then that of something which has that essence, and consequently, *is not* it (whether that "something" is regarded as a Kantian "Ding-an-sich" or as an Abhidhamma constellation-of-dhammas-with-no-self-substance, or what you will, makes no difference here): it is that special phenomenon by which I recognize what this which *has* it, *is*, and believe this to *be what it itself is*. Now this characteristic, by the utraquistic ontic metaphor of "essence" applied to it, renders it possible to appear to verbally externalized Being and so to objectivize it entirely. So it is now easier (apparently) to handle "existence" (that same thing's Being) as just another external attribute, namely that thing's ("quality-of-existence") predicatable of it. The fraud is now nearly complete; and if the logical copula is (the being assumed and agreed on as one of the basic assumptions of logic, and a logical constant) can only be passed off as quite divorced from being or existence with the mediation of the metaphor of "essence" externalized, as a characteristic and attribute, then we can forget about it, forget that it is the true verbal symbol for existential being, and forget that it contains the (hateful subjective) element of self-identification. This play with the "essence"-metaphor is possible precisely because of the actual existential miragic identity-relation of ambivalence between consciousness and being and between being-and-phenomena. This ambivalence which remains in the copula is anathema to logicians, and they seek any means to hide it away. So, now we have *split* being into two, tried to drain being away from the copula by means of the "essence"-metaphor, and now we can make believe that the copula is not really being at all (which is quite untrue) since it remains being on the verbal plane; and if it did not, statements would not correspond at all to life, and, logic could not possibly ever have any connection with existence at all), and so the copula can be exempted from all questions and analysis when we are investigating *being* and its structure, and what is more, this investigation can be handed over entirely to logic, which, since the copula (its constant) exhibits this most serious and crippling error: *cogito ergo sum* / "if *cogitatio* is, then *esse*."

(3) *The Form of the Statement*: I believe it is legitimate to paraphrase "AB implies A" by "If AB, then A", and to take them as equivalent. If that is correct,' then, in their second form, the statement looks superficially to be similar in form to "*imasmiṃ sati idaṃ hoti*" expressed in the form "If this is, then that is" or the *cogito* expressed in the form "If I think then I am." But it seems to me there are these most important differences: (1) In "AB implies A" (or "If AB, then A") the individual *natures* of A and B are completely unimportant so long as they are merely *different* and suitably combinable and they are thus level one with the other. But on the contrary, in the *cogito* (where the first person is unique) and in *imasmiṃ sati idaṃ hoti* (which is only legitimately expandable into the Paṭiccasamuppāda formula) the natures of the concepts employed are of fundamental importance; for the *cogito* would be valueless if it did not specifically employ the unique first person, and consciousness and being; and likewise *imasmiṃ sati idaṃ hoti* whose expanded from (it is not like a Law of Thought a *quelconque* generalization) the concepts' particular natures are of absolutely fundamental importance; for it includes the constituents necessary for *asmi-māno* (the first person singular "I") and consciousness, and being. So while "AB implies A" is, in its form, quite general and impersonal, both the *cogito* and *imasmiṃ sati* are inseparable from the special unique concepts they incorporate.

(4) *Self-Identification within the Cogito and the Statement.* The ontological act-of-self-identifying is quite differently treated in the *Cogito* and the *Statement.* The *Cogito* implies "When I think, then I am self-identifying self identical on return "(making be)" while the Statement implies "When A and B are combined then A remains unchanged on return to, or repetition of, A". Or the *Cogito* says "I am conscious whenever I am my self-identity" but the Statement

says "Self-identity is always valid", which is something quite different. The *Cogito* shows my self-identity of being as contingent upon consciousness as subjectivity; but the *Statement* only declares that the self-identity of A does not change on a return to self (A). (And here I remember that the "invariant of a transformation" on "Invariance in transformation", as the third characteristic of the *saṅkhata*, is, such as it is described, subject to its relation within the wider description "*Avijjā-paccayā saṅkhārā ... upādāna-paccayā bhavo*). I certainly agree with you that it is dangerous rationalist *mauvaise foi* to doubt what is certain (just as it is dangerous religious irrationalist *mauvaise foi* to believe what is uncertain), and I think we agree in regarding the *Cogito* as a true description and as unquestionably certain and verifiable by reflexion; and likewise the Paṭicca-samuppāda formula. But I do not, for the reason stated, accept "AB implies A" on this footing at all. That I, when I cognize, identify I do not doubt; but that an *identification made* can never be doubted I do most certainly non admit. *Il est dons mon être question de mon être.*

(5) *Certainty*. I do not know how far we agree on this matter. "AB implies A" assumes that A remains unchanged in the repetition, in the return to it by self identification; but how can I be certain that it has not changed meanwhile (*thitassa aññathattaṃ paññāyati*)? And if it has, then "AB does not imply A" is appropriate. For myself, I am certain that I cognize and that I am, but I am not certain *what* it *is* that I cognize, or *what* it *is* that I am. Whether I am myself or not is quite open to doubt even in ordinary usage, since I can on one day be "quite myself," on another "not quite myself," and on another "Quite beside myself." I am certain that when I see, that I see; but though I identify what I see (recognize it), I am not *certain what it* is that I see; hence the constant question "What is this that I see?" which is always liable to be reopened however well answered. I am certain that "I am doing" but my identification of "*what* I am doing is uncertain. True it (the other cases too) is, or seems, in *pure immediacy, certain* what I am doing; but any pure immediacy is only part of a wider immediacy, and so on in infinite hierarchy; so that what I am doing now, namely (certainly) writing this letter in one immediacy, is part of

spending-a-day-at-Polgasduva,[17] which is part of living-at-the-Hermitage, and so on, but ad infinitum—but N.B., the "infinite here" is "*indefinite*", so while I am unquestionably certain that "I am doing", I am only relatively certain what I am doing in any immediacy, and I am quite uncertain what it is that I am doing (in its self-identity), since that recedes always into the infinitely indefinite.

(6) *Infinity*: While the recourse to infinity gives maximum freedom of movement in proportion to the number of facts of a situation relegated to infinity and thus made indefinite, yet this infinity, owing to its *indefiniteness*, renders what is infinitized absolutely ineffectual existentially. Existence partakes of both finite and infinite, being the synthesis of both. Now grammar, though so greatly despised, is sometimes instructive: and here we find the verb has its *infinite mood*, in which it is depersonalized, relegated to a position not even admitting potentiality, and consequently quite neutralized as regards any effective (verbal) action on its part. It is perhaps one of the weaknesses of Berkeley's formula "*esse est percipi*" that it is stated in grammatical infinitives (*esse, percipi,*) and so is depersonalized and abstracted from existence. If he had, like Descartes, worked in the *finite* form, the *indicative*, he might have noticed some of its deficiencies "I am, therefore I am perceived" does not claim the unquestioned recognition as an adequate valid description of reflexion that *cogito ergo sum* does; it then appears as *être vu*, which invites completion, owing to its one-sided passivity, by involving, say God, by whom I am perceived in order that I can *be*. Infinity enters at once with double reflexion, and I think that conscious reflexion is not reducible below double reflexion. But *esse est percipi* forgets the finite *percipiens* in my definite finity. "AB implies A," if considered in this light, can only belong to (side with) the infinite type of expression, and never to the finite, and so is abstract and ineffectual, though, of course, invaluably useful within the limits of infinity.

(7) *Law*: If the Statement is regarded as a Law of Thought, then it is not a description: then the whole Legal Mode (derived as it is

---

17. The Sinhalese name for the "Island Hermitage" where the author lived. (Ed.)

from the manner of formulating laws from cases (as in English Common Law) is implied; for the mental machinery is the same, wherever laws are formulated. A court case, with the evidence and verdict or judgment, is comparable to a description, and any law *formulated* from it is comparable to a law abstracted from a *description* (or set of descriptions). Much more might be said on this, but I refrain I only remark that I regard the *Cogito* as a valid *description* free from errors (even if a little incomplete). I regard "AB implies A" as a statement of a law abstracted from (some description or descriptions not recorded). As such, it is on a different footing, and in a different mode; it is *abstract* (and in the legal sense arbitrary). If the two are confused (I do not say they are), it seems to me a mistake.

In conclusion, if you mean (as I take it you do) that the Laws of Thought and "AB implies A" are objectively valuable witnesses to how being is maintained (rather as instruments of torture are valuable witnesses to the methods of the Holy Inquisition by which the Catholic Church maintains itself on occasion) then I agree with you. But if it is suggested (and I am not supposing that you suggest this at all) that they are subjectively acceptable as instruments *for use in analysing* being and, as such, are themselves subjectively *niyyānika*, then I dissent. What I am not clear about is what you mean when you say that a reflecting logician sees "AB implies A" on reflexion and no error can arise beyond error of description. (3rd February 1959)

II

The trouble about discussing wind, I find (I here refer to discussions on this subject 'fra me e me') is that (a) they *always* ramify fantastically and (b) one *always* finds that one has not been talking about mind (either *mano* or *viññāṇa*) but only about *nāma-rūpa*. The committee called Buddhaghosa Thera made a parallel most grave and fundamental error in their *Visuddhimagga's* 14th Chapter when they set out to describe the *viññāṇakkhandha* second, next to the *rūpakkhandha*, and before *vedanā*, *saññā* and *saṅkhārā* (that is why the description of the last two is so thin there, because it is these two, not *viññāṇa* that has been described second under ***viññāṇa*** and so there is nothing intelligible left to say about them beyond mere repetition). This is quite contrary to the Suttas, which never change the order for the vital reason that it is only *after* you have exhausted everything positive by the first four that *viññāṇa* remains (MN 140) and that is indescribable except on the basis of that due to which it arises (MN 38), or on the basis of *nāma-rūpa* (MN 109) which it is—not (in the mode of not-being-what-it-is-and-being-what-it-is-not), and unlike the other four, it is the only infiniteness among them (*ānañca*—see the four *āruppas*) and so, phenomenologically it is the pure negative ("purer" than the first negation, *ākāsa* the four *ārupas* are Absolute Negation). From this you may safely infer that I quite agree with your earlier "glass-shelves" theory, with the reservation that an infinite hierarchy of infinitely extensive glass shelves is (are) *indistinguishable from nothing except dialectically* (what, by the way, does 002 signify mathematically, if anything?). This latter I regard as important. For if the *pañcakkhandhā* are *assumed* (*upādiṇṇa*)—and if they are absolutely not assumed there is no talking and no talked-about-then the assumption (consumption on the physical-material level) must, by its nature, be a dialectical assumption. But since, fundamentally all dialectic (which—in decision = anxiety—fear = pain) is *unpleasant*, one side of the basic dialectics has to be closed, more compulsively so in proportion to their existential importance (the *consumption* of *food* being one of the basic aspects), and is closed unilaterally by *taṇhā* and *avijjā*. The other side, being left open, then becomes the object of faith, which, when pure, believes absolutely it is not open to dialectic.

Here a further train of thought is, I find, waiting at the station with steam up ready to depart. Whereto? Let us see. You know my view of the necessary organic relation of faith-ignorance (*saddhā-avijjā*) in the *puthujjana*, when faith supplements, in action, the deficiency in knowledge (*ñāṇa*) truncated by ignorance, and so makes action (kamma) not only possible but inescapable: Well, my train now seems to be heading in the following direction: Given faith's intimacy with ignorance (take this in the worst sense, if you like), faith only functions well (as '*bonne foi*') when ignored (perhaps the mythico-psychological term for this would be "in the Unconscious," which, otherwise translated, would mean "in overlooked behaviour patterns as regards the Other"—but subjectively, it means "in pure, unreflective action," I think). But in proportion as faith is brought up by reflexion into full ignorance governed cognizance (i.e., knowledge of the limited, I-positional, kind that must accompany the basically still unbroken-up faith-ignorance ménage) it either dies and turns into honest doubt, or it lives on as *mauvaise foi*. I say "it dies and becomes doubt" because it is an easily verifiable fact that if one *knows* (in this way) that one is acting on faith alone, one thereby becomes inhibited (simultaneous knowledge of this type is *destructive* of faith) and the action collapses (e. g., miracles (?), or Ogden & Richards' "Centipede" or stage-fright or ordinary straight forward doubt, as, for example, one's first real attempt at swimming, etc.) This, I take it, is because action is only an *aspect* or a *function* of faith-ignorance. (When action is analyzed into *paticcasamuppāda-nirodha, saddhā* vanishes and *avijjā ceases*). The first three paths are then necessarily paradoxical and represent the opening of fundamental dialectics, of which two recognizably basic ones are consciousness/unconsciousness and being/non-being. It is these that indicate *nirodha*, I take it. The *sotāpanna's aveccappasāda* as "confidence due to undergoing" (*adhigama-saddhā*) is thus properly faith which is no more faith (MN 47) and owing to his loss of a measure of ignorance, his knowledge *ñāṇa* is no more knowledge as the simple opposite of ignorance. Confidence and understanding (*paññā*) are now *both* one *and* two until the Arahant's revolution terminates the absurdity (see also MN 95). The train of thought has now stopped. Where are we now? Where are the station name-boards? What does it *mean*?

I think you are quite right to bring out the fact that the Buddha while giving definitions, never gives a single definition as absolute, and all really basic ideas; like the *saccāni* are most delicately balanced, too, in the matter of negation. If any single definition were absolutely valid determinism must result, and then no *brahmacariya* is possible for the ending of suffering. (26th June 1959)

III

... *There are no absolute opposites.* Complexity denies the possibility of anything arising alone, since an event a always complex. If any thing or quality (is) discriminated (as) the opposite of another, each will be associated with other qualities that are not opposites, thus apparent-oppositeness is only partial. Perhaps if a complete opposite is not an impossibility, and were found, something frightful would happen.

... *What is said and thought about anything is always reflexion.* Without reflexion nothing comes to light. The moment I say 'I am doing this,' I am reflecting, not 'doing this.'

... *Complementarity* (a la Bohr), i.e., any description that claims complete coherence is incomplete by omitting to deal with incoherence. This appears in the "complementarity" of wave-particle descriptions of the percept-bodies called electrons, and again in the *ajjhattabahiddhā* aspects of the subjectively-experienced and objectively-perceived body. Perhaps this principle shadows every generalization, the more general, the closer.

... *Continuity-discontinuity*: There must be same recondite fundamental tie between the (as it were) seunction of the Quantum theory and the converse continuity, the flow, that is an *undeniable experience* (giddiness and nausea). The simile that comes to mind is that of my walking up a down-going escalator: I proceed by steps (my step-function or quanta), which conforms to the shape of the flow, but the steps flow against me and, as it were, fuse my acts. By this means I have to step and flow simultaneously to stay put. (10th September 1957)

The Essential Relation in Observing

Preamble

The assertion is made here that the *event of observing* at its simplest *must of necessity be complex.* Without comparison (confrontation) no observation could be said to have been made at all. For (a) without simultaneous (as it were 'spatial') confrontation of difference in the observed ("This—not that") no observation could be said to happen at all since there would be no way of distinguishing the alleged observation from non-observation; and (b) without difference *between* observed and observer (observable by successive, as it were, 'temporal' comparison as "difference in the new observed") no observation could be happening either, since the alleged observer could not be distinguished from the observed. An "observed that is indistinguishable from the non-observed" will be regarded as unconstitutable as likewise an "observer with no observed," an "observed with no observers" and an "observer and observed indistinguishable *inter se.*" (Fragment)

A. The Division

1. *Unless* there is division between observer and observed, no difference can be compared and no observation can take place.

2. *Unless* what is observed by the observer is itself divided (from what is not observed), no comparison can be made (and without comparison in the observed, no difference can be found between the observed and not observed)

3. The simplest, minimum, elementary division in the observed can be called the "affirmed/denied/" the "this/ not that," "yes/no." Since each counterpart excludes the other (so regarded), they can be symbolized by the signs + and —. The two elements of the observed, so divided I shall call *adjacent* to each other), and observed as such.

4. *Division* thus appears as a necessary factor (*sine qua non*) of observation: division (a) between observer and observed, and (b) in

the observed. The observer, so divided from the observed, I shall call also adjacent (to the observed), but unobserved. Since observer and observed are also mutually exclusive (but not in the same way as the two divisions of the observed) they can be respectively symbolized by 0 and 1. Each is, in fact, '0' in terms of the other—the 'divided' and the 'undivided' and my equating '0' with the observer is an arbitrary, if convenient, decision of a choice, which cannot be escaped if a statement is to be made—(it *could* be made conversely).

5. The observed, therefore, in order to be observable at all, must appear to the potential observer *at least* as a duality. (N. B.: a "potential observer without any observed" and an "as-yet-unobserved observable" are convenient fictions at this stage, but will vanish). The two divisions of the observed I shall call *the elements of the observable*, and these together with the potential observer I shall call *the elements of observation*.

6. The division in the observable allows the differentiation of "this/not-that" = +/–. The division between the observer and the observable is expressible either as the difference of nature, namely, undividedness/ dividedness, or as the observability of the observable and the unobservability of the observer: the observer *can* observe the observable but *cannot* observe himself. (The objection will be made that all this 'observer-cum-observed' is being observed by *some other observer*, e. g. the writer of this paragraph. That is legitimate, but it must wait for treatment till later (§ 20).)

Here only a mental note need be made that in symbolizing the observer by 'o' I have intended to signify also an essential *incompleteness*, which the unavoidable introduction of the observer (with his comparing) brings automatically with him. The description of the situation is thus structurally (skeletally) "completed" by the addition of "nothing" (the observer = o), but is nevertheless still incomplete since it still "lacks nothing" (an observer of the observer = oXoX...); the mere ramification by division/ confrontation in the observed 'completes nothing' in this sense. The apposition o:1 is asymmetrical. Observation is originally asymmetrical.

B. The Constitution of the Observed as a field or Unity

7. The 'observable' (+1; −1), which, to be so, must be divided (§ 2), is only constituted as a unity when the confrontation of the divisions is constituted by the presence of the observer ('o') in the Event of Observation (in which Event also the potential observer is constituted qua observer). This divided unity thus constituted I shall call the *observed field* (+1 X −1).

8. But, for this constitution to be effective, it is necessary (*sine qua non,*) that the observer should be unmistakably different by nature from the observed (i.e., unobserved) and that the two divisions of the observed should be unmistakably different by nature from each other and, in a different way, from the observer (+1 x−1, o). This can be stated, for convenience, spatially as follows the constituted duality + <->—cannot be so constituted as a line (of two points) except from a standpoint not in the same line (expressible as 'o' in terms of that line). This "linearity" of the observed field constituted from outside I shall call Rectangularity (the "*Rectangularity* of a straight line").

9. But in order that what is essentially *different* in the Event of Observation may not absolutely *fly apart*, it is also equally necessary (*sine qua non*) that all three constituents of the Event have something in common to bind them. That, in fact, is 'nothing.' The 'nothing' that the divisions of the observed have in common is their not being the observer ('o'), who while observing that they have 'nothing' in common with each other, has 'nothing' in common with them. This state of being bound together (......?) in the divided observed field as a unity I shall call *Conjunctive Adjacency*.

10. The constitutive power of the observer in binding the observed from a (rectangular) standpoint outside it (in virtue of which he is 'nothing' in terms of it) I shall call *Disjunctive Adjacency.*

11. The Event of Observation, with its three elements, so minimally constituted (by divisions and binding) I shall call the *Relation*. (There is *no relation* unless the *two observed* elements are constituted as a unity by the *third* element, the observer, who is 'nothing to them.' Therefore Relation has a minimum of three elements sine qua non).

12. That the three elements of the Relation 'have nothing in common' makes it incorrect to say that any one has an 'absolute opposite' within the Relation.

13. At this point I shall note that there are four possible confrontations (neither less nor more) to be made by the observer in the observed field. They can be symbolized as follows:

+ x +, +x–, –x+, –x–.

These can be regarded as four unoriented pairs, four "states of the observed field" (spatially simultaneous). Their stated order—an order of simultaneous pattern not in succession—is *arbitrary* (being only one of the possible permutations). But without this arbitrariness no order can be stated. It is not possible to *invert* any of them since they (as yet) lack the orientation between themselves that would make any inversion observable by comparison (+ x + inverted is undistinguishable from + X +, not inverted). "Change" and "alternative" have not so far emerged; only "and" and "difference" have emerged (space is implied, but not time). Observation, as the Event (but not an event), has now been constituted.

(The balance of the manuscript page has been left blank (for addition?), with the following pencilled note:)

Asymmetrical observer and observed are not "equal and opposite."

C. Change in the Constituted Observed Field

14. But a calamity occurs. If this Event, so carefully constituted, is expressed symbolically in the terms I took care to choose, it must appear as follows: +1 > –1) X 0. (But, as everyone knows, the result of that is 'o' ! How absurd! My sums must be wrong or else there is No Event).

15. The sums are not wrong, and there is an Event. But the act of the constitution of the Event is also the act of its annihilation. While there is, it seems, no constituting it otherwise, the constitution automatically reduces it (the Event) again to nothing. Now 'nothing' is 'o', and 'o' is the observer. But the observer cannot be an observer without an observed field. Consequently the act of annihilation must be, cannot help being, an act of

reconstitution. And so on ... (in retrospect as, it seems also, in prospect). (This "reconstitution" from 'o' cannot be expressed in mathematical terms; for mathematically a specific proposition, once reduced to zero by multiplication with 'o' cannot be resurrected). This "... constitution/ annihilation/reconstitution ..." (can it be conceived as a flow?) I shall call *Successive Adjacency*. (Time as well as space is now implied: and what cannot happen in time & space?).

16. This is another way of saying that "space without time is impossible," since, by its being observed, it is simultaneously asserted and denied. Another decision is necessary. And, consequently, it follows that time has no nature of its own beyond that of the *division* between and succession of adjacent space.

17. With simple constitution (up to § 13 end) the observational Relation I have described was only a generality, as *The event*, and no *alternative comparison* was possible. This could only be effected by another division, namely, by the introduction of succession (§ 14) expressible as 'change or difference in time.' By this means, the four pairs (see § 13) become oriented with regard to each other. This has rectangularity to the 'conjunctive adjacency' (§ 9) since it is expressible as 0 in terms of them.

18. The introduction of *succession* transforms the generality of *The Event* into a plurality of events, and adds to 'simultaneity' also alternativity, adds 'or' to 'and.' Consequently, while (in §§ 7–12) only simultaneity was possible as, for instance, "yes; no" (yes *and* no), now the alternative "yes", "no" (yes *or* no) is possible.

19. At this point the four confrontations earlier stated as unoriented pairs (§ 12) can be stated as successively oriented pairs as follows:

$$\begin{matrix} + & + & - & - \\ \downarrow & \downarrow & \downarrow & \downarrow \\ + & - & + & - \end{matrix}$$

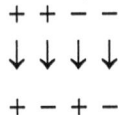

(The 'pairs' are now oriented, or, as it were, 'charged.') But whereas earlier (§ 12) the event was 'fixed' arbitrarily as to the *order*

of the four pairs though inversion made no difference, now, while the *order* can be changed, inversion makes a difference.

$$\begin{array}{ccc} + & & - \\ \downarrow & \neq & \uparrow \\ + & & + \end{array}$$

etc.

Consequently any statement of an event must, further, be an arbitrary instance of (one of the permutations of) the Event. This arbitrary element, which enters in as soon as the division comes about (§ 4) I shall call the *dialectic.*

20. However, conversely, whenever any arbitrary expression of the event is stated, the structure of the Event necessitates certain consequents and excludes others. This I shall call the *logic.*

The Dialectic and the Logic imply one another (they 'coincide' and are 'at war,', but they are never 'congruent' and no 'final peace' is possible). The Dialectic is the 'if' (if this statement of The Event is made) while the Logic is the 'then' (then it follows that the pattern of orientation will be this, not that); but the 'if' is arbitrary and 'precedes' the 'then.'

Arbitrariness (ofmode)	= the *particular* expression (which automatically excludes thealternative)
Element	= the two parts of the observed,and the observer
Adjacency	= conjunctive adjacency of the twoparts of the observed, anddisjunctive adjacency of observerand observed
Relation	= the triple relation between theduality of the observed field andthe observer
Event of Observation	= the mutual interconstitution ofobserver and observed
Division	= (rectangularity)

D. The Bracketing of the Observer 'o'

21. The four alternatives (§ 19) can be interchanged, and, being oriented, can also be turned upside down. With the constitution of

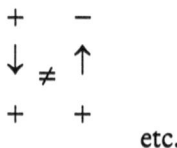

the observed field (§§ 7–13) the confrontation of "and" takes place, while with the annihilation and reconstitution (§ 14) the succession of "or" becomes possible. With the possibility of alternative, confrontations in Successive Observations the question arises, 'What of Successive Observers?' Now, while the basic division in the observed field as +:– leads to its ramification in the presence of the observer ('o'), no such ramification takes place in the observer, who is 'nothing' and, whatever is 'done to' nothing, may be –o remains 'o'. (I shall leave aside for the moment the proposition - $^{1} = \infty$). The consequence of this is that, in order to multiply the observer I must describe him in terms of his observed, since no other way is possible, and this would seem to be a fiction.

22. The observer does not appear in his observed field in any way at all, which 'lacks nothing' (§ 7), which is why he is symbolized by 'o.' While he is everywhere, while he is absolutely essential, he 'does not count' at all. Whether he is one or many it is impossible to tell except from the field or fields that are being observed. But this anticipates. Consequently, while his singularity or plurality may be a matter for consideration in an inquiry into his nature, in an inquiry into the nature of the observed he can be disregarded (so long as I remember that there I learn *nothing* about him). I shall therefore, for the moment at least, put him in brackets ('o') and forget him (remembering, of course, that I have forgotten him).

This is what all Objective Science claims to do (and often forgets to do) and for which admiration is commonly expected. (The results of this I shall call '*Solalterism*' or the 'Science of the Subject leaving himself out of his calculations'). Since He counts for zero in the observed, which is not observed without him, he can easily be reintroduced. It is, of course, the converse of the opposite procedure, where results are usually condemned without trial as detestable and are commonly called *solipsism*' or that of the 'madman who has shut himself up in, an impenetrable 'blockhouse.' [See § 369]

Here the manuscript ends with a blank page carrying only the chapter heading:

E. The Ramification of the Observed

(The following text, obviously belonging to the preceding treatise was found in a different file among the late Author's posthumous papers. The sheet was not paginated and had no paragraphing linking it with the above treatise.)

Existence is an *operation*. Operation comes into being with a *leap*, and at once extends back to infinity and forward to infinity, yet with the personal horizon that conceals both infinities.

The necessity for the observed duality (+I, –I) to be in relation with an observer (o), in order to *exist* implies:

(i) that the observer (o) has perpendicularity to the observed (+I, –I),

(ii) that *spatially* the observer has no status (=0) in terms of the observed (+I, –I),

(iii) that *temporally* the observer (=o) is structurally related to (=multiplied with = added to) the observed (+I, –I) and so spatially annihilates it by introducing change as temporalization,

(iv) that existentially (consciously) that observer (=0), having annihilated the observed (=+I, –I) *must* reconstitute it (he, the observer, cannot exist as o—cannot 'non-exist'—except against the observed), immediately reconstitutes the observed (as thus reconstitutable = ±I or ±I),

(v) that in the reconstitution of the observable (+1 or #1) by the observer (o), a choice *must* be exercised whether the observable is to be constituted as this or that alternative (i.e., + or—). N.B., the term "observable" refers to the just-annihilated observed, neither more nor less,

(vi) this unavoidable choice exercised in the reconstitution is *arbitrary*. Once exercised the world is determined logically, but subject to immediate annihilation.

* * *

Motion is spatial (change is temporal)

Motion existentially establishes space. Change existentially establishes time. In space-time, when no motion is observed there is no *time*, and where no change is observed there is no *space*.

Just as *motion* is *relative* i.e., it is impossible (purely existentially) to ascribe absolute motion (or stationariness) to any body (acceleration introduces features other than motion), so too *change* is relative, i.e., it is impossible to ascribe absolute change or stability to any state. The "absolutely motionless" and the "absolutely unchanging" (whether temporary or 'eternal') depend as such on consciousness functioning with the unique "I." (The consequence seems to be that all are relative.)

Pathways of Buddhist Thought

Buddhism: A Religion or a Philosophy?

Sometimes the question is heard: "Is Buddhism a religion or a philosophy?" And sometimes the answer comes readily: "It is a religion." "But why?" "Well isn't religion a matter of observances? And the Eightfold Path is largely observance, with Right Speech and so on. So Buddhism is a religion, like any other." Or it may come just as readily: "It is not a *religion*; it is a philosophy." "Why?" "Because it doesn't rely on blind faith but emphasises understanding. It is the way of Reason. And isn't Right View philosophy?" Or someone may say: "It is neither a religion nor a philosophy; it is an ethico-philosophical system." Who is right? Are they all right, some right, or none?

We may have read somewhere that religion is a matter of emotions and that philosophy is rational. If we fly to the dictionaries for help, we may well come away in this case more uncertain than before, as to define "Buddhism," "religion," and "philosophy" from the dictionaries is no easy matter. (But if we once begin to inquire from them what exactly the word "is" implies, we shall soon find ourselves in a pretty tangle, as anyone can see for themselves if they would like to try.)

But if we are not sure what we mean by religion or philosophy (let alone the word "is"), can we attempt to answer the question at all? Suppose we do agree on a meaning for those two words; are we right in supposing that the question is rightly put, and put in such a way that some correct answer is possible if it can be found?

Are, in fact, all religions and philosophies each just *a* religion and *a* philosophy among a crowd, and is Buddhism *necessarily* one among this crowd? What then would be the unique Olympian point of view, able to survey all those religions and philosophies, and able to class them and pigeon-hole them so readily and neatly?

There used to be a recognized type of question in ancient Greece which committed the answerer equally, whether he replied affirmatively or negatively. One was "Do you use a thick stick when you beat your wife? Answer yes or no." Now, whether the answer was "Yes" or "No," the retort was "So you *do* beat your wife, then." There are many questions of that type, and some of them not at all evidently so.

Why not pause (there is no hurry) before plumping for a one-sided answer, and take a quick glance at the way in which the Buddha handles and presents his whole *teaching*.

One thing among many others to be noticed here is that he is careful to spread a *net* with which to intercept all speculative views. This is the *Brahmajāla,* the "Divine Net," which as the first discourse of the whole Sutta Piṭaka forms as it were a kind of filter for the mind; or to change the analogy, a tabulation by whose means (if rightly used) all speculative views can be identified, traced down to the fallacy or unjustified assumption from which they spring, and neutralized. This Net, in fact, classifies all possible speculative views (rationalist or irrationalist) under a scheme of sixty-two *types.*

These 62 types are not descriptions of individual philosophies of other individual teachers contemporary with the Buddha (a number of those are mentioned as well elsewhere in the Suttas), but are the comprehensive net (after revealing the basic assumptions on which these speculative views all grow) with which to catch *any* wrong viewpoints that can be put forward. (Ultimately, these must all be traceable to the contact of self-identification in some form, however misinterpreted, but that cannot be gone into here.)

But why bring in this here, it may well be asked. Because, instead of accepting the question "Is Buddhism a religion or a philosophy?" and attempting an answer straight off, we can step back for a moment. We can ask ourselves if, by replying "It is a philosophy," we may not be making out that the Buddha was actually teaching one of the types of wrong view catchable in the Divine Net, against which that net should protect us. Then the Buddha denounces ritualism (*sīlabbata-parāmāsa*) as a vain waste of time bound to lead to disappointment. If we take practice of rites to be a religion, or unjustified and unverifiable emotional beliefs, to then say "Buddhism is a religion" is to imply that Buddhism teaches the very rite-ridden blindness of gullible credulity that the Buddha himself so plainly denounces.

There is, of course, no end to the arguments that can be churned out on both sides. The dialectic goes on oscillating with no resolution, till cut short by sheer weariness, or till some eloquent plea lulls us into thinking the matter is settled once and for all. Or we may just accept one side and forget about it for the time. But it will be reopened again for sure sooner or later, and the dialectic will resume its pendulum-swing. With the best will in the world, though, and the most tireless patience and brilliant dialectic skill, is there really anywhere to go, any solution to be found, on these lines? What are we to do, then?

In the Aṅguttara Nikāya, the Buddha divides questions into four kinds. Some can be answered unilaterally (yes or no). Some have to be analysed before answering. Others must be dealt with by a counter-question (making the questioner produce material out of himself that shows him how things are). And lastly there are some that cannot be answered at all. (They are like the one above about thick and thin sticks, for they make the answerer affirm an assumption, whatever he replies.) These must be entirely set aside.

Now a *question*, as long as it remains a question, is a *dialectic*; and when it is answered, the dialectic is unilaterally resolved.

In his fourfold classification of questions (dialectics), the Buddha may be taken to be communicating how to treat dialectics. There are two forms of communication. They have been called the "didactic" and the "existential." The first says, "This is like this; this is what has to be done," while the second tends to set forth the basic elements of a situation and leave it to the other to discover for himself the act-of-discovery that can be made on the basis of those elements set forth. Didactically one can tell someone how to cook a dish by communicating the recipe, but the satisfying of hunger, the discovery of cooking, and how good the dish is in the eating, can only be communicated existentially. It must be lived.

Now to return to the four types of questions and ways of communicating answers, as communicated to us by the Buddha:

first, any question is a dialectic. The first type of question is answerable didactically. It is the kind of dialectic where both sides are already evident, which can and ought to be resolved by a unilateral answer (the authority for such a resolution being always accurate observation with out forgetting what has been accurately observed). Examples of such unilateral decisions would be: choosing giving and not avarice; choosing kindness, not hate or anger; choosing unilateral keeping of the five precepts unbroken (since the Buddha observed that breaking them entails pain, such being the observable nature of existence for a Buddha who sees how it is), and so on. The highest form in which this unilateral decision is expressed is in the form of the Noble Eightfold Path, in choosing the Right and rejecting the Wrong. (Regarded in this way, the Path appears not as an observance, a rationalist scheme or a duty, but as a practical way to end suffering.) This is a didactic communication which communicates the unilateral resolution of a dialectic for a clear reason without mystification.

The second type of question (that answerable after analysis) can be regarded as a dialectic, one side of which is hidden or partly hidden, both sides of which need bringing clearly to light, and one whose *ambiguity* should be *displayed* didactically. Whether it can then be answered, or partly answered, unilaterally is here of secondary importance. The important thing is not to "buy a pig in a poke" by answering unilaterally a question one has not yet fully understood. The *doubleness* of the dialectic involved, until it has been brought to light by analysis, lurks concealed, can be harmful, and mislead. Such a question would be "Does the Buddha condemn all asceticism?" Before answering, the main debatable points involved should be clearly displayed.

The third type has to be dealt with by a *counter-question.* It makes the questioner dig out of his own mind the elements that prompt him to ask it. These, when thus brought to light *by himself,* give him the opportunity to discover how he went wrong in formulating his question. He can *discover* for himself that the supposed dialectic of his question is fictitious and that the truth lies elsewhere. This is not a didactic communication at all but an existential one. The questioner is not told didactically what to do;

he is existentially given the opportunity to discover for himself. (What is *discovered* may be didactically communicable, but the act-of-discovery is not.) The Buddha's teaching (that of the Four Truths together) is at heart an existential communication in this sense. (An example would be the "Gaṇaka Moggallāna Sutta," MN 107.)

The fourth type of question, which must be avoided, is that which traps the answerer, either purposely or unwittingly, into affirming an unjustifiable assumption, whether he answers negatively or affirmatively. (It is well recognized in logic how a denial necessarily implies the prior affirmation of what is denied or negated.) The best examples of such questions are this set of four: "Does the Tathāgata exist after death?" "Does he not exist after death?" "Does he both exist and not exist after death?" "Does he neither exist nor not exist after death?" None of these the Buddha consented to answer. "Was it because he was an agnostic?" some people have asked. But that very question shows that the existential communication has failed in the questioner. For besides the fact that to describe the Buddha (the Awakened One) as agnostic is rather a quaint contradiction, the point is overlooked that the four questions about the Tathāgata existing after death or not all contain an assumption which the answers yes and no alike affirm: they are all ultimately begged questions.

We may seem to have by now wandered rather far from the original query: "Is Buddhism a religion or a philosophy?" But two things have come to light. The first is that if we answer in too much of a hurry one way or the other, we may unwittingly be making out that Buddhism "is" either one of the speculative views which are caught by the Buddha's own Divine Net (the *Brahmajāla*), or that it "is" one of the ritualistic observances of blind faith condemned by the Buddha as bound to disappoint. The second is that, before undertaking to answer, we may ask ourselves which of the four types of questions this one falls under.

Yet before we start doing that, which might well involve us again deeply in dialectics, let us take another look at the way the Buddha sometimes *gives* his teaching. He was, in fact, asked a question whose essentials were much the same though the details were different. It was the night of the Buddha's Parinibbāna, and the wanderer Subhadda went to him and asked: "Master Gotama, there are these monks and divines with their congregations, teachers of congregations, famous philosophers whom many regard as saints....Have they all direct acquaintance of what they claim, or none of them, or have some and some not?" The Buddha's reply was this: "Enough, Subhadda. Let that be. I shall teach you the Dhamma." And he went on to expound the Eightfold Path. Now the Noble Eightfold Path is one of the Four Noble Truths. The Noble Truth of Suffering, the Noble Truth of the Origin of Suffering (which is need), the Noble Truth of the Cessation of Suffering (which is cessation of need), and the Noble Truth of the Way leading to cessation of suffering (which is the Eightfold Path). These four Truths- (termed "truth" (*sacca*) because they do not deceive, are founded on actual experience and nothing else, and cannot disappoint) are called the "teaching peculiar to Buddhas," (*Buddhānaṃ sāmukkaṃsika-desanā*), since it is precisely this teaching by which a Buddha is recognizable and distinguished.

Religion tends to rely upon faith alone, and *philosophy* on understanding alone. But the Buddha, in his teaching of the Truths, stresses the even balancing of *five* faculties. They are those of faith, energy, mindfulness, concentration, and understanding. While mindfulness can never be overdone, the others, if one-sidedly overdeveloped or repressed, may distort the character, outlook, and spiritual health that resides in their even balancing. Faith alone is blind credulity and gambles against disappointment. Overexerted energy agitates and distracts. Too much concentration tends to sleep and quietism, while understanding unsupported by the others degenerates into craftiness and cunning. When all are being properly managed, faith functions as confidence in the ability of the others to resist opposition and to reach their fulfilment in liberation from suffering.

All the five are perfectly familiar because they are present to some extent, however small, in everyone. No one can act at all without at least faith that his act will bring the desired result. Everyone has the energy to show life. Without mindfulness nothing at all could ever be remembered or recognized. Every time we hold a thought for the shortest space of time we concentrate. And no one could ever place their faith at all, however strong or weak, without making some judgment, however bad, where to place it. Such are these five faculties at their bare inescapable minimum. And these same faculties, the Buddha says, "end in the Deathless," which is the end of greed, hate, and delusion, the end of suffering. They are with us always.

The Eightfold Path has eight factors: right view, right intention, right speech, right action, right livelihood, right effort, right mindfulness, and right concentration. The five faculties are (to repeat) faith, energy, mindfulness, concentration, and understanding. What has the one set to do with the other? Faith (which is faith in the other four faculties) undertakes the three path factors that constitute virtue, namely right speech, action and livelihood; for these are first undertaken (like any other action) in the faith that they will lead to the development of the rest and to the ending of suffering. Energy is right effort. Mindfulness is right mindfulness. Concentration is right concentration. Understanding is right understanding and right intention. In this way, the five faculties correspond to the Eightfold Path. They are the Path's raw material. In this way too the Eightfold Path is clearly faith alone, and so is not adequately or rightly described as an observance (observance of ritual), that is, as a *religion*. It is equally clearly *not* understanding alone, and so is not adequately or rightly described as purely rationalistic in the sense of limited to logic (suffering is not a logical category, nor is liberation), that is, a philosophy. Again, while it certainly has its ethical and philosophical aspects (the first steps in the Path are right intention, speech, action, and livelihood; the second, mundane right view), and is certainly systematic, not chaotic or incoherent, yet it is not adequately or rightly to be pigeon-holed as *an* ethico-philosophical *system*. The Buddha said, "I teach only suffering and the liberation from suffering," and he said, "As the ocean has only one taste, that of salt, so my teaching has only one taste, that of liberation." That seems hardly *a* mere *system*.

But is Buddhism a religion or philosophy? Would the reader not like to deal with this for himself?

Does Saddhā Mean Faith? Part I

Sheer ignorance, gullibility, credulity, belief, faith, trust, confidence, certainty, knowledge--set out like that, the words seem to form a sort of spectrum with faith (most disputed of all the shades) somewhere in the middle.

Perhaps it is that very middle aspect of *faith* which makes it so liable to distortions in opposite directions; for not only is it in the middle in that sense, and not only is it an essential mediating relation between subject and object, but also it stands in between lack of knowledge and the need to know. So some see it only as pure limpid spontaneity of Truth and the noblest Human Faculty, for which no price is too high to pay, while others deride it as a wretched, even worthless, substitute for knowledge. Many try a hand at defining it, arriving at oddly diverse conclusions.

Bewildered from time to time in this way by his betters, some ordinary man (whose knowledge is limited and who wants to believe something) may ask, "But what does the word 'faith' *mean*? What are we talking *about*?" At once the extremists chip in again: "Faith is the Noblest Attribute of Man," "Faith is a drug for fools," "It must be cherished for ever," "It wants chucking out good and proper," they cry. Then the ordinary man, looking for a compromise, mostly uses his native faith in order, ostrich-like, to hide his head in a dune of euphemisms, saying perhaps something about "needing confidence." But "You can't always trust your own ears," he mutters incredulously to himself.

Others less procrustean may say (driving wedges between words) "To believe only in possibilities is not faith," (Sir Thomas Browne after Tertullian), or (making specious definitions of the faculty itself), "Belief, like any other moving body, follows the path of least resistance," (Samuel Butler), or (attempting to define its object), "The essential characteristic of a materialist doctrine is 'belief in something not dependent on our knowledge of it,'" (W.W. Carington, quoting Prof. J.B.S. Haldane, in *Mind, Matter and Meaning*), or else (painting word-pictures), "I've caught belief like a disease; I've fallen into belief like I fell in love," (Graham Greene), and so on. Fanned by these doldrum gusts, the ordinary man drifts this way and that; he doubts here, puts his faith there, and sometimes he is right and often wrong.

Now a dispassionate glance into matters of the heart is notoriously difficult. But, if the effort is made, it *can* be perceived that exclamations about "Noblest Attributes" and "wretched substitutes" are just evocative haranguings, ways of trying to push people into thinking as one does oneself, or as one thinks they ought to think (as the case may be), perhaps with the best of motives. They appear as an aspect of human behaviour telling quite a lot about the speaker's personal attitude, but precious little about faith considered as a component of experience: whether it is, for example, good or bad in itself or unavoidable. Tending covertly as they do to the extremes of rationalism or irrationalism, none of them (not even the subtle ones) examine experience or even attempt an inquiry into why the ordinary man does not just gullibly do as he is told. Why does he not? Is it because, when pushed too far, his common sense tells him that he can't?

Let us look a little closer. Let us consider for a moment the question of action (of doing, or even saying or thinking, something). An ordinary man sees the past as decided ("What's done can't be undone."), but the future as semi-foreseeable though undecided ("You can never be sure how it will turn out."). So when he acts purposively, intending to do what he does (which always happens now), he seems to do so guided by what he remembers of the past and by some measure of faith (or expectation) that his present acts will not have a too inappropriate result in the rather uncertain future. Still he can never be quite sure: doubts haunt him constantly.

That indeed is the pattern of the ordinary human situation: a state of being committed in a changing scene, of (moral) certainty about a definite-seeming past, of present knowledge of acts by restricted free choice which there is no escaping, and of guessing at a more or less indefinite future potentiality, which one hopes (with a grain of justification) to influence because one believes that things will go on happening roughly as they have done. That too is the pattern which makes life valuable and tolerable for the gambler. And who never gambles in his heart?

On that basis, if such a very rough sketch is provisionally accepted, faith—or call it what you will—give a dog a bad name and hang it, but a rose by any other name is just as sweet) as a chancy expectation of results is, it seems, inevitably present in some form in every act done; there would be no doing anything without it. While one has *knowledge* of *what* one is doing now, even if it is only that one is sitting still and doubting, *faith* alone can cope with the unknown future (as it is apprehended) and decide *why* one does what one does. Such humdrum faith as that neither needs any special advertising as "noble" nor can it be "chucked out." It is simply a commonplace necessity.

So it is that parents send children to school in the faith that what is taught there will help the children to make a living. Those same children, when adults, delegate some of their influence by vote to governments in the faith that society will thus cater better for their needs. Through faith in the order of Nature those same adults, when old, sense death edging nearer: an impending ambivalent catastrophe that as surely blots out from their certainty all form of the future as it seems an inescapable plunge into it.

Faith is left a free hand here though men have a general intellectual certainty that their physical death will take place (regardless of any considerations of immortality). Other people's bodies are seen to die, but, it is pointed out by Freud, the Unconscious, while accepting that, absolutely rejects its own mortality. Though material bodies only too publicly die and disintegrate, at the same time no materialist theory is capable of *proving* (in any sense of that word) that physical death is the end, or physical birth the beginning, of conscious activity. Hence the ambivalence of the catastrophe. Hence too the fact that faith is forced willy-nilly to exercise a free hand here.

Faith normally manifests itself as one of three particular types of belief, that is, it must absolutely take on one of them so long as there is ignorance and action. It is, (1) a dogma asserting that something of them will survive the catastrophe, or (2) a dogma asserting that nothing of them at all will survive, or (3) radical agnosticism denying that any knowledge beforehand is possible. Depending on which of the types of belief people assume (and one of the three apparently *must* be assumed) their behaviour will vary. Any act whatsoever, then, involves (where there is ignorance) one of these three assumptions indirectly or directly. To be born is to die, and to live as the ordinary man does is to act; to be in space-time is to be unsure of a future one is sure to encounter.

The reservation "where there is ignorance" has been made, for ignorance, as we shall see, has an organic relation with faith (which is what the ignorant have to rely on in the acts they are obliged to perform). Will anyone deny that the ordinary man is constantly bothered by immediate ignorance (about the weather tomorrow; the contents of an examination paper; what the person he is talking to is thinking; the price of goods next week; whether his memory can be trusted or not; what will happen to him), or that he is ever without some measure of it, let alone ignorance of what is going on beyond his horizons, and may burst into his world? Then since he cannot avoid doing things ("But what are we going to *do*, if something happens?"), he has to take risks, to supplement by faith his lack of certain knowledge, to act *as if* the weather *will* be such and such tomorrow, and this kind we may call first degree ignorance, which goes with simple faith. "Take what you will, but pay the price," says Emerson.

But the ordinary man is also subject to desires, needs, fear, and pain. Because he attaches importance to the results of his acts, the lack of certainty inherent in faith is often odious to him (for all that he may like a gamble now and then). Whenever facts do not prohibit his doing so, his desires prompt him to treat the faith, by which he acts, *as if it were* knowledge ("It's a dead cert!"), and he may well quite honestly forget that he does not know. His defence against fear and pain is forgetting (a mode of ignorance, which, at its deepest, takes the form of death). But if he cannot quite forget, if his forgetting mechanism fails him, he may dope himself with self-deception, refusing both to question his faith and to test its object. This we may call second-degree ignorance, which loses sight not only of the limits of knowledge but of truth as well. With that, his faith has become bad faith. "If bad faith is possible at all," says a modern writer, "it is because it is an immediate and constant threat to every human project; it is because consciousness hides within its very being a permanent risk of bad faith." Bad faith, however, is not a lie, since the essence of a lie implies that the liar is completely aware of the truth which he dissembles. "One no longer lies when one deceives oneself." Bad faith, in short, both refuses to face all one knows and vetoes any investigation into whether the faith is well placed or not. "O take the cash and let the credit go," says Omar Khayyam's translator. (And if the cash runs out, they'll sure let us live on tie!)

At any time an ordinary man may become fed up with the consequences of misplacing his own faith or by seeing the silly things other people sometimes do out of faith. Blaming the faith instead of the misplacing of it, he may decide to throw it overboard altogether (away with all bath water and babies too), and become a Cynic or a Rationalist. But has he not merely deceived himself once more in fancying it can be jettisoned like that, for he still has ignorance and still has to act? Even despair is no more than a mode of bad faith: faith that the situation is irremediable with refusal to seek an escape. The self-gulling goes on, and so does the risk of disappointment, anger and frustration. If he is healthy, young, and lucky, perhaps he can forget about it and begin all over again. Forgetting is a very *useful* kind of ignorance: it wipes the bad sums off our slates.

What is the answer, then? Must one either leave the baby unbathed or bottle the bath water? Surely not. The first thing to be done is to reduce ignorance to the "first degree," to become aware that one *is* ignorant and *how* one is ignorant, facing up to it courageously and remembering it, regardless of hopes and fears. That is enough for the Goal, isn't it? What more *can* be done? After all, faith has been shown to be a practical necessity for the ordinary man. Without it indeed all profitable and unprofitable action, as well as all possibility of remedying suffering, must be paralysed. And how richly it ennobles! It is the source of all inspiration. The rapturous leap of faith at Great Moments exhilarates, uplifts, and transfigures. Faith attends all good things. Faith that the very ground will receive one's foot prevents the vertiginous sensation of falling into a chasm every time one steps forward. Faith is Life, and it must be good in itself. How can it be otherwise? If the right dogma can be found, is not that the answer, the realistic answer? Why cry for the moon?

True, faith is a practical necessity for the ordinary man. That is indeed what we have been trying to show. But how can the Right Dogma ever be found, and can it be absolutely trusted without a grain of bad faith as we have described it? And is faith then to be the *goal*, in which case is ignorance to remain with us for ever more? Examination of what both the theists and the atheist materialists have offered as dogma from the dawn of history down to the present day, a long time and a wide choice, is far from encouraging (consoling, doubtless but utterly inconclusive). The rather arid alternative seems to be Radical Agnosticism, which is what is usually meant by the phrase "no faith"; no faith, that is, in the heaven the theists offer only after death, or in the substance of matter here and now which the materialists admit can inherently never be known at all and doesn't matter after death anyway.

Why bother, though? Perhaps the world is not such a bad place after all. They say there is plenty of good in it if you look, so forget about the unpleasant side of it. Agnosticism tomorrow, then, and dogma today. "Gather ye roses while ye may," as luck may be on our side.

Dogma or agnosticism. But before we choose, before we risk our faith going bad on us, let us take one more look.

(Editor's Note: The following paragraph in handwriting was found among the late author's papers, together with this essay and carrying the note "above at the end of Pt. 1." Since the insertion of it would have necessitated adjustments in the given manuscript, it was preferable to reproduce this paragraph separately. Its fitting place would be before the second last paragraph of the above text.)

Then if neither dogma nor agnosticism will do, why not be satisfied with some form of the critical humanism of 18th to 19th century Europe? Criticism has been incalculably productive, and we owe to it all the material advances we enjoy today. It is criticism that has allowed science a free hand to question and experiment. Granted that Criticism (as Inquiry) merits all that praise and far more. But that is as a means. If Criticism is to be made the goal, the *summum bonnum*, against what can it be tested? A fundamental weakness always remains in the position of the critic: if he discloses his own standpoint, that standpoint is open to criticism from some other. That is why it is rare that the academic scholar, who employs the so-called "higher criticism" can afford to state his own position in positive terms. When the English Prime Minister Disraeli was asked what his religion was, it is said that he replied "My religion is that of all wise men." "But what is that, Mr. Disraeli?" "Wise men never say." Criticism requires that the critic be uncommitted, that he is, or pretends he is, outside what he criticises. The professional critic's very being depends on dialectics, the food that keeps him alive is other people's standpoints. As a means this may be invaluable; as an end it can never amount to more than an ordered form of agnosticism.

Does Saddhā Mean Faith? Part II

To "Gather ye roses while ye may," would be fine if there were "roses, roses all the way." But will our simple faith really stretch that far? Hardly.

Soon after the Buddha had attained enlightenment he surveyed the world with the new vision he had achieved. He did not see only roses. He uttered this exclamation: "This world is racked by exposure to the contact [of pain]. Even what the world calls self is in fact ill; for no matter upon what it bases its conceit [of self], the fact is ever other than these [which the conceit conceives]. To be is to become: but the world has committed itself to being, delights only in being; yet wherein it delights brings fear, and what it fears is pain. Now this Life Divine is lived to abandon pain" (Ud 3.10). He was not alone in this estimation of the world: "Here, bhikkhus, some clansman goes forth out of faith [saddhā] from the home life into homelessness [considering] 'I am a victim of birth, ageing and death.... I am exposed to pain. Surely an end to this whole aggregate mass of suffering is described?" (MN 29).

Now in this situation how does the Buddha show the function of faith? "One who has faith [*saddhā*] succeeds, Mahānāma, not one who has no faith" (AN 11:12).

Here the question at once intrudes: Is the translation of "*saddhā*" by "faith" justified? Let us try it out and see, for the contexts in which it appears will be the test. We shall be strictly consistent in our renderings. The Buddha speaks of five Faculties, or human potentialities, through whose means an ignorant ordinary man may emerge from ignorance to right understanding, and so from suffering to its cessation. They are faith (*saddhā*), energy, mindfulness, concentration, and understanding (as "mother wit" to start with). If they can be maintained in being against opposition, they are called Powers (SN 48:43). Managed by reasoned attention (*yoniso manasikāra*, awareness of the organic structure of experience), and carefully balanced, they build each other up. Maintained in being and cultivated, they merge into the Deathless (SN 48:57).

The Buddha speaks of faith as one of the Seven Noble Treasures (AN 7:4), one of the Seven True Ideas (DN 33), one of the Five Factors of Endeavour (MN 8), as an Idea "on the side of enlightenment" (SN 48:51), as a Fount of Great Merit (Aṅguttara Ṭīkā 41), as one of the Three Forms of Growth (Aṅguttara Ṭīkā 48), which "brings five advantages" (AN 5:38).

And then, "Where is the faith faculty to be met with? Among the four Factors of Stream-entry." (SN 48:8). "A Stream-enterer [of whom more below] has absolute confidence [*pasāda*] in the Enlightened One, in the True Idea [the Dhamma], and in the Community, and he has the virtue beloved of Noble Ones" (SN 55:1). Four other factors of Stream-entry are frequenting True Men, hearing the True Idea, reasoned attention, and the putting into practice of ideas that are in accordance with the True Idea (SN 55:5).

"What is the faith faculty? Here a noble disciple who has faith places his faith in a Tathāgata thus: 'This Blessed One is such since he is accomplished and fully enlightened, perfect in true knowledge and conduct, sublime, knower of worlds, incomparable leader of men to be tamed, enlightened, blessed.'" (SN 48:9) "If these five faculties are absolutely perfected, they make an Accomplished One [Arahant]; if a little weaker, a Non-returner; if a little weaker still, a Once-returner; if a little weaker still, a Stream-enterer; if a little weaker still, One Mature in Faith or One Mature in the True Idea" (SN 48:12). "Those who have not known, seen, found, realized, touched with understanding, may go by faith in others that [these five faculties] when maintained in being and developed merge in the Deathless ... but on knowing, seeing, finding, realizing, and touching with understanding, there is no more doubt or uncertainty that when maintained in being and developed they merge in the Deathless" (SN 48:44).

But then, does not the Buddha say in the Kālāma Sutta, "Come, Kālāmas, [do] not [be satisfied] with hearsay-learning or with tradition or with legendary lore or with what has come down in scripture or with conjecture or with logical inference or with weighing evidence or with choice of a view after pondering it or with someone else's ability or with the thought 'The monk is our teacher'"? Is not that an injunction to have nothing to do with faith, to "throw away your books," as Marcus Aurelius says, and listen to no one at all?

If that statement of the Buddha's is taken as a general instruction to disregard instruction, it is then impossible to carry out. For then one could only carry it out by not carrying it out (a well-known logical dilemma). But that is not what is intended, as is shown by the rest of the passage: " ... or with the thought 'The monk is our teacher.' When you know in your-selves 'Certain ideas are unprofitable, liable to censure, condemned by the wise, being adopted and put into effect, they lead to harm and suffering,' then you should abandon them .... When you know in yourselves 'Certain ideas are profitable, not liable to censure, commended by the wise, being adopted and put into effect, they lead to welfare and happiness,' then you should abide in the practice of them" (Aṅguttara Ṭīkā 65).

The ordinary man is affected by ignorance, and he cannot dispense with simple faith, though in good faith he may grossly misplace it, or dissipate it, and be said to have no faith (*asaddhā*). But if he places it honestly and reasonably, he is called faithful (*saddhā*). In the Buddha's words, "A bhikkhu who possesses understanding founds his faith in accordance with that understanding" (SN 48:45), to which words may be added also those of the venerable Sāriputta: "There are two conditions for the arising of right view: another's speech and reasoned attention" (MN 43). From this it emerges that an ordinary man has need of a germ of "mother wit" in order to know where to place his faith and a germ of unsquandered faith in order to believe he can develop his understanding. That is the starting position.

Faith thus begins to appear as a fusion of two elements: confidence (*pasāda*), and what the confidence is placed in. Faith as confidence is elsewhere described as a clearing of the mind, like water cleared of suspended mud by a water-clearing nut, or as a launching out (*pakkhandana*), like a boat's launching out from the near bank to cross a flood to the further bank, or as a hand that resolutely grasps. (A grain of "mother wit" is needed to recognize the nut, to avoid launching out into a flood that has no other shore, to refrain from grasping a red-hot poker as a stick to lean on). Just as "Seeing is the meaning of the understanding as a faculty," so also "Decision [*adhimokkha*] is the meaning of faith as a faculty." (*Paṭisambhidā Ñāṇakatha*). When faith is aided by concentration, "The mind launches out [to its object] and acquires confidence, steadiness and decision" (MN 122).

Choice of a bad object will debauch faith by the disappointment and frustration it entails. Craving and desire can corrupt it into bad faith by the self-deception that it is not necessary to investigate and test the object, and then, as well as error, there is disregard of truth. In one of his great discourses on faith the Buddha says, "Bhāradvāja, there are five ideas which ripen in two ways [expectedly and unexpectedly] here and now. What are the five? They are faith, preference, hearsay, learning, weighing evidence, and choice of a view after pondering it [compare the Kālāma Sutta quoted above]. Now [in the case of faith] something may have faith well placed in it [*susadahita*] and yet it may be hollow, empty and false; and again, something may have no faith placed in it, and yet it may be factual, true and no other than it seems. In such circumstances it is not yet proper for a wise man to make the conclusion without reserve 'Only this is true, anything else is wrong.' ... If a man has faith, then in such circumstances as these he preserves truth when he says, 'My faith is thus'; but then too he still does not, on that account alone, make the conclusion without reserve, 'Only this is true, anything else is wrong.' He preserves truth in that way too" (MN 95). The other four cases are similarly treated, after which it is shown how "preserving of truth" can be developed successively into "discovery of truth" (path of Stream-entry) and "arrival at truth" (fruit of the path of Stream-entry). The element of confidence has then become absolute because its object has been sufficiently tested by actual experience for the principal claims to be found justified. Another discourse concludes by showing how the value of rightly placed faith serves (as the means rather than the end) in the progress from ignorance to liberation: "Bhikkhus, I say that true knowledge and deliverance have a condition, are not without a condition. What is their condition? The seven Factors of Enlightenment [Mindfulness, interest in the True Idea, energy, happiness, tranquillity, concentration, and onlooking equanimity]. ... What is the condition for these? The four foundations of mindfulness [contemplation of the body, of feelings, of cognizance, and of ideas] .... What is the condition for these? The three kinds of good conduct [of body, speech and mind] .... What is the condition for these? Mindfulness and full awareness .... What is the condition for these? Reasoned attention .... What is the condition for that? Faith .... What is the condition for that? Hearing the True Idea [the true object of faith, the *saddhamma*] .... What is the condition for that? Frequenting the company of True Men [*sappurisa*]" (AN 10:62).

This shows plainly the need for a reliable guide. How is he to be found? One should be an Inquirer (*vīmaṃsaka*) and make the Tathāgata the object of research and tests in order to judge whether confidence in him is rightly placed. The Buddha says "Now bhikkhus, if others should ask a bhikkhu [who is an inquirer] 'What are the evidences and certainties owing to which the venerable one says "The Blessed One is fully enlightened, the True Idea is well proclaimed, the Community has entered upon the good way"?' then, answering rightly, he would answer thus: 'Here, friends, I approached that Blessed One for the sake of hearing the True Idea [Dhamma]. The teacher showed me the True Idea at each successively higher [level], at each superior [stage], with the dark and bright counterparts. According as he did so, by arriving at direct knowledge here of a certain idea [namely, one of the four paths] among the ideas, [taught] in the True Idea, I reached my goal: then I had confidence [*passaddhi*] in the teacher thus: "The Blessed One is fully enlightened, the True Idea is well proclaimed, the Community has entered on the good way."' When anyone's faith in a Tathāgata is planted and rooted and established with these evidences, these phrases and these syllables, then his faith is called supported by evidence, rooted in vision, sound, and invincible by Monk or Divine or Māra or Divinity or anyone in the world" (MN 47).

Faith as the indispensable means, but not the goal, transparent in itself, is debased or ennobled by the mode of its employment and by its goal. As understanding grows, it approximates to knowledge, while the risk of its degenerating into bad faith diminishes with the diminishing of craving.

But there are still two problems. First, it was argued earlier that faith involves not knowing the future. So if faith becomes knowledge, does that not imply that the future can all be known and is therefore predetermined? Second, with craving unabated would not knowledge of everything be unbearable; would it not be Hell itself? How does craving diminish?

The key to these two locks on the gate of liberation lies in the Contemplation of Impermanence. Let us take the second problem first. It is part of the constraint imposed by ignorance and craving together that an ordinary man is led to speculate on time and permanence, and to ask such questions as, "What was I?," "What shall I be?," "What am I ?" (MN 2), unanswerable questions to which philosophers go on furnishing many an unquestionable answer, disproving each other as they do. But progress towards liberation from ignorance transforms and transfigures the world. One who is liberated asks no more questions (*akathaṃkathī*). The Buddha tells his listeners, "Bhikkhus, material form [and likewise feeling, perception, determinations, and consciousness] are impermanent, changing and altering. Whoever decides about, and places his faith in, these ideas in this way is called Mature in Faith. He has alighted upon the certainty of rightness. He has alighted upon the plane of true men and left behind the plane of ordinary men. He can no more perform action capable of causing his rebirth in the animal world or in the realm of ghosts and he cannot complete his time in this life without realizing the fruition of Stream-entry" (SN 25:10). Such faith decides in advance that nothing arisen can reveal any permanence at all, however brief. Since all subsequent evidence supports the decision, if that evidence is not forgotten, craving is progressively stultified in the impossibility of finding any arisen thing worth craving for, and is progressively displaced by the joy of liberation. The first problem, though, that of time, is properly a matter for insight (*vipassanā*) and can only be dealt with here by hints and pointers because of lack of space. As has already been said, the ignorant man questions, but one who is liberated does not. The Buddha tells his listeners, "Let not a man trace back a past or wonder what the future holds .... Instead with insight let him see each idea[18] presently arisen" (MN 131). He includes the Contemplation of Impermanence under the Four Foundations of Mindfulness: "He trains thus: 'I shall breathe in . . . breathe out contemplating *impermanence*"' (MN 10).

Now it is in the very nature of ignorance to perceive the bare conditions for consciousness in terms of things, persons and hypostases, and to project upon these percepts a varying degree of permanence, a misperception which it is the task of true vision and mindfulness to correct. During the period of transition, while understanding that "to be is to be otherwise" is still immature and helped out by faith in the impermanence of every-thing that is, the faith must be tested and the outcome of the tests remembered. This needs concentration and energy.

"When one gives attention to impermanence, the faith faculty is outstanding." And in the cases of attention to pain and not-self the faculties of concentration and understanding are outstanding respectively. These are called the "Three Gate-Ways to Liberation," which "lead to the outlet from the world" (*Paṭisambhidā Vimokkhakathā*). When the Stream-entry path is reached, a new, supramundane faculty, the I-shall-come-to-know-the-unknown

18. Dhamma: "thing" or phenomenon, material or mental. (Editor)

faculty (*anaññātaññassāmītindriya*) appears, to be subsequently followed by the new and supramundane final-knowledge and final-knower faculties (*aññindriya, aññātāvindriya*). These are gained in this life with the attainment of Arahantship.

Meanwhile, however, "The characteristic of impermanence does not become apparent [as universal] because, when the constant rise and fall of determinations[19] [things] is not given attention, it is concealed by continuity (*Visuddhimagga* Ch. 21). In fact the Buddha said, "There is no matter or feeling, perception, determinations, or consciousness whatever that is permanent ... not inseparable from the idea of change...[20] Taking a small piece of cow dung in his hand, the Blessed One said, "If there were even that much ... that were permanent ... not inseparable from the idea of change[21] ... the living of the Life Divine[22] could not be described as for the exhaustion of suffering. It is because there is not ... that it is so described" (SN 22:96).

Now that statement can be taken to imply that if time were an absolutely independent objective reality, there would be no liberation.

Permanence and *impermanence* on the one hand, and time on the other, are but two modes of the same view. The appearance of the three new supramundane faculties signals profound changes in the apprehension of *permanence* and *impermanence*, that is, of time, and consequently in actual experience itself.

To question the objectivity of time is not new even to Western philosophy. While objective reality of time and space still remains one of the assumptions made by scientists for which they have no proof, Immanuel Kant argued irrefutably for the pure subjectivity of both. But almost a millennium and a half before him, Ācariya Buddhaghosa wrote, "What is called 'time' is conceived in terms of

---

19. *Saṅkhāra* is usually translated as "formations," or, in the case of the 5 Aggregates, "mental formations."(Editor)
20. *Viparināmadhamma*, usually translated as "subject to change." (Editor)
21. Ibid.
22. *Brahmacariya* is usually translated as "Holy Life" or "Life of Purity." (Editor)

such and such dhammas ... But that [time] should be understood as only a mere conceptual description, since it is non-existent as to any individual essence of its own." (*Atthasālinī*. Space is analogously treated elsewhere). A century or two later it was observed that "Nibbāna [extinction] is not like other dhammas. In fact because of its extreme profundity it cannot be made the object of consciousness by one who has not yet reached it. That is why it has to be reached by change-of-lineage cognizance [*gotrabhū*], which has profundity surpassing the three periods of time" (*Mūlaṭīkā*). When the seen, heard, sensed and cognized (see Ud 1.10), are misperceived to be (this that I see ... that *I* think about, *is* that *man*, so-and-so, that *thing* of *mine*, to have temporal endurance and reality, it is because the three periods of time, these three modes by which we subjectively process our raw world in perceiving it, have been projected outwards by ignorance on the raw world and misapprehended along with that as objectively real. That is how we in our ignorance come to perceive things and persons and action.

These fragments are merely pointers. The *contemplation* of impermanence, which, when fully and *unreservedly* developed, necessitates the contemplations of suffering (pain) and not-self, involves the whole field of insight. (There is no space to deal with it here.) However, the inquiry has already led us away from the apparent either-or choice between faith in dogma-as-the-goal or agnosticism. By establishing a structural interdependence between faith and ignorance, it has opened up a new line. In the pursuit of that line it has uncovered an unexpected association between faith and the temporal mirage of *permanence* and *impermanence*. And so it has been possible to sketch a practical outline of the way to end here and now this whole aggregate mass of suffering. The adventure is waiting to be tested.

"Fruitful as the act of giving is ... yet it is still more fruitful to go with confident heart for refuge to the Buddha, the Dhamma, and the Sangha, and undertake the five precepts of virtue .... Fruitful as that is ... yet it is still more fruitful to maintain loving-kindness in being in the heart for only as long as the milking of a cow .... Fruitful as that is ... yet it is still more fruitful to maintain perception of impermanence in being for only as long as the snapping of a finger" (AN 9:20).

But does saddhā really mean faith? Let the reader judge for himself.

Cessation of Becoming

(With a Note on *Faith*)

Why do normal people normally react with panic and horror to the idea of cessation of becoming, or cessation of consciousness? There are at least two reasons. There is first the failure to see both sides of life, the negative/destructive as well as the positive/constructive, which are (as it were) the obverse and reverse of each piece of experience. It is a refusal to face the ambivalence of experience, and a putting on of blinkers to shut out, as far as one can, what is disturbing. It is by this that life is made to look nice, and appears tolerable. The process is largely automatic and subconscious, so it is seldom ever enquired into. With the blinkers on one does not see what is unwelcome and one quickly forgets the unwelcome that intrudes.

And here I want to distinguish two kinds of suffering: (1) enjoyable suffering and pain (the arduousness of exhausting sports, self mortification, "being ill," masochism and sadism, etc.), which are not properly suffering because they are enjoyed and welcomed; and (2) horror or nausea, which is all those things (whatever they may be, and they vary with different people) that produce horror, nausea, and vertigo, because they are absurd and menace the core and pattern of our personal existence. Everyone knows that border across which he cannot go, even in thought, and it is that, not the former, that people automatically shut out and cannot face. Yet one knows at times (in the middle of the night, perhaps, when one is sleepless, or on encountering some revolting experience) that this horror haunts every form of experience (always and ever), and hastily one readjusts the blinkers that had slipped. Put the beautiful before you and the horror behind you. Yes, but then I shall not dare to turn round.

The world is a bad place. Is it? But it seems that this haunting, this self-delusion by wearing blinkers, is not an attribute of the world. The haunting is in consciousness itself, in its very nature. Just as when I set up any object in the sunlight a shadow is cast (because it is the nature of sunlight to cast shadows), so anything that comes into the light of consciousness casts a shadow of the unknown. It is in the unknown that the horror resides in the dark of knowledge where the patterns can no longer be traced, where chaos resides, and whence utterly hostile systems may emerge, devour, and digest us.

Again this insecurity resides in consciousness because it cheats. It lives between the past and the future like a reflection between two opposing mirrors. I put my head between the opposing mirrors and I see the reflection of the reflection of the reflection ... which suggests recession to infinity. But I cannot see that infinity because (even if the glasses were clear enough) my head and its reflections are in the way. But then if I slightly displace one mirror so that my head is no more in the way then the series of reflections passes out of the field of the mirrors at some stage of the reflections which it must now do (unless the mirrors are made of infinite size). So I am forced by this set of experiences to infer an infinity of which the very circumstances deny the possibility of my experiencing. That is one essential aspect of consciousness: it cheats.

Another example is the moon. I see as an experience an existent crescent, an existent half-moon, or full moon, and there are perceptions of existents that are repeated (which are in fact over and done with as soon as experienced). Consciousness groups together these repeated experiences and forms a concept that transcends all these possible existents, and which it presents as "the moon." But "the moon" can never be experienced, and even when visualized it is only as one of its aspects. It is a fake. This concept "the moon" is then projected upon the objective world where it appears to lurk behind existence as Kant's "*Ding an sich*," or, say, Eddington's "reality," that the physicists are trying to discover behind what they investigate. Suppose a man gets lost in a desert and he wanders all night. When the sun comes up he may see lots of tracks in the sand all pointing the way he is going. He thinks, "Marvellous! I am on the high road. Lots of people have gone this way already. I am alright." So he follows them. They are, in fact, his own tracks made in the night by his walking in circles (which people actually do). If he does not stop to consider and goes on following them, he will get nowhere. He will die. If he put aside his assumption and looked about him, it is possible he might find the way of escape.

This is what I mean by the failure to see both sides of life, to see things and ourselves as they and we really are, in their relationship. This is what Māra (if we like personification) tries his utmost to keep us from seeing, for it is by this that we can slip out of his clutches. Māra is Death, but he is also Life, for "all that is subject to arising is subject to cessation," "all that is born and lives dies." Byron said somewhere:

> Sorrow is knowledge: they who know the most
> Must mourn the deepest o'er the fatal Truth.
> The Tree of Knowledge is not that of life.

But it is Māra that makes us mourn because he makes his living by that, just as a rubber estate owner makes his living by the trees that he cultivates and bleeds, and cuts down when they are old.

But there is another, equally fundamental, reason that makes people shy away from the notion—their notion—of cessation. This is a very deep-rooted double misconception: (1) there is the idea that by "cessation," by "extinction," something "good" and "valuable" and "lasting" will be "lost forever," and (2) there is an uncritical assumption that consciousness will somehow continue to survive—will be "there"—to be aware of this as an "everlasting privation." "Does all this" they say "only end in extinction? But a state of nothingness is horrible!" and there the whole double misconception lies like a pair of Siamese Twins in a bed. But there is, in the last analysis, no "entirely good" and "lasting" individual thing or state discoverable anywhere. Whatever appears good melts away in the end. The subconscious cheating of the mind seizes on the good, rejects and forgets it, and it melts away. By a "sleight of mind" that is one of consciousness's essential functions, the idea is presented that it is possible to skim the good off the world, like cream on a bowl of milk, and live in that cream in "eternal bliss." But, alas, like the cream, the bowl of heavenly bliss is not permanent. Such is the "good" that is supposed to be "lost." And then there is the instinctive feeling, the uncritical automatic reaction that takes cessation somehow to mean a survival of conscious awareness of that loss, in spite of the fact that the proposition was in the first place "cessation of consciousness." This is the verbal-mental subconscious cheating that has only to be examined fearlessly to see it as a mere self-contradiction. If consciousness ceases and with it its objects, there is no question of conscious awareness of privation. If there is awareness of loss and privation, consciousness has not ceased, and it is not such cessation that is being talked about. This misconception (often enough believed in due to uncritical acceptance) is often used to deride Buddhists without seeing that it hurts only him who uses it. And not only Buddhists, for Saṅkāra in his commentary to the Bṛhadāraṇyaka Upaniṣad says: "The Buddhists themselves do not deny the existence of gods and heavens [or hells]—they are not atheists—but only that the gods are omnipotent or everlasting: they change and die, let one down, make one let oneself down, because they cannot help it, because consciousness and its objects, with its disease of impermanence, are there too."

Consciousness without object is impossible, not conceivable, and objects without consciousness, when talked about, are only a verbal abstraction. One cannot talk or think about objects that have no relation to consciousness. The two are inseparable and it is only a verbal abstraction to talk about them separately (legitimate of course in a limited sphere).

But it is in the consideration of this cessation as the goal that the real comfort and safety are to be found. There is no cheating here, and no anxiety to exclude haunting opposites. All else, however good it seems, is only temporary, because there is consciousness there to know and to change. So there is no permanent safety of attack or harm, and there is no permanent safety from one's being led to do harm, even if that harm is merely changing.

Regarding *the matter of faith*, it is commonly felt and often stated that faith is a weakness, a mere substitute for knowledge, a "blind belief in dogma" and "unnecessary." But the point overlooked is that there is an element of faith in every conscious act. It is another of the false aspects inherent in all consciousness: the presenting of objects in such that the perception of them necessitates inference about what is hidden. This is in fact an aspect of faith. Without this faith nothing can be done at all, viz. faith that things will repeat themselves and happen as one expects. But the case is most clearly seen in the case of death. Death is an obvious fact. Described in terms of life, it is meaningless (like a blank featureless wall, or a black chasm to vision), but nevertheless by its very existence, by its basis in experience, necessitates inference about it. The three main inferences are that life of some sort continues after death, that it does not, or plain agnosticism. Whichever I adopt is a matter of pure faith (I leave out "evidence" for and against other alternatives here). But I cannot avoid adopting one of the three.

On the other hand, faith about, say, "phoenixes rising from their own ashes" is simply this same universal attribute of consciousness applied to a fantasy, an assumption (the phoenix) that has no basis in experience. What is unnecessary here is not the faith but the assumption. Now many faiths place faith in baseless assumptions. And when people discover this, they not only reject the assumption (rightly), but, because they fail to discriminate, they deceive themselves into thinking that they can do without the faith too. All that has happened to them, though, is that they have transferred their faculty of faith to the basis of experience and have simultaneously forgotten that they are using it. Now to forget that one has a sharp knife in one's hand is dangerous.[23]

Consciousness and Being

What follows will have to be stated in terms of ordinary speech, though that necessarily involves the word "is" and logical constructions, because speech is hardly possible without them. Nevertheless they have to be regarded here as a makeshift, and the

23. Here the manuscript ends. This undated fragment (which in the manuscript, follows immediately after the preceding essay) may have stimulated the author to treat the subject more fully in the essay "Does Saddhā mean Faith?" included in this publication. (Editor)

whole of what follows tends to undermine the ultimate value of speech, retaining it, however, as a necessity for communication in conditions where separateness and individuality predominate.

The word "consciousness," it seems to me, can only refer to what one might define provisionally as "the knowing that cannot know itself without intermediary and that cannot function in experience (of which it is an indispensable component) except negatively."

To the question "What *is* consciousness," then, a low level provisional answer might be "It is the pure subjective" or "It *is* the bare knowing of what it *is not* that constitutes (orders) experience and allows it being." It must be added that, when consciousness *is*, it seems to be individualized by what it knows. But on another (higher) level the "is" in the question has still to be questioned, and so the low-level (and logical) answer is only a conventional makeshift, a conventional view, nothing more. And this qualification applies not only to logically inductive and deductive statements necessitating use of the word "is," but also to descriptive statements that appear in "logical" form, using that term, or any equivalent.

When I ask myself, "What does the verbal expression 'universal consciousness' refer to?," I confess to be unable to find an answer, because, in spite of its "attractive" form, I cannot distinguish it from non-consciousness (see below). So I seem to have no alternative but to regard the phrase as one of those abstract expressions that appear on the surface to mean something, but when more closely examined, do not. (This, I know, may seem shocking, but I am more interested here in finding the facts than in avoiding shock.)

The more I examine and observe experience (What else can one do? Build castles?), the more I find that I can only say of consciousness (and in this I find a notable confirmation in the Pali Suttas) that it seems only describable (knowable) "in terms of what it arises dependent upon" (i.e. seeing-cum-seen ... mind-knowing-cum-mind, known or mind cum-ideas), that is, negatively as to itself. And so, instead of being said to *appear*, it should rather be called that negativeness or "decompression of being" which makes the appearance of life, movement, behaviour, etc., and their opposites, possible in things and persons. But while life, etc. cannot *be* or *not be* without the cooperation of the negative presence of consciousness, which gives room for them (and itself) to "come to *be*" in this way (gaining its own peculiar form of negative being, perhaps from them)—the only possible way of *being*—they are, by ignorance, simultaneously individualized in actual experience. Unindividualized experience cannot, I think, be called experience at all. Thus there *appears* the positive illusion also of individual consciousness: "illusion" because its individuality is borrowed from the individualness of (1) its percepts, and (2) the body seen as its perceiving *instrument*.

Unindividualized perception cannot, any more, I think, be called perception at all. The supposed individuality of consciousness (without which it is properly inconceivable) is derived from that of its concomitants. This illusory individualization of consciousness, this mirage, manifests itself in the sense both of "my consciousness" and of "consciousness that is not mine" (as e.g. in the sensation of *being seen* when one fancies or actually finds one is caught, say, peeping through a keyhole, and from which the abstract notion of universal consciousness develops). The example shows that the experience of being seen does not necessarily mean that *another's consciousness is seeing one*, as one may have been mistaken in one's fancy owing to a guilty sense (though the experience was just as real at the time), before one found no one was there. To repeat: my supposed consciousness seems only distinguishable from the supposed *consciousness* that is not mine on the basis of the particular non-consciousness (i.e. material body, etc.) through which its negativity is manifested and with which it is always and inevitably associated in some way. It is impossible, I think, to overemphasize the importance of this fact. So of the concept, "universal consciousness," I at present think that the word "universal" misleads. (Perhaps some hidden desire for power to "catch all consciousness in the net of one's understanding," and so escape the horrors of the unknown, seduces one to catch at this seemingly attractive term.)

Again it may be asked: What knows universal consciousness? Would not individual consciousness (if the "universal" is accepted) be held inadequate to judge it? And how can it know itself, or what are the means by which it can know itself and distinguish itself from non-consciousness and individual consciousness? I can find no answer to that and so I conclude that, if I ask it, that is simply because I must have started out with an unjustified assumption about the nature of consciousness (which, platitudinous as it may seem, is horribly difficult to understand and handle in view of its negativity; when one talks about "consciousness" normally, one finds on examination that one has not been talking about it at all but about the positive things like pleasure and pain, action, perception, etc., that always accompany and screen it). Is the question then really necessary? Consciousness, of course, cannot be denied as a necessary constituent of experience, but the trouble starts when we begin to ask what *consciousness* (or its nature) *is*. We have assumed the individuality of consciousness, apparently unjustifiably, because of the observed individuality of the objective part of experience through which we say it is manifested; and the assumption of its individuality logically leads to the further assumption of some universal form. Why?

Now, as I said earlier, when I begin to ask what something *is* (*is*, say, consciousness individual, universal, both, or neither?), we have taken *being* for granted and failed to examine the nature of a part of my question. In one sense consciousness seems correctly describable as functioning (that is in its true negativity) by putting everything in question: What *is* this? What *am* I? What *is* life? What *is* consciousness? What *is* being? Now here the emphasis must be removed from "what" and "this" and placed squarely on "is." Suppose I suggest this: for "is" read "belief-attitude" (as a mode of craving combined with ignorance). In other words, it is the nature of consciousness to *make be* (with the aid of *desire-for-being* and of ignorance-of-how-anything-comes-*to-be*) and the nature of being to depend on consciousness. The multiplicity and the contradictoriness of the answers normally given to these questions ought to be sufficient evidence for something of the sort, or at least for the suspicion, that all the methods of answering them in the way normally done are radically wrong in some way. In fact the contradictory answers in all their variety, as usually given, each bolstered up by logic, betray, it seems to me, just that form of ignorance-craving combination which make perception/non-perception, change/immortality, time/eternity, life/death, action/inaction, choice/fatality, unity/variety, individuality/universality, seem not only possible but real. (It then seems necessary or "right" [here we have craving] to determine what among these *is* [*here we have ignorance*] real and what *is not*.) And the trouble begins again: I begin asserting "I *am* this, I *am not* that," "This *is* that," "A *is* B," "Consciousness *is* life," "Truth *is* beauty," "Life *is* good," "Killing *is* right," "The end *is* the justification of the means," "I *am*," "God *is*," etc., all of which others may deny. Perhaps we get angry and come to blows. How many more people in history have been killed for the sake of opinions about what *is* and what is *not* than have been killed for the sake of facts? *View-points*, interpretations, and opinions about the raw material of experience differ, less or more, from individual person to individual person. The more consistent and logically strengthened any moral, religious, or philosophical system becomes, the more possible it becomes for it to be contradicted by an opposing system. And then bare craving has to arbitrarily choose and bash the opponent on the head if it can. That is why Buddhism (especially Nāgārjuna, but also Theravada) favours a dialectic that pulls down all such positivistic-negativistic systems (the positive is always haunted by the negative, and so there is really no true *via negativa* or *via positiva* in any absolute sense). It pulls them down using their own premises.

Of whatever I can say that it *is*, by that very fact I imply that it *is not*: It *is* this, *is not* that. It then is in virtue of what it is not, being so constituted by the consciousness that determines it thus. But the *consciousness* on which its being depends is negative, whose negativity appears in objective things as their temporality and change, the change in their being. But while the *being* of whatever is objective to it appears as positive, even though it may change, its own being appears as a negation of itself and a denial, flight or movement, the temporalizing of the temporalized objective world.

Now, perhaps, you will understand why it is really impossible for a Buddhist to answer the questions, "Does Buddhism teach the extinction of consciousness? *Is* nibbāna the extinction of consciousness?" On the basis of what has been said above, could it be answered yes or no without examining each term of the question?

There is, of course, another, different approach to the analysis of (not the answer to) that question: Why should consciousness (however conceived) seem preferable to cessation-of-consciousness (however conceived)? Consciousness of deprivation, of an "abyss of nothingness," is not cessation of consciousness. Would not any *preference* (absolute one-sided choice) for one over the other show craving in the aim if that were set up as the ultimate aim? The desire-to-end-craving, as I see it, is a provisional measure adopted while craving is still present in order to use craving to terminate itself, while the aim is absence-of-craving and consequently ending of suffering. Use of the word *is* (which implies presence of ignorance) in *this* way is also use of present ignorance to terminate itself, while the aim is (to me in this state) liberation from ignorance.

Second, suppose a state of consciousness without suffering. Would it not have to be entirely without change since the slightest change in the state must imply a degree of suffering intruding. But can a state of consciousness absolutely without change be distinguished at all from absence of consciousness? I do not see how it can. However a mixture of longing for the incompatible (craving) and fear of or disinclination to face the facts of the association and complexity which are inseparable from conscious experience (ignorance) can make it seem as possible and realizable as the catching of the red in a rainbow with a butterfly net. So out we go with our butterfly nets chasing colour ... and get wet instead. Craving and ignorance persist in heaven, though suffering may be suspended there for a time.

That is how I see Emerson's "Take what you will but pay the price," viz. "Pay death as the price of life," or "Pay suffering as the price of consciousness." May get it on loan, but if one does not pay up when the bill comes in, the bailiffs distrain. But that does not mean that I think one should counter with undiminished craving and ignorance and use them to denounce life, consciousness, etc. I say one should take them as they *are* and develop understanding of them. That, as I see it, and only that, along with the sharing of it, is the true source of joy, not joy of life haunted by fear of *loss-of-consciousness*, and so on. This you know, so I am not saying anything new.

If I ask myself "Is it possible for me to end consciousness?" I have to reply to myself that I see no possibility at present. (*What* might happen *if* I succeeded in ending craving and ignorance, of which I see no prospect at present, is, of course, hard to say!) If the possibility were available now, I at present see no sound reason why I should not avail myself of it. Pure speculation! Yes, but at least it prevents me coming down one-sidedly in favour of consciousness or in favour of non-consciousness in the crude mode. I do regard death (my life's end, murder, or suicide) as the ending of consciousness: to presume that conscious continuity (negativity) ends because a particular continuity of its material objective world (including its body) ends seems to me a pure assumption whose opposite is just as valid, with possibly better logical arguments in favour of it if the evidence is observed without bias. However, what happens to me at death cannot be known. Consequently I am at liberty to assume (since I cannot avoid assuming something about it) what seems most reasonable. Death seems above all to be forgetting. I do not know. But since I have to believe something about it whether I like it or not, I do not believe that consciousness ends with death. Memory may well do so. I don't, however, know that this is what I *want* not to believe.

It is, I think, rather important to bear in mind one thing in regard to what has been said above. With this view there are two scales of value (not so much divorced as crossing at right-angles) which must be carefully discriminated. The physical world of consciousness-being-action in which we *live* and *are*, biased by ignorance and propelled by craving, is governed by perception of being and the practical values based on that. But any positive metaphysical system, whether based only logically or emotionally on it, which is founded on that, is haunted by the shadows that it cannot avoid casting and that it cannot itself see (like the Sun). It acts in virtue of cause and effect and its thought is logical by its dependence on the word "is." As far as we live *in* this world we have to live its mode and by its values, or we risk falling into wells through star-gazing. But *none* of its laws are made *absolute* (without divorcing idea from experience). The Void, of which it cannot be said that it is or is not, nor that it has consciousness or has none, while it denies absoluteness to any experiential value (alike to being and to consciousness) cannot be identified. And that is the doctrine of not-self (*anattā*) as I see it in one aspect at present. This voidness cannot be "is-ed" and so introduced into the worldly scheme, except as the denial of absoluteness of all particular values. It has no more effect on ordinary life than the theory of relativity. But just as that theory completely alters calculation of enormous speeds, so, as I see it, this void-element completely alters calculations of extraordinary situations, of death (as killing, suicide or the partner of old age).

Written in June 1957

The Sukkhavipassaka

It is the aim here to ascertain the meaning of these three terms, and especially of the last with respect to the minimum of concentration (*samādhi, samatha*) implied by it as indispensable. The material for this inquiry is the Pali texts and their commentaries.

Samathayānika ('one whose vehicle is quiet'): see, e.g., *Visuddhimagga* Ch XVIII. 'Quiet' (*samatha*) stands here for the four *jhānas* and four *āruppas* ('Formless Attainments').

Vipassanāyānika ('one whose vehicle is insight'): see, e.g., Vism Ch XVIII. 'Insight' here means investigation intended to lead to the attainment of the Noble Eightfold path in any one of its 4 stages. The *suddhavipassanāyānika* ('one whose vehicle is pure insight') in Vism Ch XVIII is probably equatable with the next.

Sukkhavipassaka ('bare-insight worker'): see quotations in Appendix I; since the term is often used to explain the Piṭaka term *paññāvimutta*, an examination of the meaning of that term is required before attempting to fix a meaning for *sukkhavipassaka*.
As will be seen from the Sutta references summarized in Appendix I, the term *paññāvimutta* is given a number of widely varying descriptions. The word *descriptions*, rather than *definitions* is used purposely here; for numerous differing descriptions can, and should, be made of a single thing or person from various angles as, say, of a fig-tree from above, from the side, etc.), with different emphasis, in alternative terms, and so on; but a definition is properly only a single strict delimitation, usually of a quality or set of qualities. The Buddha makes great use of multiple descriptions as well as of definitions. (See. e.g., App. I § 8). So, taking these descriptions of the *paññāvimutta* as complementary and not contradictory, they can be used as the basis for *ad hoc* definitions, if required.

However, *paññāvimutti* ('understanding-deliverance') emerges as the particular distinctive quality (*guṇa*) or idea (*dhamma*), found in *all* arahantship, of being liberated by the permanent deliverance from ignorance (*avijjā*) given by understanding. This quality (or idea) has in itself no grades (only the four unrepeated stages of the Path—the '8 stages of insight' in Vism Ch XX and XXI are not relevant here, see § 5). But in the formal statement of the 6th (supramundane) *abhiññā*, that is Arahantship as exhaustion of taints (see. e.g. M I 35–6 and App. I § 8), both *paññāvimutti* and *cetovimutti* ('heart-deliverance') appear always together. *Cetovimutti*, however, *alone*, is the temporary liberation from need (*taṇhā*) provided in anyone, Arahant or ordinary man, by the eight attainments (4 *jhānas* and 4 *āruppas* ; see e.g., MN 29, and *Paṭisambhidāmagga Vimokkhakathā*), and at its lowers is the first *jhāna*. *Cetovimutti* thus has grades, is temporary, and is the particular field of quiet (*samatha*), while *paññāvimutti* has no grades, is permanent (in each of its four stages in its removal of ignorance) and is the particular field of knowledge of the Four Truths. In combination with *cetovimutti* of some grade, *paññāvimutti* gives the Arahant permanent unassailability to his deliverance from both ignorance and need.

Now while *paññāvimutti* is thus the quality (or idea), the word *paññāvimutta* is used of the 'person' (i.e., 'type of person') possessing that quality. Arahants, as 'persons' vary, not in *paññāvimutti* but in the grade of development of their *cetovimutti*, and on this general basis two kinds of Arahant are contrasted, that is, the *ubhatobhāgavimutta* ('Both-Ways-Liberated') and *paññāvimutta* ('one liberated by understanding'); see MN 70, *Puggalapaññatti* etc.). The former, at maximum, has the highest grade of *cetovimutti* with the five mundane *abhiññās*, while the latter, at minimum, has only one or the four *jhānas* (this will be shown later): a possessor of the five mundane *abhiññās* is never, then, called a '*paññāvimutta*' (though he of course has *paññāvimutti*), and one with only the jhānas for *cetovimutti* is never called *ubhatobhāgavimutta* (thought he of course has some cetovimutti). However, the two terms overlap in the intervening grades of *cetovimutti* (the 8 *vimokkhas*, 4 *āruppas*, etc.), and the line of demarcation varies according to the terms to the terms of description and contrast (see App. I). The lower the grade of *cetovimutti* the more emphasis comes to be laid on *paññāvimutti*, though the former is never and nowhere stated to be quite dispensable with. The *paññāvimutta* 'person' (*puggala*)—'persons' being a convention (*vohāra*)—is thus not strictly or uniquely definable in the way that the quality of *paññāvimutti* is. Hence the treatment of him by multiple descriptions.

At this point the question arises: Does the Tipiṭaka allow any interpretation of *paññāvimutta* to the effect that, at the very minimum, he *can* reach Arahantship quite without *jhāna*, even as a factor of the Eightfold Path? Does the *Satipaṭṭhāna* method suggest this?

A careful examination of the Suttas summarized in Appendix I and of other relevant Tipiṭaka passages shows quite clearly that not one of them furnishes ay information on the question: the four *jhānas* are not mentioned either collectively or singly in connection with *paññāvimutta*. In fact nowhere in the Tipiṭaka is it said that Arahantship (or any stage of the Path) can be reached without *jhāna*. In the particular case of the *Susīma Sutta* (App. I § 4) the specific omission of the *jhānas* from the list of attainments not necessary for the *paññāvimutta* is, however, particularly striking. If the Buddha intended that *jhāna*, too, was not necessary, why did he not say so outright, which he never did? But in other Suttas, too, such as those at SN 35:70 & 152, no mention is made of *jhānas*: might that not show that the Buddha may have wanted perhaps to hint that *Satipaṭṭhāna* made *jhāna* unnecessary? Let us see. Those two Suttas do relate specifically to the fourth *Satipaṭṭhāna*, the contemplation of Ideas as Ideas of the *Mahāsatipaṭṭhāna sutta* (DN 22). And in that Sutta the Noble Eightfold Path is defined in full with *sammā-samādhi* ('Right Concentration'), its eight factor, clearly and unequivocally as jhāna. That is the answer.

The Suttas' answer to the question is thus perfectly definite: there is no dispensing with *jhāna*. And this is also confirmed equally decisively by the Abhidhamma, where the *Dhammasaṅgaṇī's* comprehensive list of 89 types of cognizance contains no type of Path-Cognizance without supramundane *jhāna*.

In view of this, then, if the Commentaries say the contrary if, for instance we think that they assert or suggest that a *sukkha vipassaka* can become an Arahant *without any jhāna-concentration at all–*, then, if we are not mistaken, they must be in irreconcilable conflict with both the Suttas and the Abhidhamma: there is really no escape. If that is right, they disregard the instructions of the *Mahāpadesa Sutta* (A II 167) and their own criterion, which is that of a statement in commentaries conflicts with the Tipiṭaka, it must be rejected. Let us see if, in act, they actually do so.

The commentaries often use their term *sukkhavipassaka* to explain the Piṭaka term *paññāvimutta*, though they are not at all synonymous. That being so, since the Tipiṭaka, as already shown, does not allow the omission of *jhāna* from the indispensable qualities of he *paññāvimutta* or from the factors of the Path (and consequently Arahantship), this meaning must ne conveyed also by the commentaries either explicitly or implicitly, of they are not to contradict the Piṭakas. Let us take five representative statements—the most awkward we can find from the commentaries, which at first glance most clearly seem to state the contrary.

Mayaṃ nijjhānikā sukkhavipassakā (App. I § 4a).
So (paññāvimutto) sukkhavipassako ca catūhi jhānehi vuṭṭhāya arahattaṃ pattā cattāro cā ti imesaṃ vasena pañcavidho hoti (App. I § 5a).
Paññābalen'eva ... vimutto ti attho (App. I § 7a).
Jhānābhiññānaṃ abhāvena (App. I § 8a).
Anuppāditajjhāno āraddhavipassako (App. I § 8a).

What are we to make of these?

Do they, especially § 4, not show incontestably that the commentator held that *jhāna* was unnecessary altogether? That quotations out of context can be misleading is so obviously true that it is constantly forgotten and has always to be reiterated. The full immediate contexts will be found in Appendix I with English translations. But let us take each statement individually and examine it closely in the light of its proper context, of the text commented on, of possible alternative grammatical solutions, and of the teaching as a whole.

(1) The word *nijjhānika* here (as described in the note to App. I § 4a) does not mean "*no jhāna,*" but on the contrary unmistakably alludes to the term *dhammanijjhānakhanti;* for the appearance of

this expression in the sutta (MN 70) where the *paññāvimutta* is described makes this allusion inescapable. The word thus means 'ponderers' indeed there appears to be no usage anywhere of *nijjhāna* in any form in a negative sense, the prefix being here augmentative, not privative. As to the words that follow in the same passage (§ 4a), namely *vināsamādhiṃ evaṃ ñāṇuppattiṃ dassanatthaṃ*, these simply state what is, in fact, the essence of the Buddha's teaching: that concentration alone does not provide final liberation, which is only attainable by the intervention of insight leading to Path-attainment (see § 2 above). The words *Vinā samādhiṃ* belong properly to *dassanatthaṃ* not to *ñāṇuppattiṃ*. And this does not imply in any way *jhāna*—concentration (*cetovimutti*) has no part to play at all.

(2) The addition of the *sukkhavipassaka* to the four distinguished by the *jhāna* they have emerged from (*vuṭṭhāya*) might seem to suggest that he does without *jhāna* at all times. If that were actually intended, though, it would be odd, given that the *Susīma Sutta* here being commented on omits, specially and pointedly, any mention of jhāna (see § 2 above) from the dispensables, that the commentator should leave such an important point not cleared up (and it is not cleared up anywhere else). But this oddness here vanishes if we take proper account of the word *vuṭṭhāya*; for that means 'having emerged' and so applies only to the time *before* reaching the Path, but conveys nothing about the composition of the Path reached. The *samathayānika* first develops *jhāna*, on the basis of which, *after emerging* from it, he develops insight, till he reaches the Path whose eighth factor is supramundane *jhāna*. The *vipassanāyānika* (including the *sukkhavipassaka*) places *jhāna* second, or works without it at all, till the attainment of the path whose eight factor is likewise supramundane *jhāna*. This passage therefore gives us information about the practice of *vipassanā*, but none at all about the composition of the path or the indispensability of *jhāna* (see also § 5 below).

(3) This simply restates what is said in the later part of App. I § 4a, namely that the attainment of the path, as such and considered apart from the necessary accessory concentration, is the peculiar

field of understanding (and of it were not, understanding would have no part to play.)

(4) This might seem at first conclusive, explicit and incontrovertible evidence in favour of the view that the commentaries did reject *jhāna* as indispensable. However, let us take a close look at the wording of the sutta commented in (see App. I § 8, 1st para). The commentary (§ 8a) says *jhānābhiññānāṃ abhāvena*: but in the sutta passage being commented on we find the words *sayaṃ abhiññā sacchikatvā* (which are actually the basis for this formula being called the 'sixth, supramundane, *abhiññā*'). So here in the sutta we have the sixth, supramundane, *abhiññā* alone without the other five, mundane, *abhiññā*. Now while the 'five' are the exclusive product of the fourth jhāna and so belong only to *samatha* (see e.g. Vism Ch XII and XIII), the 'sixth' is, considered alone, the exclusive product of understanding (as explained under (i) above). If we, then, uncritically take the commentary's compound *jhānābhiññānaṃ* to be what the grammarians call a *dvandva*-compound, resolve it into *jhānānañ-ca abhiññānañ-ca*, and translate the whole phrase by 'with the absence of *jhānas* and *abhiññās* we have made the commentator contradict flatly the very passage in the sutta he is commenting on—the sutta assets the presence of an *abhiññā* and the commentator has been made to deny sweepingly both *jhānas* and *abhiññās*—which is plainly absurd. The proper and only way here is to take the compound as a *tappurisa*-compound, resolve it into *jhānena abhiññānaṃ*, and translate the whole phrase by 'with the absence of *abhiññās* du to *jhāna*' (i.e., of the five mundane, which are due to the perfecting of the 4th *jhāna*). Further confirmation is provided by the presence, in this same sutta passage, of the word *cetovimutti*: and there is no *cetovimutti* without *jhāna*. It is also said in this same sutta passage that this Arahant 'has not... the Eight Liberation's. Now the first three of these are *jhāna* collectively in three aspects, the remaining five being the four *āruppas* and cessation. In this connection the commentaries (App. I § 5b and 6a) are at special pains to show that 'having the Eight Vimokkhas' is a collective statement allowed of one who has gained any one *āruppa* but *not* of one who has only *jhāna*: having *jhāna* is thus compatible with the eighth 'having no

Eight Vimokkhas'. Such an explanation would indeed be futile of the commentators held that *jhāna* was dispensable for Arahantship.

(5) The expression *anuppāditajhāno āraddhavipassako* means simply 'one who begins his insight without first arousing *jhāna*' and so is interpretable under (ii) above.

So here too all the commentarial passages describing the *paññāvimutta* and exhibiting their use of *sukkhavipassaka* tell us nothing about *jhāna* not being necessary for the path.

There is, in fact, nothing here to tell; for that has already been told unequivocally in the suttas and Abhidhamma in the appropriate place (see § 2). It would also be quite absurd to suppose that Ācariya Buddhaghosa forgot the *Dhammasangaṇī's* definition, since he uses its 89-fold classification of all cognizance as one of the main pillars of his exegetical system, and equally absurd to suggest that he forgot that the *Mahāsatipaṭṭhāna sutta*, commented upon by him in such detail, contains the sutta definition of Path-*samādhi* as *jhāna* (also repeated elsewhere). But it would be reasonable to suppose that he remembered them well—well enough for him not to suspect that these passages which he wrote could possibly be interpreted to mean that *jhāna* could be dispensed with, for him not to refer here to definitions that he must have regarded as too well known to need repetition in every instance. For in the *Visuddhimagga* (p. 666–7 / Ch xxi) he wrote the words—repeated in the *Atthasālinī* (p. 228–9)—*Sukkavipassakassa uppannamaggo ... paṭhamajjhāniko va hoti*: 'The bare-insight worker's Path ... always (only) has the first *jhāna*'.

Examples of omission for the sake of emphasis of other aspects will be found, for instance, in *Majjhima* sutta 121 (omission of the 4 *jhānas*), in *majjhima* sutta 125 (omission of only the first *jhāna*), etc., etc., and these too are not to be taken as 'hints that what is omitted is unnecessary'.

This inquiry would not be complete without observing that several types of concentration (*samādhi*) are distinguished in the commentaries. The *Visuddhimagga* (p. 85) lists, among other sets, two kinds, namely *upacāra* and *appanā*. Elsewhere it is explained that by *upacāra samādhi* ('access-concentration') is intented the concentration of *kāmāvacara* ('sensual sphere') type that accompanies strong *vipassanā* ('insight'), which arises when the five hindrances (*nīvaraṇa*) have been suppressed but before the *jhāna*-factors have arisen (based on the passage at M I 21, lines 31–3: 'my energy was aroused, ... my heart was concentrated and unified', which theme is developed differently at *Paṭisambhidā* I 99). *Appanā-samādhi* ('absorption-concentration') is defined as *jhāna* (with the jhāna factors arisen), and as *rūpāvacara* ('from sphere') or *arūpāvacara* ('formless-sphere'). However, in another context (Vism 289) a third type called there *khaṇika-cittekaggatā* ('momentary unification of cognizance') is introduced but not developed. Of this the *Paramatthamañjūsā* says *khaṇikacittekaggatā ti khaṇamattaṭṭhitiko samādhi; so pi hi ārammaṇe nirantaraṃ ekākārena pavattamāno paṭipakkhena anabhibhūto appito viya cittaṃ niccalaṃ ṭhapeti*:

"Momentary unification of cognizance" is concentration that is steadied for only a moment; yet when that occur in one mode uninterruptedly on an object without its being overcome by opposition, it steadies cognizance (making it) motionless as through it were absorption' (p.278 Hewavitarane ed.). This, in its context of a sub-comment on a comment on the sutta-phrase *samādahaṃ cittaṃ assasissāmī ti pajānāti* ('he understand " I shall breathe in concentrating cognizance"), might seem to half-open the door to some form of substitute for *appanā* (to use the commentarial terminology, which is not in the Piṭaka) Remembering, however, that both suttas and Abhidhamma define Path consciousness unequivocally as inseparable from *jhāna* (paraphrased in the commentaries by '*appanā*') what is '*as though it were* absorption' can never be the actual supramundane *sammāsamādhi* of the path (see e.g., *Atthasālinī* p. 214). Though it is doubtless a perfectly legitimate way of describing certain aspects of the necessary degree of *concentration* without which no insight can take place at all, this passage cannot be taken, and was never intended to be taken, to have any bearing on the composition of the Noble Eightfold Path.
In these contexts it needs also to be remembered that the term *vipassanā*, whether in the Piṭakas or the Commentaries, whether by itself or as a component of the commentarial term *sukkhavipassaka*, is used specifically for that kind of examination of experience

which leads up to attainment of the Path, but not for the understanding (*paññā*) contained in the actual path under supramundane *sammādiṭṭhi* ('Right View'). *Vipassanā* is thus only that kind of understanding that *precedes* the Path, its last states before the actual Path itself being called *vuṭṭhānagāminī vipassanā* ('insight leading to emergence' Vism 661), and the Path itself being called *vuṭṭhānaṃ* that is, 'emergence' of Right View from wrong view (and so with other seven factors: see Paṭisambhidāmagga I 69). It would therefore seem that any use of the term *Vipassaka* (whether *sukkha* or not) as synonymous with *maggalābhī* ('path-obtainer') would be incorrect. It that is so, then whatever is said about a *sukkhavipassaka*, as *vipassaka*, tells us nothing about the composition of the path which he may attain, for which we must look to the proper definitions in the proper places .

It is perhaps allowable to infer that, at minimum, a *sukkhavipassaka* need not develop *jhāna* at any time *before* he actually reaches the supramundane *jhāna* of the Noble Eightfold Path, but unless his Path contains at least the supramundane first *jhāna* it is not, in fact, the Path but only *dhammuddhacca* ('overestimation of ideas') in the form of a *vipassanūpakkilesa* ('imperfection of insight') see App. II; also Vism Ch XX end).
With the reservations already made about the difficulties of defining 'persons' (§2 above), the following general definitions can perhaps be made.

(i) *Samathayānika* ('one whose vehicle is quiet'); one who in his work to reach the path (in each of its four stages) habitually first arouses *jhāna*, then emerges from it, and practises insight on the *jhāna* emerged from. This leads him, if successful to the 'emergence' of the path with supramundane *jhāna* (at minimum the first as its eighth factor.)

(ii) *Vipassanāyānika* ('one whose vehicle is insight'): one who habitually practices insight before *jhāna* on his way to the Path. If he makes no use of, or does not attain *jhāna* before he reaches the path, he is called a *suddhavipassanāyānika* ('one whose vehicle is pure insight'), in which case he can be taken as equivalent to the next.

"(iii) *Sukkhavipassaka* ('bare-insight worker'): one who never emerges from *jhāna* (or any attainment of *samādhi*) before the time he reaches the supramundane *sammāsamādhi* of the Path—in his case the supramundane first *jhāna* (Vism 666–7; *Atthasālinī* 228–9). Unlike the *paññāvimutta*, which term describes the Obtainer of the Fourth Stage of the Path and its fruit, the term *sukkhavipassaka* (like the other two commentarial terms (i) and (ii) above) is only applicable to one who is trying for, but has not yet reached, the path in any one of its four stages, and so it can be, and is, used for the ordinary man who has not yet reached even the Stream-Entry Path as well as for those trying for the other stages of the Path. The term *sukkhavipassaka-khīṇāsava* (App. I § 8a) then properly means 'one whose taints are exhausted, who has arrives at the Path by the way of the Bare-insight worker'. Since his insight is called 'bare (dry), impoverished' (App. I § 7b), his way is probably not the easiest.

(iv) *Paññāvimutta* ('liberated by understanding'): since all Arahants are, strictly speaking 'liberated by understanding', this term, when used to distinguish one kind from another has only a relative or comparative meaning: in this sense, a *paññāvimutta* is contrasted with a *Buddha* as not having *discovered* the path he *follows* (App. I § 1.), or he is contrasted with an *ubhatobhāgavimutta* ('both ways liberated') Arahant by his not having fully exploited to the full the field of *samādhi* (*samatha*: App. I § 2 etc.), while at minimum the *ubhatobhāgavimutta* must have one of the four *āruppas* (App. I § 5b, 6a), a *paññāvimutta* can at minimum have only the first *jhāna*. What is the latest point to which his attainment of it can be put off is not stated. If called (collectively) 'without the Eight *Vimokkhas*' (App. I § 6, cf. § 8) he can still have *jhāna* (App. I § 5b, 6a). Both *paññāvimutta* and *cetovimutti* (the last in some degree) are present in all Arahants (App. I § 8.).

(v) The Suttas (notably the *Mahāsatipaṭṭhāna sutta*) and the Abhidhamma (*Dhammasaṅgaṇī*) state unequivocally that there is no Noble Eightfold Path without supramundane *jhāna*. This is confirmed in the commentaries (specifically with the words 'the bare-Insight Worker's path ... always (only) has the first *jhāna* (§ 3 end). Commentarial passages that at first glance seem to state the contrary can be found after proper investigation, not to do so.

(vi) The general spirit of the Buddha's teaching in relation to *samatha* is expressed by the following sutta: "Bhikkhus, these two ideas partake of true knowledge. What two? Quiet and insight. When quiet is maintained in being ... a pure heart is maintained in being ... (and) lust is abandoned. When insight is maintained in being, ... understanding is maintained in being, ... (and) whatever ignorance there is abandoned. No heart defiled by lust is liberated, and no understanding defiled by ignorance is maintained in being. This heart-deliverance is due to fading of ignorance' (AN 3:10/I 61). Other suttas expressing this are far too may to refer to here. Consequently, such suttas as the *Satipaṭṭhāna sutta* (MN 10), or those at, say, *Saṃyutta* 35:70 and 152, have to be taken as emphasizing the essential part played by insight in developing understanding, without, however, implying that the minimum *jhāna* of *cetovimutti* can ne dispensed with.

* * *

Appendix I

(For discussion and justification of translations see § 3.)

§ 1. *Paññāvimutta* (at maximum) distinguished from *sammāsambuddha* only by the fact that the *paññāvimutta* follows the way that a *sammāsambuddha* discovers (SN 22:58/S III 65–6).

§ 2. *Paññāvimutta* contrasted with *ubhatobhāgavimutta* in terms of the '9 attainments' (4 *jhānas*, 4 *āruppas*, and cessation): the *paññāvimutta* can have all these, but what distinguished him then from the other is that he has not fully exploited them (in their aspect of *samatha*). No *paññāvimutta* is without one of these attainments. (AN 9:44/A IV 452–3).

§ 3. *Paññāvimutta* contrasted with *tevijja*, *chaḷabhiññā*, and *ubhatobhāgavimutta*: he is less than these, but no mention that he can dispense with *jhāna*. (SN 7:7/S I 191).

§ 4. *Susīma sutta*: the *paññāvimutta* need not have the five mundane *abhiññās* (supernormal powers) or the 4 *āruppas* (formless attainments): specific omission of *jhāna* from the attainments that can be dispensed with. Compare the wording of attainments here with that in, say, MN 6. (SN 12:70/A II 121–7).

§ 4a. Commentary to *Susīma Sutta: mayaṃ nijjhānikā sukkhavipassakā paññāmatten'eva vimuttā ti ... "Ājāneyyāsi vā" to ādi kasmā vuttaṃ? Vinā samādhiṃ evam-nāṇuppattim dassanattham. Idañ hi vuttam hoti: Susīma maggo vā phalaṃ vā na samādhinissando na samādhi-ānisaṃso na samādhissa nipphatti, vipassanāya pana so nissando vipassanāya ānisaṃso vipassanāya nipphatti ...*

Translation: (note: *nijjhānikā* fr. *nijjhāna* ('pondering'), and alludes directly to *dhamma nijjhānaṃ khamati* ... *dhammanijjhānakhanti* (MN 70/M I 480), cf. also *nijjhatti* & *nijjhāpenti* (M I 320); no instance of this term in any form as negative of *jhāna*, prefix *nir-* being augmentative, not privative, here). "We are liberated by understanding, friend": we are ponderers, bare-insight workers, liberated simply by understanding ... "Whether you understand or ..." and the rest: why is this said? In order to show without (reference to) concentration the arising of knowledge thus. What is meant is this: 'Susīma, neither the Path nor (its) fruit are the outcome of concentration, or the benefits of concentration, or the productions of concentration, rather they are the outcome of insight, the benefits of insight, the production of insight'. (Note: this simply states the fact that concentration alone does not, as susīma seems to have supposed, produce true liberation, which is the field of understanding; but nothing is said here to the effect that *jhāna* can be dispensed with).

§ 5. *Paññāvimutta* contrasted with *ubhatobhāgavimutta* in terms of the 4 *āruppas* only, the difference then being that the *paññāvimutta* need not have these. (MN 70/A I 477–8). No mention of *jhāna*.

§ 5a. Commentary to MN 70: *Paññāya vimutto ti paññāvimutto. So sukkhavipassako ca jhānehi vuṭṭhāya arahattaṃ pattā cattāro cā ti imesaṃ vasena pañcavidho hoti. Pāḷi pan' ettha aṭṭha-vimokkha-paṭikkhepavasen'eva āgatā* ... (cites *Puggalapaññatti* 14; see § 6 below, and particularly reservations in this respect in both § 5b and 6a).

Translation: (resolution of compound not rendered) 'He (one liberated by understanding) is of five kinds namely the bare-insight worker and those (four) who have reached arahantship after emerging from the four respective *jhanas*. Now here (in this particular aspect of the *āruppas*) the text is also stated in terms of rejection of the Eight Liberations' (as in the *Puggalapaññatti*) but see commentary to that, § 6a below).

§ 5b. Sub-commentary to MN 70 (cf. § 6a below): *"Paññāvimutto" ti visesato paññāya eva vimutto na tassa paṭṭhānabhūtena aṭṭhavimokkhasankhātena sātisayena samādhinā to paññāvimutto—yo ariyo anadhigata-aṭṭhavimokkhena*[24] *sabbaso āsavehi vimutto/ tass'etam adhivacanam // adhigate pi hi rūpajjhānavimokkhena1 so sātisayasamādhinissito ti na tassa vasena ubhatobhāgavimutto hotī ti vutto vayaṃ attho/ arūpajjhānesu pana ekasmim pi sati ubhatobhāgavimutto yeva nāma hoti/ tena hi aṭṭhavimokkhekadesena tannāmadānasamatthena aṭṭhavimokkhalābhi tveva vuccati samudāye hi pavatto vohāro avayave pi dissati yatha sattisayo ti// ... Aṭṭhavimokkhapaṭikkhepavasem'eva ti avadhāraṇena paṭikkhepavasen'eva āgatabhāvaṃ dasseti/ ten'āha "kāyena phusitvā viharatī" ti.*

Translation: 'Liberated distinctively by means of only understanding; not by means of any concentration with extra (development), entitled (collectively) the "Eight Liberations" and made the basis for that (understanding), thus 'liberated by understanding" ; this is a synonym for the (type of) Noble One (i.e., Path-attainer) liberated altogether from taints with respect to a Liberation (i.e., form-*jhāna*—see note at the end for the 'Liberations') that has not arrived at (the collective title of) "the Eight". For even when (that title is) arrived at (by his developing a formless *jhāna* (as in § 2 above) yet since (the *paññāvimutta* is here regarded specifically) with respect to (some) form-*jhāna* Liberation (of his), he (thus) has for support (the form-*jhāna*) concentration "with extra" (i.e., with extra formless-*jhāna*), and so the meaning is that he is not then called *ubhatobhāgavimutta* in virtue of that (extra formless-*jhāna*), though when there is even one of the formless *jhānas* he is called an *ubhatobhāgavimutta* too (as in MN 70, see § 5 above). For he is called an "Obtainer of the Eight

24. It is not clear whether we should read locative and negative *vimokkhe na* or instrumental *-vimokkhena*. Whichever is right—probably the latter—both should be the same, probably. Fortunately the sense is clear from No. 6a, from which this is expanded.

Liberations" in virtue of the ability of a part (i.e., one of the last five) of the Eight Liberations to confer that name since the usage is found to occur with respect to the whole and to a member, as in the case of (the term) *sattisayo*... "Also stated in terms of rejection of the Eight Liberations" points out how it is stated in terms of rejection on account of emphasis'.

§6. *Paññāvimutta* contrasted with *ubhatobhāgavimutta* in terms of possession of the Eight Liberations (collectively: § 5 above and § 6a below). The *Paññāvimutta* need not have the Eight Liberations collectively. (N.B. the insistence of the commentary here and the *Sub-commentary* in § 5b above on the *collectiveness* of the term 'Obtainer of the Eight Liberations' and that it can only be gained by attaining one of the *āruppas*, but not by attaining *form-jhāna* clearly shows that the commentators were fully aware of the indispensability of *jhāna* for the attainment of the Noble Path). (*Puggalapaññatti* 14 & 73).

§6a. Commentary to Pug: Reproduces § 5a up to '*Pañcavidho hoti*', and adds *etesu hi eko pi aṭṭhavimokkhalābhī na hoti// ten'eva "na h'eva kho aṭṭhavimokkhe" ti (*Pug. text*) ādim āha// arūpāvacarajjhānesu pana ekasmiṃ sati ubhatobhāgavimutto yeva nāma hotī ti.*

"Translation: For not even one among these [five (see 5a)] is (called) an "attainer of the Eight Liberations" (collectively), hence "without (having touched with the body) the Eight Liberations" and so on is said. But when there is any one of the formless-sphere *jhānas* (i.e., the four *āruppas*) he (i.e., this 'obtainer of the Eight Liberations') is also called "*ubhatobhāgavimutta*" (Note: this means that an "obtainer of the Eight" can be called an *ubhatobhāgavimutta* in contrast to a *paññāvimutta* who has no *āruppas* and he can also be called a *paññāvimutta* in contrast to an *ubhatobhāgavimutta* who has, say the five mundane *abhiññās* (see § 2 above). The *Mūlaṭīkā* adds nothing extra).

§7. *Paññāvimutta* described in contrast with the *ubhatobhāgavimutta* in terms of 'seeing with understanding the 7 standing-points for consciousness (*viññāṇaṭṭhiti*) and two bases (*āyatana*), namely those of the non-percipient and neither-percipient-nor-non-percipient. He lacks the 8 *Vimokkhas* (see Nos. 5b and 6a), this tells us nothing about *jhāna* (DN 15/D II 70).

§7a. Commentary: *'Paññāvimutto' ti paññāya vimutto; aṭṭhavimokkhe asacchikatvā paññābalen'eva nāmakāyassa ca rūpakāyassa ca appavattim katvā vimutto ti attho. So sukkhavipassako ca paṭhamajjānādīsu aññatarasmiṃ ṭhatvā arahattaṃ patto cā ti pañcavidho* (see § 5a) hoti.

(There follows quotation from Pug. As in § 5a)

Translation: '... without having reached the Eight Liberations (collectively, see nos. 5b and 6a), he is liberated by causing, through the power of understanding alone (see § 4a), the non-occurrence of the name-body and the form-body. He (the *paññāvimutta*) is five fold as the bare-insight worker and the four who reach arahantship by having already steadied themselves in one of the *jhānas* beginning with the first (before they reach their Path)'. (Note: no more is said here than in § 4a and 5a)."

§7b. Sub-commentary: *Paṭhamajjhānaphassena vinā pari jānanādippakārehi cattāri saccāni jānato paṭivijjhanto. Tesaṃ kiccānaṃ matthakappattiyā niṭṭhitakiccatāya visesana mutto ti vimutto. So paññāvimutto ... samathabhāvanāsinehābhāvena sukkhā lūkhā asiniddhā vā vipassanā etassā ti sukkhavipassako.*

Translation: 'One knowing, penetrating, the four Truths in the (four) modes of diagnosing (suffering), etc., without (having already had) the experience of (even) the first *jhāna*. He is freed distinctively by these four functions being brought to their culmination and to their function-completion, thus he is liberated. It is he that is "liberated by understanding" ... He has insight that is bare (dry), impoverished, owing to the absence of the moisture of maintenance of quiet in being, or is unmoistened, thus he is a "bare-(dry)insight worker" (Note: Since this passage deals explicitly with *insight* (*vipassanā*) alone, nothing can be deduced from it about the composition of the Path: see § 5).

§8. The Arahant without the Eight Vimokkhas has both *paññāvimutti* and *cetovimutti*: *Kathañ ca bhikkave puggalo samaṇapuṇḍarīko hoti? Idha bhikkhave bhikkhu āsavānaṃ khayā anāsavaṃ cetovimuttiṃ paññāvimuttiṃ diṭṭhe 'va dhamme sayaṃ abhiññā sacchikatvā upasampajja viharati, no ca kho aṭṭha vimokkhe kāyena phusitvā viharati.* (AN 4:87/A II 87)

Kathañ ca bhikkhave puggalo samaṇapuṇḍarīko hoti? Idha bhikkhave bhikkhu sammādiṭṭhiko hoti ... sammāsamādhī hoti sammāñāṇī hoti sammāvimuttī hoti, no ca kho aṭṭhavimokkhe kāyena phusitvā viharati. (AN 4:89/A II 89)

Kathañ ca bhikkhave puggalo samaṇapuṇḍarīko hoti? Idha bhikkhave bhikkhu pañcas' upādānakkhandhesu udayabbayānupassī viharati: Iti rūpaṃ iti rūpassa samudayo, iti rūpassa atthaṅgamo; ... iti viññāṇassa atthaṅgamo ti, no ca kho aṭṭha vimokkhe kāyena phusitvā viharati. (AN 4:90/II 90)

Translation: 'And what, bhikkhus, is a *samaṇapuṇḍarīka*? Here, bhikkhus, a bhikkhu by realization through his own direct-acquaintance (*abhiññā*) here and now enters upon and abides in the heart-deliverance (*cetovimutti*) and understanding-deliverance (*paññāvimutti*) that are taintless owing to (complete) exhaustion of taints; and yet he has not touched with the body the Eight Liberations (*aṭṭha vimokkha*) and abode in them'. (AN 4:87).

'And how, bhikkhus, is a person a *samaṇapuṇḍarīka*? Here, bhikkhus, a bhikkhu has Right View, ... has Right Concentration (*sammāsamādhi*), has Right knowledge, and has Right Deliverance; and yet he has not touched with the body the Eight Liberations and abode in them'. (AN 4:89)

'And how, bhikkhus, is a person *samaṇapuṇḍarīka*? Here, bhikkhus, a bhikkhu abides contemplating rise and fall in the five categories of consumption thus: Such is form, such its origin, such its disappearance; such is (feeling... perception... determinations...) consciousness, ... such its disappearance; and yet he has not touched the Eight Liberations and abode in them'. (AN 4:90)

§8a. Commentary: *Samaṇapuṇḍarīko ti puṇḍarīkasadiso samaṇo; puṇḍarīkam nāma ūnasatapattam saroruham, iminā sukkhavipassaka-khīṇāsavaṃ dasseti. So jhānābhiññānaṃ abhāvena aparipuṇṇaguṇato samaṇapuṇḍarīko nāma hoti. Samaṇapadumo ti ... jhānābhiññānam bhāvena paripuṇṇaguṇattā samaṇa-padumo nāma hoti.* (ad. 87).

Dasaṅgikamaggavasena vā arahattaphalañāṇa-arahattaphalavimuttīhi saddhim aṭṭhaṅgikamaggavasena vā sukkhavipassakanīṇāsavo kathito. (89).

Anuppāditajjhāno āraddhavipassako appamādavihārī sekhapuggalo kathito. (90).

Translation: "*Samaṇapuṇḍarīka*" is a *samaṇa* like a *puṇḍarīka*; a *puṇḍarīka* is a waterlily with less than a hundred petals. By this he shows a bare-insight worker; and he is called a *samaṇapuṇḍarīka* because his qualities are incomplete with the absence of (those kinds of) direct acquaintance (*abhiññā*) due to *jhāna* &. "*Samaṇapaduma*" ... is so called because his qualities are complete with the presence of (those kinds of) direct acquaintance due to *jhāna*[25].' (87).

(Here) the bare-insight worker is expounded by means of the ten-factored path or by means of the eight-factored path together with arahant-fruition knowledge and arahant-fruition deliverance.' (98).

(Here) an initiate person (i.e., not an arahant, but who has at least reached stream-entry) who abides in diligence as one who initiate (his) insight without having aroused jhāna (already)'.

* * *

Appendix II

A sutta in the Aṅguttara Nikāya Fours (AN 4:170/A II 156–7) gives four ways of arriving at Arahantship, apart from which, no Arahantship—final knowledge' (*aññā*)—can be arrived at. They are:

Samathapubbaṅgamaṃ vipassanaṃ bhāveti—he maintains in being insight preceded by quiet.

Vipassanāpubbaṅgamaṃ samathaṃ bhāveti—he maintains in being quiet preceded by insight.

Samathavipassanaṃ yuganaddhaṃ bhāveti—he maintains in being quiet and insight yoked together.

25. The reason for treating *jhānābhiññānaṃ* as a *tappurisa*-compound and not as a *dvandva*-compound are given in § 3(iv) and need not be restated here, except to repeat that to threat it as a *dvandva* makes the comment contradict the passage commented on which is absurd).

Bhikkhuno dhammuddhaccaviggahitaṃ mānasaṃ hoti. So ... samayo yaṃ taṃ cittaṃ ajjhattaṃ yeva santiṭṭhati sannisīdati ekodi hoti samādhiyati; tassa maggo sañjāyati—a bhikkhu's mind is misled by overestimation of ideas. On that occasion cognizance (then) become steadied in himself again, clarified, becomes single, and is concentrated. (Then) the path is born in him. (AN 4:170/A I 157; *Paṭisambhidā Yuganaddhakathā*).

As to the fourth instance, the commentaries explain *uddhacca* here by '*vikkhepa*' ('distraction') and *viggahita* by *virūpagahita* and *virodhagahita* (respectively 'seized by deformation' and 'seized by opposition') and paraphrased by *taṇhāmānadiṭṭhi* ('need, conceits, and wrong views'). *Uddhacca* as one of the ' 5 Hindrances to concentration' is properly 'agitation', but here the meaning is more literal in the sense of being 'distracted' from fact, and is 'thrown up' (*ud+hata+ya*), i.e., 'overestimates' ideas. He thus overestimates what he has achieved and mistakes it for the Noble Eightfold Path when it is not.

Now these four 'ways' are not *four alternatives*: the first three are alternatives, and need no comment, since they are three alternative ways of arriving at the Noble Eightfold Path *without mistake in the way*. The fourth, however, *makes a mistake* on the way, whichever of the three ways he is following, and afterwards sets himself right and eventually reaches the Noble Eightfold Path. The *mistake* he makes is to fancy some mere advance in *Vipassanā* ('insight' in the sense of §5, 9.v.) is the Noble Path. That mistake is called in the *Paṭisambhidāmagga*

Yuganaddhakathā, a *vipassanūpakkilesa* ('imperfections of insight') and is divided into ten different kinds, which are also treated in detail in the *Visuddhimagga*, Ch XX.

The conclusion to be drawn from this sutta, in the light of the definitions of the supramundane *sammāsamādhi* of the Path given in the *Mahāsatipaṭṭhāna sutta* and the *Dhammasaṅgaṇī*, is that if someone fancies he has obtained the Noble Eightfold Path but not even the first *jhāna* as a component of it, he has in fact, simply exhibited *dhammuddhacca* ('overestimation of ideas'), the remedy for which is further practice in elimination of need, conceits, and wrong views.

WORKS OF THE AUTHOR

THE VENERABLE BHIKKHU ÑĀṆAMOLI

Minor Readings and Illustrator. The Khuddakapāṭha and Commentary. Transl, from the Pali. 1960.

The Guide (Nettippakaraṇa). Transl. from the Pali. 1962.

Piṭaka-Disclosure (Peṭakopadesa). Transl. from the Pali. 1964.

The Path of Discrimination (Paṭisambhidāmagga). Transl. from the Pali, 1982.

The Path of Purification (*Visuddhimagga*) by Bhadantācariya Buddhaghosa. Translated from the Pali. First edition 1956. 3rd ed. 1991.

Dispeller of Delusion. Transl. from the Pali. 1987 & 1991.

Mindfulness of Breathing (Ānāpānasati). Buddhist Texts from the Pali Canon and Extracts from the Pali Commentaries. First published 1964. Fifth edition 1991.

The Life of the Buddha, as it appears in the Pali Canon, *the oldest authentic record.* (369 pp.) First printing 1972, fifth printing 2007.

The Practice of Loving-kindness (Mettā)" as taught by the Buddha in the Pali Canon. Compiled and translated 1958. Published in *The Wheel* No. 6/7. First printing 1958. Sixth reprint 2005.

A Pali-English Glossary of Buddhist Technical Terms. Edited by Bhikkhu Bodhi. First edition 1991. Second edition 2007.

Three Cardinal Discourses of the Buddha. Translation with Introduction and Notes. First printing 1960; third reprint 1981 as *The Wheel* No. 17.

Pathways of Buddhist Thought. Four Essays (from Posthumous papers). 1963, 1983—(The Wheel No. 52/53.) Reprinted in an anthology of *The Wheel* publications, published by George Allen & Unwin, London, 1971 under the same title).

The Three Refuges. 1959. (Bodhi Leaves No. A. 5). Available online at http;//www.bps.lk/onlinelibrary_ bodhileaves.html

"Anicca-Dukkha-Anatta. According to the Theravāda." Three Essays in *The Three Basic Facts of Existence* (*The Wheel* Nos. 186/187, 191/193, 202/204), 1973–74,

The Pātimokkha. 227 Fundamental Rules of a Bhikkhu. Translated from the Pali. 1969

Of Related Interest from the BPS

The Path of Purification: Visuddhimagga
Translated by Bhikkhu Ñāṇamoli

The Visuddhimagga is the most important non-canonical work of Theravada Buddhism. Written in the 5th century by Ācariya Buddhaghosa, the book serves as a systematic encyclopaedia of Buddhist doctrine and a detailed guide to meditation. The translation by Ven. Nanamoli itself ranks as an outstanding scholarly achievement.

BP 207H 950 pp.

A Pali-English Glossary of Buddhist Technical Terms
Bhikkhu Ñāṇamoli

This glossary, compiled by the erudite British scholar-monk, includes renderings for technical terms from the Pali Canon and selected commentaries, as well as words and meanings not included in the PTS Pali-English Dictionary. With textual references.

BP 608S 161 pp.

The Life of the Buddha According to the Pali Canon
by Bhikkhu Ñāṇamoli

Among the numerous lives of the Buddha that have been written, this work with its comprehensive material and original method of presentation claims a place of its own. Composed entirely from texts from the Pali Canon, the oldest and most intact authentic record, it portrays an image of the Buddha which is vivid, warm and moving. An inspiring and informative work.

BPS 101, 375 pages.

MINDFULNESS OF BREATHING
Bhikkhu Ñāṇamoli

This book brings together the most important suttas from the Pali Canon and extracts from the commentaries dealing with ānāpana-sati the meditative practice of mindfulness of breathing.

BP 502S 126 pp.

THE DHAMMAPADA
THE BUDDHA'S PATH OF WISDOM
Translated by Ācariya Buddharakkhita

The Dhammapada is the best known scripture of Theravada Buddhism, and one of the most beloved spiritual testaments of all time. An anthology of 423 verses spoken by the Buddha, the Dhammapada serves as a perfect compendium of his teachings for study, reflection and contemplation.

This compact, handy volume is not only ideal for personal use, but will also make a beautiful gift which can bring to others the light of the Dhamma in one of its most inspiring expressions.

Available in book size and pocket sized editions.

BP 203, 116pp.

BEGINNINGS
COLLECTED ESSAYS
S. Bodhesako

This book contains all the known published and unpublished essays by S. Bodhesako: *Beginnings, Change, The Buddha and Catch-22, The Myth of Sisyphus, Faith, and Being and Craving.* The thought-provoking, witty, essays investigate the relation between the Pali Canon and modern, especially existentialist, Western philosophy and literature. This collection is of interest to those who like to learn about the Buddha's Teaching from the perspective of modern Western philosophy and literature as well as those who like to learn about alternative, modern interpretations of traditional Buddhist concepts.

BP 425, 252pp.

Prices according to latest catalogue (http://www.bps.lk)

BUDDHIST PUBLICATION SOCIETY

The BPS is an approved charity dedicated to making known the Teaching of the Buddha, which has a vital message for people of all creeds. Founded in 1958, the BPS has published a wide variety of books and booklets cover-ing a great range of topics. Its publications include accurate annotated translations of the Buddha's discourses, standard reference works, as well as original contemporary expositions of Buddhist thought and practice. These works present Buddhism as it truly is—a dynamic force which has influenced receptive minds for the past 2500 years and is still as relevant today as it was when it first arose. For more information write to:

The Administrative Secretary
BUDDHIST PUBLICATION SOCIETY
P.O. Box 61
54 Sangharaja Mawatha
Kandy • Sri Lanka
Tel: 0094 81 223 7283 • Fax: 0094 81 222 3679
E-mail: bps@sltnet.lk
Web site: http://www.bps.lk